What People Are Saying About This Book

The Career Pathways Effect brings ideas, facts, and best practices into one resource for educators and policymakers who want to improve student academic and career success. It makes the case that Career Technical Education has become a valued player in today's educational and economic landscape, where business and industry have a major role in bringing personalized education to life. This book brings together the research and practical applications that can be used to improve the nation's education system.

Kathy D'Antoni
Assistant State Superintendent of Schools
West Virginia Department of Education

In our fractured American education system, too many potentially successful students drop through the cracks or sleepwalk through an irrelevant curriculum. This important book brings together voices from diverse organizations to guide us in creating a system that supports all students in preparing themselves for success in school or in the workplace.

George "Pinky" Nelson
Former NASA astronaut
Director of Science, Mathematics, and Technology Education
Western Washington University

The Career Pathways Effect is a must read for anyone interested in "re-engineering" the U.S. educational system. And hopefully, that's more than just a few of us. From innovative curriculum design approaches to constructing solid partnerships with business, this book provides great insight and examples of how it can be done.

Anthony M. Landis
Director of College & Career Transitions
Ohio Board of Regents

Our nation must regain the status it once held as the most advanced technological nation on earth...the nation that landed on the moon over forty years ago. To regain that status, we must have people who are both trained and motivated. We will not motivate our students unless we can provide the relevance between the study of tough subjects and rewarding career pathways. This book starts to significantly move the needle in that direction.

Ben T. Robinson
Brig Gen, USAF, Retired
Owner/President, Sentry One LLC

D0206318

"Why do I have to learn this?" *The Career Pathways Effect* answers this question in a comprehensive and immediately useful learning tool for current and aspiring educators who seek to develop and implement initiatives designed to assist students and adult learners in answering this age-old question.

  Jeraline Marsh
  President
  National Association for Career Pathways Leadership

Based on a revitalized vision of Career Technical Education, *The Career Pathways Effect* is an essential evidenced-based resource and motivational tool for all educators, civic leaders, employers, and policymakers dedicated to transforming the U.S. education and workforce system into a new, more productive one.

  Ellen Hewett
  Director
  National College Transition Network
  At World Education, Inc

The *Career Pathways Effect* provides clear and visionary guidance that will assist educators in implementing innovative career pathways and programs designed to help develop the workforce that our country so desperately needs. It is chock full of realistic and achievable advice for policy, professional development, accountability systems, instructional design, and more.

  Betsy Brand
  Executive Director
  American Youth Policy Forum

This book touches on the right topics to set the stage for helping students achieve success. We need more teachers and administrators at the high school and college levels who understand how it all fits together. I am also very glad to see the chapter on partnerships since we could not be an award-winning school without an active business advisory board.

  Angela Reiher
  Dean of Academies
  A.J. Moore Academies at University High School
  Waco (Texas) Independent School District

The Career Pathways Effect is a culmination of what is right about our Tech Prep, CTE, and career pathways efforts over the past two decades. I recommend that you share the book with your educational and community partners, as well as policymaking stakeholders. Its processes and models should be used to improve and implement successful career pathways.

  Brenda Abbott
  Director
  Center for Secondary Students
  Laramie County Community College (Wyoming)

The Career Pathways Effect

Linking Education and Economic Prosperity

A joint publication of the Center for Occupational
Research and Development (CORD) and the National
Association of State Directors of Career Technical Education
Consortium (NASDCTEc)

Published by
  CORD Communications
  4901 Bosque Blvd.
  Second Floor, Suite 280
  Waco, Texas 76710
  800-231-3015
  Fax 254-776-3906
  www.cordcommunications.com

Cover design by Joy Ty Design and Erin Uy

ISBN 978-1-57837-706-4

CONTENTS

V. Ensure

Foreword

The Boeing Company is no stranger to the power of strategic partnerships and collaborations. In seeking the best of innovation and production for its own aerospace products through collaboration with secondary and postsecondary education, Boeing is second to none. From top management to our technicians, Boeing has been a willing partner, inextricably involved in initiatives designed to improve the effectiveness of Career Technical Education (CTE).

Seeing CORD and NASDCTEc partnering to publish the newest book on Career Pathways is exciting. CORD's *Career Pathways: Education with a Purpose* (2005) and its over 30 years in the CTE field give it a solid platform for this new book. NASDCTEc's leadership role in CTE and its body of work in support of CTE, including years of effort with the U.S. Department of Education in developing the Career Clusters™, Programs of Study, and industry-validated knowledge and skills standards, bring further credibility, depth, and dimension to this new book. CORD and NASDCTEc have partnered to provide CTE and all of education with the most current roadmap for developing Career Pathways programs.

A central tenet of the book is that CTE has now gained much of the data to show all of education that utilizing context in coursework, providing students real-world experiences and creating partnerships throughout the community are among the CTE techniques that can excite students about the potential of their futures and cause them to learn more readily by staying engaged in their education. That is precisely what education, business and industry, and the nation need to regain global competitiveness.

In my work at Boeing, I have had the privilege of advising the National Career Pathways Network and am familiar with several of the chapter authors in this book. I am exceptionally pleased to support their work and their efforts to assist you in shaping and improving our collective futures, encouraging economic development, and ensuring that our students are college and career ready.

Mark N. Turner
Enterprise Learning Strategy
Learning, Training & Development
The Boeing Company

Introduction

In 2005 the Center for Occupational Research and Development (CORD) published *Career Pathways: Education with a Purpose,* just as the Career Pathways concept was beginning to be widely discussed and the Career Technical Education (CTE) field and policymakers were beginning to use their experiences with Tech Prep programs to enhance the effectiveness of CTE. The book has been used for professional development and pre-service teacher education across the country. Several state-specific editions were created to support the varying strategies for Career Pathways implementation at the state and local levels. In 2007 CORD produced a second Career Pathways book, *Adult Career Pathways: Providing a Second Chance in Public Education* (second edition 2011), to support applications of the Career Pathways concept to the special circumstances of adults returning to the workforce. The two books have provided valuable information to states, regions, and communities as they have developed their own Career Pathways models.

The Career Pathways Effect, initially envisioned as an updated version of CORD's first Career Pathways book, is an entirely new book, co-published by CORD and the National Association of State Directors of Career Technical Education Consortium (NASDCTEc). With its extensive leadership experience in working on the U.S. Department of Education, OVAE Career Clusters™ projects, NASDCTEc has developed significant resources to support CTE, such as its Programs of Study, Career Clusters™, Common Career Technical Core, and the Knowledge and Skills bodies of work. Working together, CORD and NASDCTEc are strongly positioned to provide CTE and general education with the recent data, examples, processes, and models necessary for effective Career Pathways implementation.

CORD and NASDCTEc take the position that *The Career Pathways Effect* will meet a need for evidence-based support for the concepts and principles associated with Career Clusters™, Career Pathways, and Programs of Study, and will provide a template for more uniform implementation across the nation. It is hoped that the book will stimulate conversation on topics such as new models, collection of evidence-based data, and how the successes achieved by CTE can improve all of education. Surely all of education can be improved through the wide application of the proven strategies of Career

Pathways—contextualized teaching and learning, partnerships among education and community stakeholder groups, integrated curriculum, and transportable academic and technical credentials—strategies that the book discusses in detail. CTE, delivered via Career Pathways models, provides a powerful means of reaching the goals that today's educators and policymakers seek: implementation of new college and career readiness standards and common core curriculum models, elimination of the need for (and high cost of) remediation, increasing graduation rates (both secondary and postsecondary), and ensuring that American employers have access to a well-prepared and highly skilled workforce, to name a few.

The first edition of *The Career Pathways Effect* will be followed by frequent updates as called for by changes in the field (e.g., the next reauthorization of The Carl D. Perkins Career and Technical Education Act of 2006). We welcome your comments and pledge to do our utmost in giving you the best tools available as you carry out your essential and meaningful work with our nation's students of all ages.

The Career Pathways Effect:
Linking Education and
Economic Prosperity
Team Leaders
Dean Folkers, NASDCTEc
Kimberly Green, NASDCTEc
Richard Hinckley, CORD
Debra Mills, CORD

Acknowledgements

The CTE community is rich with dedicated and talented individuals who have given their careers to improving the lives and ensuring the futures of our children and young adults. It is wonderful to work with so many across the country and to touch each others' lives through print and electronic media, and occasionally in person.

When considering authors and contributors to this book, there was no shortage of ideas and suggestions. But with only so many chapters, we had to make hard choices, knowing that only a small sampling of many worthy potential contributors would be represented. We are certainly grateful to our authors, who took valuable time to write and edit, and rewrite so that their message would be clear and compelling. Each and every author drew upon the work and experiences of others and thereby richly extended their message. Please keep in mind that opinions and conclusions are their own and do not necessarily reflect those of each other or of CORD or NASDCTEc.

As you look over the list of contributing authors, know that we value them greatly and at some point may tap you on the shoulder for your contribution. Thank you for all you do and will do to improve the field of education.

Chapter Authors

BRYAN ALBRECHT, ED.D., serves as President of Gateway Technical College's (WI) multi-campus facilities, which serve nearly 26,000 students. Under Dr. Albrecht's guidance, Gateway has become nationally recognized for leadership in stimulating economic growth through business and education partnerships, demonstrated commitment to environmental sustainability in all aspects of the community, and innovation in improving students' academic and career success. He serves on over 50 local boards impacting education and workforce preparation. Nationally he serves on the boards of the National Occupational Competency Testing Institute, Center for Occupational Research and Development, National Manufacturing Institute, National Manufacturing Skill Standards Council, National Career and Technical Education Foundation, Biopharmaceutical Technology Center Institute, National Coalition of Certification Centers, and the National Coalition of Advanced Technology Centers.

KATE BLOSVEREN KREAMER is an Associate Director at Achieve, a bipartisan nonprofit organization that helps states raise academic standards, improve assessments, and strengthen accountability to prepare all young people for postsecondary education, careers, and citizenship. In this role, she leads research in the areas of advocacy, career readiness, and critical college and career ready policies, supporting Achieve's and the American Diploma Project network's strategic communications and outreach efforts. Before joining Achieve, Ms. Blosveren Kreamer was a policy advisor at Third Way, where she acted as a policy liaison between the organization and its corporate leadership committee. Prior to her work at Third Way, she was a research assistant at the Progressive Policy Institute, focusing exclusively on education policy issues. She is also the founder and president of Young Education Professionals-DC (YEP-DC), a DC-based network created by and for young professionals who want to connect around their common interests in education policy, research, and practice in a nonpartisan environment.

DAVID BOND, ED.D., is CORD's Senior Vice President for Career Pathways and Director of the National Career Pathways Network. He has been with CORD since 1993. Prior to that Dr. Bond served as a U.S. Army officer and as an administrator at Missouri Baptist College and at Baylor University. He has directed 20 national conferences, conducted statewide and local evaluations on program effectiveness, made numerous presentations at education conferences, written numerous articles for the NCPN *Connections* newsletter, and was a contributing author to *Career Pathways: Education with a Purpose* and *Adult Career Pathways: Providing a Second Chance in Public Education.*

JAN BRAY serves as the Executive Director of the Association for Career and Technical Education (ACTE), a not-for-profit association representing over 30,000 professionals across the United States. Ms. Bray represents the Career Technical Education profession and ACTE on a number of boards and advisory groups, including the U.S. Department of Labor Apprenticeship Advisory Committee, the Home Builders Institute Board of Trustees, the Manufacturing Skills Standards Council, the National Coalition of Certification Centers, Friends of the National High School Center, the America's Promise Alliance Board of Trustees, and the board of the U.S. Partnership for Education for Environmental Sustainability. Ms. Bray has been an active participant in the ACTE community, serving on the American Society of Association Executives Education Foundation Board of Directors, the Greater Washington Society of Association Executives Board of Directors, and numerous association-related committees and councils. She has spoken at numerous ACTE conferences and seminars and has authored articles on CTE and related topics.

NANCY CONNEELY, J.D., is the Public Policy Manager at the National Association of State Directors of Career Technical Education Consortium (NASDCTEc). In this role, she develops public policy, advocates for career technical education and funding, and tracks and monitors legislation and initiatives that affect career technical education. Prior to joining NASDCTEc, Ms. Conneely had several legal internships in the government and nonprofit sectors related to education law and policy. She has interned for Catholic Charities USA in the social policy and government affairs office; the U.S. Department of Education in the Office of General Counsel; and the Senate Heath, Education, Labor and Pensions Committee in the Office of Oversight and Investigations.

HOPE COTNER is CORD's Vice President for Community College Initiatives. Since coming to CORD in 1991, she has directed a wide variety of faculty and curriculum development projects at both the secondary and postsecondary levels. Current projects range from administering statewide professional development networks for community college faculty to developing customized course materials for industry. She leads many of CORD's regional Career Pathways and Adult Career Pathway projects. Ms. Cotner was project director for STEM Transitions, funded by the U. S. Department of Education's Office of Vocational and Adult Education (OVAE) to develop learning modules that integrate science and math with workplace contexts. In partnership with Kratos Learning, Ms. Cotner coordinates CORD's work in support of *Designing Instruction for Career Pathways,* an OVAE-funded project dedicated to assisting state and local adult education providers in the development of Adult Career Pathway programs.

LYLE COURTNAGE, ED.D., is Project Manager for the Montana University System's Rigorous Programs of Study (RPOS) project, a partnership between the U.S. Department of Education Office of Vocational and Adult Education (OVAE), Montana's Office of Public Instruction, the Office of the Commissioner of Higher Education, and four school districts. Dr. Courtnage previously served as co-director of Montana's Tech Prep program and taught business classes at both four-year and two-year colleges. Dr. Courtnage's industry experience includes marketing management, owning television and radio stations, and managing a tax accounting firm.

SETH DERNER is the President and Development Leader for Vivayic, an agency specializing in human capital development through the design of effective learning solutions. Vivayic provides strategy, consulting, design and implementation services related to training and development initiatives for corporate, nonprofit, and governmental agencies. Mr. Derner has been a professional development consultant for the National Career Technical Education Foundation (NCTEF) for projects related to the National Career Clusters™ Framework, including the 2008 and 2011 revisions of the Knowledge and Skills Statements. Mr. Derner draws from his experience as a secondary CTE teacher, program manager for a national career and technical student organization, and director of FutureForce Nebraska—an organization designed to facilitate partnerships between education and workforce and economic development. He has co-authored the books *Strategies for Great Teaching* and *Strategies to Integrate NOW: Academics in Career and Technical Education*.

DEAN FOLKERS, D.M., is the Deputy Executive Director for the National Career Technical Education Foundation (NCTEF) and the National Association of State Directors of Career Technical Education Consortium (NASDCTEc). His responsibilities include work involving the National Career Clusters™ Framework, Knowledge and Skills Statements and products and professional development that support the Career Clusters™ and Career Technical Education. Prior to his current role, Dr. Folkers served as the Assistant State CTE Director for Nebraska Career Education, worked as a high school agricultural education instructor, and served as a team leader for the National FFA Organization.

JOHN FOSTER, PH.D., has served public Career Technical Education as a tradesman, teacher, director, teacher educator, and state director. After his experience as a construction contractor, Dr. Foster spent the early part of his career with the Carlisle Area School District's Career and Technical Education Center. He eventually became director of that program, delivering over 20 technical programs and managing one of the largest adult education centers in the area. Later he worked as a career and technical teacher educator for the Pennsylvania State University. He then worked as the Pennsylvania State Director of Career and Technical Education under two governors and served in a leadership capacity for the National Association of State Directors of Career Technical Education Consortium. In 2005, Dr. Foster became CEO and President of NOCTI (formerly the National Occupational Competency Testing Institute) and its subsidiary, NOCTI Business Solutions. He has written and researched data-driven curriculum improvement in CTE and served as a core member of the National Research Center for Career and Technical Education. He was also a founding member of USATVET, an organization that promotes CTE internationally.

KURT GEISINGER, PH.D., is Director of the Buros Center on Testing and W. C. Meierhenry Distinguished University Professor at the University of Nebraska. He has previously been Professor and Chair of the Department of Psychology at Fordham University, Professor of Psychology and Dean of Arts and Sciences at SUNY-Oswego, Professor of Psychology and Academic Vice President at LeMoyne College, and Professor of Psychology and Vice President for Academic Affairs at the University of St. Thomas in Houston, Texas. He was elected to the American Psychological Association's Board of Directors in 2010. Previously he was an APA delegate and chair of the Joint Committee on Testing Practices (1992–1996), a member of APA's Committee on Psychological Testing and Assessment, Chair of the Graduate Record Examination Board, Chair of the Technical Advisory Committee for the Graduate Record Examination, a member of the SAT Advisory Committee, and a member of NCME's Ad Hoc Committee to Develop a Code of Ethical Standards Committee. For two years he coordinated a CTE consortium of state members interested in CTE and sponsored by the Council of Chief State School Officers (CCSSO). He has edited several titles published by APA Books.

KIMBERLY A. GREEN, Executive Director of the National Association of State Directors of Career Technical Education Consortium, has worked over nineteen years on federal policy impacting Career Technical Education. Working closely with Congress, the Administration, and a broad range of stakeholders, she represents the interests of and seeks support for Career Technical Education. In addition to this policy work, she helped establish, implement, and grow the national Career Clusters™ Initiative, which is designed to transform Career Technical Education so that it can meet the needs of the nation and its economy, employers, and students. Ms. Green represents the state directors on a variety of boards and committees, including the Manufacturing Skills Standards Leadership Council, the Executive Committee of the National Career Academy Coalition, and the Technical Advisory Groups for Adult Career Pathways, Employability Standards, and 21st Century Community Learning Centers.

JoANN HARRIS-BOWLSBEY, ED.D., has enjoyed a long and distinguished career in the field of career development that has included positions as high school counselor, director of guidance, university professor, career counselor in a university counseling center, developer of DISCOVER® (a computer-based career planning system), and Executive Director of ACT's Educational Technology Center. She is currently Executive Vice-President of Development for Kuder, Inc., and in that role works with state departments of education and labor in the conceptualization and implementation of career planning websites that serve as a virtual center for both students and adults across the life span as they engage in educational and career planning. She is also involved in the development of international career planning systems that include implementation of a highly customized career planning website and paraprofessional-level training for those who use it with students and clients. Dr. Harris-Bowlsbey is the author or co-author of many journal articles and several books including *Take Hold of Your Future* (a college-level career planning curriculum) and *Career Interventions in the 21st Century* (a graduate-level textbook authored with Dr. Spencer Niles).

KARA HERBERTSON is an Education Policy Analyst at the National Association of State Directors of Career Technical Education Consortium (NASDCTEc). In this role, she provides research and policy analysis to support advocacy efforts. Previously, Ms. Herbertson worked as a teacher in Washington, DC, and in education research and evaluation roles in Philadelphia. While in graduate school, she focused on the distinct role of community colleges within the higher education system and contributed to a program that helps first-generation community college students transition into four-year colleges and universities.

SCOTT HESS is the Vice President of Community Partnerships – Career Readiness and Technical Markets for Ascend Learning. Prior to joining Ascend Learning, he served as an Educational Program Specialist at the U.S. Department of Education, Office of Vocational and Adult Education (OVAE). Responsibilities at OVAE included Chief of the College and Career Transitions Branch and project manager for national activities including: Career Cluster Development, the College and Career Transitions Initiative (CCTI), and both Rigorous Programs of Study projects focusing on statewide articulation and implementation of the Programs of Study Design Framework. Prior to working at ED, Mr. Hess was with the Utah State Office of Education, where he served as an Educational Coordinator; State School-to-Careers Coordinator; Adult Education Director; and State Specialist for Health Sciences, Health Education, Physical Education, and HIV Education. Mr. Hess also has healthcare industry work experience in respiratory therapy and has taught medical anatomy and physiology and other health science related courses at the high school and university levels.

RICHARD HINCKLEY, PH.D., has been CORD's President and CEO since 2006. Dr. Hinckley served public education as a teacher, principal, superintendent, and college dean, spending his early career with the Illinois Department of Corrections School District 428. Later he served Moraine Valley Community College in Palos Hills, Illinois, as Dean of Workforce Development and Community Services and led the formation of the local Tech Prep consortium, the Moraine Area Career System. He was instrumental in the creation of one of the earliest advanced technology centers on a community college campus and, in 2000, became Executive Director of the National Coalition of Advanced Technology Centers. He is co-author of *Adult Career Pathways: Providing a Second Chance in Public Education.*

ANTHONY J. IACONO, PH.D., is the Vice President of Academic Affairs at Indian River State College (IRSC), where he has worked since 1999. His administrative responsibilities include operation of IRSC's academic programs, including developmental and adult education, tutorial centers, library services, Career Pathways, and minority affairs. He also serves on a number of state and national committees that involve secondary and postsecondary educational program development with a focus on Career Pathways.

PRADEEP KOTAMRAJU, PH.D., is the Deputy Director, National Research Center for Career and Technical Education (NRCCTE), University of Louisville, Louisville, Kentucky. Prior to 2009 he was the State Director for Career and Technical Education in Minnesota. Dr. Kotamraju has written several publications and monographs and made numerous presentations in the areas of student success in Career Technical Education, workforce development in the United States, and economic progress in the developing world. His current research focuses on measuring the engagement, achievement, and transition of Career Technical Education secondary and postsecondary students.

Dr. Kotamraju's research also includes examination of a variety of labor market information and workforce development issues that connect occupations, skills and careers, as individuals transitioned back and forth between employment and education. Before working in the public sector, Dr. Kotamraju taught college- and university-level economics and statistics at several higher education institutions in Minnesota.

LIBBY LIVINGS-EASSA serves as Assistant Dean of Adult Education for the Indian River State College system in Florida overseeing the institution's secondary transition initiatives. She served on appointment to the U.S. Department of Education and worked with the Division of Academic and Technical Education from September 2010 until November 2011. While at the U.S. Department of Education, she served as Program Director for nationally funded Rigorous Programs of Study state grants and served on the Perkins monitoring team while providing technical assistance to states. A staunch supporter of local, state, and national educational initiatives, Ms. Livings-Eassa has served as the President for the National Association of Tech Prep Leadership, President of the Florida Career Pathways Network, and as a member of the National Career Pathways Network national advisory board. Programs under her direction are consistently recognized as "best practices" by state and national organizations, and she is a nationally recognized speaker for Career Pathways systems implementation.

RONALD D. MCCAGE, ED.D., is the President of the Career and Technical Education Consortium of States (CTECS; formerly VTECS), a not-for-profit organization that specializes in performance-based instructional design and assessment strategies for Career Technical Education. From September 1970 through September 1980, Dr. McCage served as Director of the Research and Development Section, Department of Adult, Vocational and Technical Education, Illinois State Board of Education. He has written several articles and papers and has served on numerous state and national committees. He was Chair of the AVA (now ACTE) Legislative Task Force on State and National Program Improvement from 1979 to 1983. From 1986 to 1989 he served as Vice President of the New and Related Services Division of AVA and as Chair of the AVA Board's Subcommittee on Legislation for two of those years. These committees had a significant impact on the 1984 and 1990 versions of the Carl D. Perkins Amendments to the Vocational Education Act of 1963. Dr. McCage has made numerous presentations at state and national conferences and worked with Chile and Uruguay to implement competency-based vocational and technical education in the early 1990s. He was directly involved in the efforts of the U.S. Department of Education and U.S. Department of Labor to develop voluntary skill standards and certification systems during the 1990s and has been heavily involved in the recent Career Clusters Initiative™, as well as the first cycle of Career Clusters™ in the 1970s.

RANDY A. MCPHERSON, ED.D., LPC, NCSC, NBCT, serves as Director of Counseling Services and College Prep for Memphis City Schools. Dr. McPherson supervises 300 school counselors in over 200 K-12 schools. He has extensive experience in Career Technical Education, alternative education, and urban education. He has served on numerous nonprofit boards and was named the 2011 American School Counseling Association Counselor of the Year and received a Lifetime Achievement Award from the Tennessee School Counseling Association. Dr. McPherson also serves as adjunct faculty at The University of Memphis and Harding University.

DEBRA MILLS serves as CORD's Vice President for Partnerships. Her focus areas include secondary-to-postsecondary transitions, community engagement for the success of adult learners, curriculum development, staff development, and business-education partnerships. Ms. Mills has delivered numerous keynote speeches at state education conferences. She is a subject matter expert for the DOLETA/ OVAE *Career Pathways Technical Assistance Initiative* (2011) and OVAE *Rigorous Programs of Study* project (2011) and was part of the *College & Career Transition Leadership Team* (OVAE Project 2007). She has written or contributed to several publications and articles including NCPN's *College and Career Readiness Toolkit* and *Career Pathways Advisory Committees Toolkit; Tech Prep: The Next Generation Planning Guide,* and *Adult Career Pathways: Providing a Second Chance in Public Education.* In addition, Mills was a contributing author to *Career Pathways: Education with a Purpose* and *The Pathway from Baghdad to Tech Prep: A Success Story.*

AGUSTIN NAVARRA, PH.D., is CORD's Vice President for International Operations. He has been with CORD since 1992. He was the foreign team leader of the World Bank funded project Feasibility Studies on Secondary Education Development in the country of Turkey, but his main work is in Latin American countries. His projects have involved curriculum and textbook design and development, professional development, and the creation of business-education partnerships. Dr. Navarra has trained more than 2500 teachers in contextual teaching and has supported staff development and implementation of career pathways-like models across the Latin American region. He is author of college-level contextual mathematics textbooks in both Portuguese and Spanish and has written articles (English, Spanish, and Portuguese) about the CORD educational model that have been published in Brazil, the Dominican Republic, and internationally via the NCPN *Connections* newsletter.

REBA POULSON is the principal consultant at Poulson Consulting. She served as Louisiana's State Director for Perkins Programs. Ms. Poulson has extensive experience with secondary-to-postsecondary transitions and building pathways for Career Technical Education programs. She has served as a board member for the National Association of State Directors of Career Technical Education Consortium and the Center for Occupational Research and Development. Ms. Poulson has many years of experience with curriculum/program development, grant development, evaluation and instructional support with the Louisiana Community and Technical College System (LCTCS), Southern University, the Louisiana Board of Regents, and Kalamazoo Valley Community College (Michigan).

ANNETTE SEVERSON, ED.D., serves as the Associate Vice President, Office of Instruction at the Wisconsin Technical College System Office. In that role she is responsible for managing the new degree program approval process and course/curriculum approval for over 1200 associate of applied science and technical diploma degrees and apprentice programs offered at the sixteen technical colleges in Wisconsin, which serve 400,000 students annually. Under her leadership and in collaboration with the Wisconsin Department of Public Instruction (K-12) and the Technical Colleges, the Office works to implement Career Prep strategies designed to enhance CTE across the state. Dr.

Severson currently acts as the Co-Principal Investigator in the multi-year Rigorous Programs of Study (RPOS) grant funded by OVAE. Her presentations at the 2011 Career Cluster Institute, as part of the RPOS grant, focused on Wisconsin's implementation of the 10 Framework Components, including the use of a statewide standard RPOS implementation guide and website design and communication tool, and the implementation of technical skill attainment in the manufacturing cluster. She has extensive experience in health care, having several leadership roles in health care management, and in education, most recently as the Associate Dean for Nursing at Waukesha County Technical College.

WILLIAM C. SYMONDS is Director of the Pathways to Prosperity Project at the Harvard Graduate School of Education, a position he has held since the Pathways Project was launched in the fall of 2008. He was the lead author of the project's report — *Pathways to Prosperity: Meeting the Challenge of Preparing Young Americans for the 21st Century* — which was released in February 2011. Since then, he has been invited to speak about the report in more than half the states, as well as in Canada and New Zealand. Mr. Symonds helped create the Pathways Project while he was a senior fellow at Harvard's Kennedy School in 2007–2008. Prior to that, he spent nearly 25 years as a bureau chief and senior correspondent for *Business Week Magazine*. During his career with *Business Week*, he served as the magazine's chief education correspondent and wrote widely about business in the U.S. and abroad. He also led bureaus in Pittsburgh, Denver, Boston, Toronto, and Rome, Italy.

MARK WHITNEY, PH.D., is CORD's Manager of Publication Services. In that capacity he has provided editorial control and quality assurance on hundreds of CORD documents, including curriculum materials (both printed and online), reports, surveys, proposals, books, and articles. He has played an important editorial role in several recent CORD books, including *Career Pathways: Education with a Purpose* and *Adult Career Pathways: Providing a Second Chance in Public Education* (in which he also served as a contributing author) and is editor of *Connections*, the newsletter of the National Career Pathways Network.

The Career Pathways Effect: An Introduction

Hope Cotner and Dean Folkers

We live in challenging times. Recent events have shaken the foundations of our economic system. Today, as never before, Americans look to our nation's businesses and industries to create innovative strategies for providing jobs and bolstering American competitiveness in the global marketplace. To fulfill that task, business and industry must have access to an abundant pool of well-qualified workers, which in turn requires that our public school system produce graduates who are college and career ready. Unfortunately, that is not happening. Despite the efforts of countless dedicated teachers and administrators – not to mention billions of dollars spent on education reform – American public education continues to fall short of its potential.

Thriving in Challenging Times: Connecting
Education to Economic Development[1]

The Center for Occupational Research and Development (CORD) and the National Association of State Directors of Career Technical Education Consortium (NASDCTEc) have collaborated on the development of a book that offers solutions to major education and economic problems facing the United States today. Significant thought and intentionality are reflected in this compendium of tested results, best practices, and promising approaches. This

1 National Career Pathways Network and the Institute for a Competitive Workforce, *Thriving in Challenging Times: Connecting Education to Economic Development*, April 2012 (http://www.ncpn.info/thriving-in-challenging-times.php).

book is intended to serve as a resource that can inspire ideas, foster innovation, and create a sense of possibility about how we can collectively accomplish a brighter future for American students.

In this opening chapter we discuss the evolution of Career Pathways, its intersection with Career Technical Education (CTE), and ways to use the strategies shared in the book to improve education throughout the country.

The Harvard University Graduate School of Education's report *Pathways to Prosperity* calls for a robust Career Pathways system that leads students beyond the high school diploma. The report highlights significant and growing skills and earnings gaps that are due, in part, to changes in the workplace. "Over the past third of a century," the report notes, "all of the net growth in America has been generated by positions that require at least some postsecondary education." The solution is not to increase bachelor's degree attainment but to increase the number of high school graduates who go on to earn associate degrees and postsecondary occupational certificates — the credentials of preference in many workplace settings. Lack of college enrollment is not the problem. The problem is lack of completion. Fewer than half of American college enrollees complete their programs.[2]

The call to action for a Career Pathways system provides a unique opportunity. As identified in *Thriving in Challenging Times*, the Career Pathways concept offers "an educational model that creates relevant, challenging learning environments and, if widely implemented, has the potential to significantly increase American employers' access to high-quality, home-grown employees." Career Pathways systems offer communities the tools they need to prepare tomorrow's workforce today. Important elements of these systems are identified below.

Career Pathways systems benefit educators, students, employers, and communities by offering:

- **Context**—Demonstrating for students how academic concepts are used outside the classroom.

---

2 William C. Symonds, Robert B. Schwartz, and Ronald Ferguson, *Pathways to Prosperity: Meeting the Challenge of Preparing Young Americans for the 21st Century*, Pathways to Prosperity Project, February 2011, Harvard University Graduate School of Education (http://www.gse.harvard.edu/news_events/features/2011/Pathways_to_Prosperity_Feb2011.pdf).

- **Purpose** — Motivating students and giving them a desire to stay in school.

- **Focus and flexibility** — Guiding students toward personal and professional goals while providing the flexibility to change focus areas at any time.

- **Rigor and relevance** — Integrating academic subjects with workplace context.

- **A level playing field** — Supporting diverse student learning styles.

- **Guidance for career selection and a foundation for career pursuit** — Giving students a sense of direction and sequence of courses that supports identified interests and goals.

- **Opportunities for interdisciplinary problem-solving and critical thinking** — Producing "knowledge workers" who understand systems and can solve problems in teams.

- **A foundation for lifelong learning, and lifelong earning** — Building for a future that allows students to fulfill their potential on the job, at home, and within communities.[3]

The Career Pathways concept, whether applied to coordinated secondary-postsecondary programs or to "second chance" programs for adults, calls for a high level of involvement on the part of employers and community organizations and a commitment to collaboration between secondary and postsecondary educators.

The Interconnectedness of Career Pathways and Career Technical Education

Career Pathways has become widely accepted as a vehicle for the continued evolution of CTE. Building upon Tech Prep, Career Pathways not only continues to improve the delivery of CTE programs and services, but has been gathering empirical support for the use of many of its elements throughout general education.

A growing number of education professionals are embracing CTE to increase high school graduation rates and "on time" high school graduation, to provide logical pathways from secondary to

---

3 *Thriving in Challenging Times.*

postsecondary, to help reduce the need for remediation, to increase the number of high school graduates who meet high-performance standards, and to increase the number of American workers with postsecondary credentials.

CTE programs at the secondary, postsecondary, and adult education levels are preparing individuals for a wide range of careers in health care/biomedical, renewable energy, hospitality, nanotechnology, engineering, logistics, law enforcement, information technology, and a myriad of other fields. In short, CTE programs reflect the modern workplace. Because the majority of careers require postsecondary credentials, high-quality CTE programs incorporate rigorous academic and technical standards, as well as critical workplace skills such as problem solving, communication, and teamwork, to ensure career and college success for its students. Because it has demonstrated a positive return on investment, CTE is also a trusted, long-standing partner with the employer community. With programs in rural, suburban, and urban communities in every state in our nation, CTE has the capacity and infrastructure to prepare students of all ages to be successful in today's ever-changing global marketplace. Yet, while many CTE programs have evolved in the ways described above, not all have.

The forecasted needs of the 21st century, the pace of technological change, demographics, the challenges of student engagement and achievement, and growing global competition have created an urgent need to reevaluate the trajectory and role of CTE in the United States. In the spring of 2010, state and national CTE leaders, advocates, and partners committed to a new vision that would help guide the future of education for all students. In keeping with its leadership role and responsibility, NASDCTEc authored *Reflect, Transform, Lead: A New Vision for Career Technical Education,*[4] a collection of five guiding principles to propel CTE forward. The ultimate goal of the vision is to prepare students, of all ages, to succeed in education and careers and enable the United States to flourish in a dynamic and increasingly competitive global economy.

---

4 National Association of State Directors of Career Technical Education Consortium, *Reflect, Transform, Lead: A New Vision for Career Technical Education,* April 2010 (http://www.careertech.org/career-technical-education/cte-vision.html).

The **principles** are interdependent and offer a progressive, challenging agenda that seeks to ensure CTE's potential is fully realized:

1. *Lead*: CTE is critical to ensuring that the United States leads in global competitiveness.
2. *Succeed*: CTE prepares students to succeed in further education and careers.
3. *Partner*: CTE actively partners with employers to design and provide high-quality, dynamic programs.
4. *Deliver*: CTE is delivered through comprehensive Programs of Study aligned to the National Career Clusters™ Framework.
5. *Ensure*: CTE is a results-driven system that demonstrates a positive return on investment.

In adopting the new vision of CTE in the 21st century, the CTE community rededicated itself to working together at every level to transform the U.S. education and workforce system into an even more productive one that:

- Rewards innovation,
- Supports different learning styles,
- Values different student interests and talents equally,
- Adapts and responds to technology and workplace needs, and
- Prepares all students (secondary, postsecondary, and adult) for career success through Career Pathways.

Career Pathways and CTE's Connectedness to Programs of Study

Career Pathways has evolved to take on many different forms over the past several decades. The introduction of the term *Programs of Study* (POS) most recently occurred as part of the Carl D. Perkins Career and Technical Education Act of 2006. The legislation provided a general expectation for POS in delivering high-quality CTE using a seamless educational path from secondary to postsecondary that reflected economic and workforce development priorities.

A federal demonstration project to support statewide implementation models around the POS expectation of postsecondary credits resulted in the vernacular expression *Rigorous Programs of Study* (RPOS). Following the demonstration project, to promote consistency in implementation at the local level, a POS design framework was developed that defined 10 components, each with one or more subcomponents, of high-quality POS:

1. Legislation and Policies
2. Partnerships
3. Professional Development
4. Accountability and Evaluation Systems
5. College and Career Readiness Standards
6. Course Sequences
7. Credit Transfer Agreements
8. Guidance Counseling and Academic Advisement
9. Teaching and Learning Strategies
10. Technical Skills Assessments

The terms *Programs of Study, Rigorous Programs of Study,* and *POS design framework* are often commingled throughout this book, reflecting the evolution of the POS concept, a structured and strategic opportunity for students and adults to successfully navigate Career Pathways systems.

How to Use This Book

The Career Pathways Effect will guide and encourage your journey in designing and implementing Career Pathways. The essence of this book provides a deeper look at challenges facing and recommendations for America's education system. Each of the major book sections reflects the underlying principles of a vision for the future that will enable practitioners to *Lead, Succeed, Partner, Deliver,* and ultimately *Ensure* the future. The sections of the book are also aligned to the POS design framework components, with headings indicating which components are supported by each section. A checklist is provided at the end of each section for reflection on your Career Pathways program goals.

The chapters were written by a well-informed, diverse group of authors whose broad range of experiences and perspectives provide thought-provoking challenges, models, and strategies for consideration. The chapters are interrelated but also stand alone. Begin with one that applies to a specific area of interest and you will probably soon recognize a need for insight on another chapter topic. Or, you may prefer a sequential journey through each of the five sections. No matter your approach to using this resource, the most effective demonstration of success is *action*. The book is intended to offer insight to policy leaders, practitioners, educators, and others with an interest in education and the economy.

The structure of the book is outlined in the following chart. Best wishes on your journey of discovery. We look forward to including your examples of innovation and success in a future edition.

Alignment of CTE Vision Principles and POS Design Framework Components to the Chapters

NASDCTEc Key Principles of CTE Vision	POS Design Framework Components	The Career Pathways Effect Supporting Chapters
I. Lead—CTE is critical to ensuring that the United States leads in global competitiveness.		**Chapter 2.** The National Condition and Career Pathways **Chapter 3.** Comparative International Approaches
II. Succeed—CTE prepares students to succeed in further education and careers.	Legislation and Policies	**Chapter 4.** National Policy Trends **Chapter 5.** Legislation and Policies: Levers to Drive Change
III. Partner—CTE actively partners with employers to design and provide high-quality, dynamic programs.	Partnerships	**Chapter 6.** Leadership Roles and Responsibilities **Chapter 7.** Partnerships
IV. Deliver—CTE is delivered through comprehensive Programs of Study aligned to The National Career Clusters™ Framework.	College and Career Readiness Standards Course Sequences Credit Transfer Agreements Teaching and Learning Strategies Guidance Counseling and Academic Advisement Professional Development	**Chapter 8.** The National Career Clusters™ Framework **Chapter 9.** Standards **Chapter 10.** Course Sequence and Delivery Systems **Chapter 11.** Teaching and Learning **Chapter 12.** Career Guidance and Counseling
V. Ensure—CTE is a results-driven system that demonstrates a positive return on investment.	Technical Skills Assessments Accountability and Evaluation Systems	**Chapter 13.** Certificates and Certifications **Chapter 14.** Using Data for Decision-Making, Accountability, and Evaluation

Section I. Lead

CTE is critical to ensuring that the United States leads in global competitiveness.

Nations need a skilled workforce at all levels and in all occupations to maintain strong business and industrial activity and overall competitive living standards. They need an educational system that provides well-rounded citizens and well-prepared scientists, engineers, technicians, and managers ready to add value to their professions and their lives. CTE's goal is to create that skilled workforce by giving students a variety of choices and opportunities, indeed Career Pathways, to enjoyable and rewarding careers.

To gain and maintain a competitive advantage, a nation must support CTE through smart policy decisions, and it must do so with an understanding of the conditions at home as well as throughout the world. A global economy calls for a global approach to legislation and policymaking.

This section includes a chapter on the national condition that offers data-supported evidence of economic conditions, workforce issues and needs, and the condition of public education relative to creating an informed, educated, and skilled citizenry. The section also includes a chapter on international approaches that key off of Harvard University Graduate School of Education's *Pathways to Prosperity*. The chapter discusses the nation's educational performance within the context of the global economy and suggests alternatives and shifts in delivery systems to regain competitive advantage.

The National Condition and Career Pathways

Debra Mills and Mark Whitney

The Waning of the American Century

One of the most basic responsibilities of any society is to prepare its young people to lead productive and successful lives as adults. This means helping all young people acquire a solid foundation of language, mathematics, and thinking skills that will equip them for responsible citizenship, prosperous careers, and lifelong learning.[1]

Since the beginning of the 20th century, the United States has led the world in providing the education that its young people need for success in adult life. The resulting boom in educational attainment laid the foundation for the monumental rise in American wealth and power that came to be known as the American Century. By 2000, per capita income, adjusted for inflation, was up to six times as large as it had been in 1900. Yet as we make our way through the second decade of the 21st century, there are deeply troubling signs that the United States is failing to meet its fundamental obligation to prepare its young people for careers and adult life. In an age in which education has never been more important to personal and career success, the

---

1 William C. Symonds, Robert B. Schwartz, and Ronald Ferguson, *Pathways to Prosperity: Meeting the Challenge of Preparing Young Americans for the 21st Century*, Pathways to Prosperity Project, February 2011, Harvard University Graduate School of Education (http://www.gse.harvard.edu/news_events/features/2011/Pathways_to_Prosperity_Feb2011.pdf), p. 1.

United States has fallen behind several other countries in educational performance and degree attainment.[2]

For many years, the United States had a considerably higher rate of college completion than any other country. In the 1960s, a majority of U.S. citizens, between 50 and 60 percent of each age cohort, attended postsecondary institutions; approximately 35 percent would complete degrees.[3] Other countries followed our lead and expanded their educational systems, thus narrowing our advantage. By 2008, the United States had fallen to second place (after Norway) in the share of its workers with four-year degrees, and to third place (after Canada and Japan) in the attainment of college degrees among "prime age" adults (25 to 64 years old). The U.S. ranking among adults age 25 to 34 is lower still (seventh in bachelor's degree attainment; ninth in all tertiary degree attainment). The unmistakable trend is that the United States is losing ground in relation to other industrialized countries.[4] Figure 1 shows how college degree completion among 25- to 34-year-olds in the United States compares to other OECD (Organisation for Economic Co-operation and Development) countries.

America's decline in postsecondary educational attainment has created a two-fold problem. First, with too little postsecondary-educated talent to meet demand, the United States is falling far short of its potential for productivity. Second, the scarcity of high-level skills has raised the cost of postsecondary-educated talent sharply, thus widening the income gap between workers with and workers without postsecondary credentials.[5]

Because all economies are dynamic, fluctuations in labor market demand are natural. This is due in part to rapid advances in technology that increase the demand for certain skills while rendering others obsolete. The rise of global commerce is likewise a driver of change, as more and more workers are required to have skill sets that equip them for global competition. Fluctuations in the labor market are also due to the fact that labor markets are driven by all other

---

2 Symonds et al., *Pathways to Prosperity*.

3 Anthony P. Carnevale and Stephen J. Rose, *The Undereducated American,,* June 2011, Georgetown University Center on Education and the Workforce (http://cew.georgetown.edu/undereducated/).

4 Carnevale and Rose, *The Undereducated American*, p. 12.

5 Carnevale and Rose, *The Undereducated American*, p. 8.

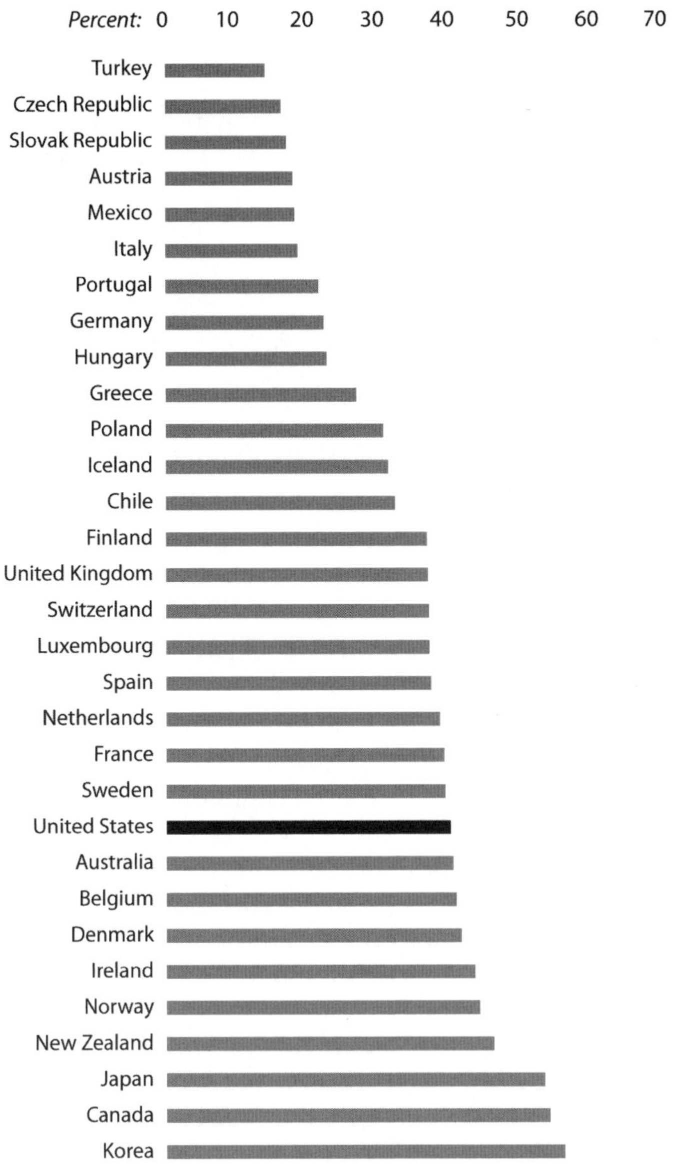

Figure 1. Attainment of College Degrees, 25- to 34-Year-Olds in OECD Countries (Source: Carnevale and Rose, *The Undereducated American*, p. 14)

markets. Labor markets naturally change over time, for instance, when the volume of online purchases increases, thus increasing the demand for workers with the skills necessary to fill those orders. At the same time, some jobs will be lost because they are no longer the most profitable way to meet consumer demand. It is easy to see how skill shortages naturally arise in a market-based economy. *Though such changes are normal, they can become crippling if not quickly addressed.* When the labor market changes, public education and workforce and economic development agencies must be able to help workers transition from areas of skill surplus or where skills are obsolete into areas of skill shortage.[6] This is one of the greatest challenges our nation faces as we enter the second decade of the 21st century.

Too Many Americans Are Undereducated

The recent decline in America's international rankings is evident not only in postsecondary outcomes but in high school graduation rates. "We have lost enormous ground over the last 15 years," according to a recent report by the Pathways to Prosperity Project of the Harvard Graduate School of Education. "The problem is that while we have been standing still, other nations have leapfrogged us."[7]

In addition to lagging high school graduation rates, the United States finds itself facing widespread *delays* in high school graduation. In 2008–2009, only about three-quarters of public high school students graduated on time with regular diplomas, as shown in Figure 2. The average freshman graduation rate for the years 2008–2009 was 75.5 percent. That figure represents approximately three million young people who graduated on time, leaving another approximately one million who did not—a troubling number.

---

6 Brian Points, "A Detailed Look at Skill Shortages," July 2011, Economic Modeling Specialists Inc. (http://www.economicmodeling.com/2011/07/26/another-look-at-skill-shortages/).

7 Symonds et al., *Pathways to Prosperity*, p. 16.

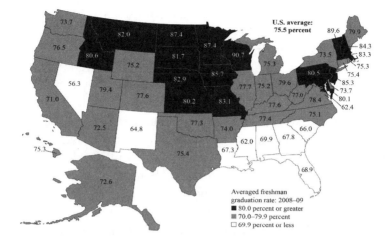

Figure 2. Averaged Freshman Graduation Rate for Public HS Students, by State: 2008–2009 (Source: C. Chapman et al., *Trends in High School Dropout and Completion Rates in the United States: 1972–2009*, NCES 2012-006 [nces.ed.gov/pubs2012/2012006.pdf], p. 25)

Among American high school graduates who go on to enroll in postsecondary education, the need for remediation is extremely high.

In 2007–2008, about 36 percent of undergraduate students considered to be in their first year reported having ever taken a remedial course, while 20 percent had taken one in that same year. At public two-year institutions, about 42 percent of students had ever taken a remedial course.[8]

Unfortunately, in the majority of cases, remediation does not lead to the desired result—college graduation. According to a recent publication by the Community College Research Center, "less than one quarter of community college students who enroll in developmental education complete a degree or certificate within eight years of enrollment in college."[9]

---

8 Susan Aud et al., *The Condition of Education 2011*, May 2011, National Center for Education Statistics (http://nces.ed.gov/pubsearch/pubsinfo. asp?pubid=2011033), p. 70.

9 Thomas Bailey and Sung Woo Cho, *Developmental Education in Community Colleges*, Community College Research Center, 2010 (http://www2.ed.gov/ PDFDocs/college-completion/07-developmental-education-in-community-colleges.pdf), p. 1.

For many Americans, mathematics continues to be a stumbling block in the pursuit of higher education. Comparison of mathematics skills with skills in reading and science literacy shows that this is a troubling weakness among many U.S. students. Relative to other countries, U.S. scores in reading and science literacy are not a cause for concern. According to the U.S. Department of Education, in 2009, among American 15-year-old students the average combined reading literacy and science literacy scores were not significantly different from the average scores of the 34 OECD-member countries. But *mathematics* continues to be troubling. The average U.S. mathematics literacy score for 15-year-old students during the same year was below the average score of the 34 OECD member countries.[10]

While nearly 70 percent of American high school graduates pursue postsecondary education within two years of graduating, only about four in ten Americans have obtained either an associate or a bachelor's degree by their mid-twenties (Figure 3). Approximately another 10 percent have earned postsecondary certificates. This is a troubling reality. Of those who enroll in four-year colleges only 56 percent attain bachelor's degrees after six years, and less than 30 percent of those who enroll in community colleges obtain associate degrees within three years.[11]

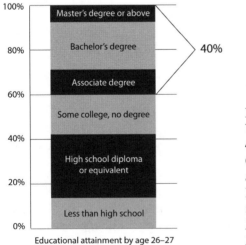

Figure 3. The Current U.S. Reality: Only 40 Percent of 27-Year-Olds Have Earned an A.A. Degree or Higher (Source: Symonds et al., *Pathways to Prosperity*, p. 10)

---

10 Aud et al., *The Condition of Education 2011*, p. 54.

11 Symonds et al., *Pathways to Prosperity*, p. 6.

The continuing decline of our "on time" college completion rates to alarming lows represents a great cost to students and to the nation as a whole.

Economic Growth Linked to Postsecondary Education

A recent publication by Anthony Carnevale et al. of Georgetown University's Center on Education and the Workforce forecasts the demand for "high school through college jobs" for the years 2008–2018.[12] According to the authors, the surest path to the middle class involves a postsecondary education. Opportunities for workers with only a high school diploma still exist, and will continue to do so in the foreseeable future, but in dwindling numbers and with lower earning potential, partly because of the steady rise of computer automation in virtually every type of workplace. Unfortunately, not everyone has the means to go directly from high school to college. Many experience delays and must work to pay their college expenses. Some lack motivation or are not prepared to attend postsecondary education.

Carnevale and his coauthors identify three general clusters of opportunities for future job seekers:

1. **High school jobs:** For those with high school diplomas or less

   - Opportunities for workers with only a high school diploma or less are declining—from 72 percent in 1973 to just 44 percent in 1992. And they are projected to drop to just 37 percent in 2018.

   - By 2018 only a third of the jobs available to those with a high school diploma or less will pay enough to meet the lower limit of the "minimum earning threshold" (MET).[13] The other two-thirds will pay less than this, suggesting

---

12 Anthony Carnevale et al., *Career Clusters: Forecasting Demand for High School Through College Jobs, 2008–2018,* November 2011 (http://cew.georgetown.edu/clusters).

13 Carnevale et al., *Career Clusters,* define the MET as "an absolute poverty-based definition of the earnings level that equals 150 percent of the federal poverty level (FPL) for a family of four. It can also be considered the wage level necessary to enter into the middle class" (p. 11).

that many workers with a high school diploma or less will struggle financially.

- Most of the jobs for workers with a high school diploma or less will be in hospitality and tourism (27 percent); transportation, distribution, and logistics (13 percent); architecture and construction (11 percent); and manufacturing (9 percent).

2. **Middle-skill jobs:** For those with some college but no degrees (including postsecondary vocational certificates) or associate degrees

- More than half of workers with associate degrees or better will earn above the MET threshold—even though their education typically costs far less than a four-year degree. Some of these jobs also offer significant job security and/ or are not in danger of being outsourced. Good examples are many jobs in health care; commercial construction; and the skilled operators needed to maintain oil refineries, chemical plants, and other industrial facilities.

- The best jobs for workers with some college but no degree, or associate degrees or postsecondary certifications, will be in health care; manufacturing; and business, management, and administration.

3. **Bachelor's-plus jobs:** For those with bachelor's degrees or better

- Almost 70 percent of workers with bachelor's degrees will earn above the MET; over 80 percent of holders of graduate-level credentials will earn above the MET.

- Essentially every job category is open to holders of bachelor's degrees or higher, especially the categories that are experiencing most rapid growth (e.g., health care).

Carnevale et al. assess both the positives and negatives of coming labor market trends:

On the hopeful side of the ledger: Once the economy has recovered from the recession, towards the end of the decade, there will be good employment opportunities for the entire range of educational attainment. Middle class aspirations need not die if, for some reason, college is out of reach for particular job seekers. . . . [G]ood paying jobs can still be found, even if the range of occupational clusters is relatively narrow.

On the sobering side of the ledger: The window is closing on such opportunity. Economic trends show that more and more jobs are requiring postsecondary credentials—especially those that pay a living wage. The days of workers graduating from high school, nabbing a job in the mail room of a big company and then working themselves into a corner office are pretty much gone. In their place is a demanding economy that puts a premium on education, training, and flexibility.

So, while high school graduates should not despair if they cannot go on to college, neither should they be satisfied with their diploma alone if they can further their education. . . . [G]oing to college pays off—not just in higher wages, but in better jobs, wider opportunity and a shot at achieving the American dream.[14]

The trends analyzed by Carnevale et al. do not merely impact individuals and the educational choices they make. They impact many American businesses and industries and the American economy as a whole. As the United States emerges from the current recession and hiring recovers to more robust levels, employers across the country may discover that there are not enough college graduates to go around. By 2018, according to a study by Carnevale, Smith, and Strohl, the American labor market will require 22 million new college degrees (about three million more than will be available, if current trends continue) and 4.7 million new workers with postsecondary certifications.[15] It's also becoming increasingly apparent that not all college degrees are created equal. While engineering graduates are in high demand, for instance, graduates who majored in fields like political science or psychology currently face more daunting prospects. This issue will become more pronounced as the cost of a four-year degree—along with the amount of debt held by recent graduates—continues to escalate.

---

14 Carnevale et al., *Career Clusters*, pp. 8–9.

15 Anthony Carnevale, Nicole Smith, and Jeff Strohl, *Help Wanted: Projections of Jobs and Education Requirements Through 2018*, June 2010 (http://cew.georgetown.edu/jobs2018), exec. summary, p. 1.

If we continue to underproduce workers with postsecondary credentials, the large and growing gap between the earnings of Americans
of different educational attainment will grow even wider.[16] Figure 4
shows the percentage of adults ages 25–34, by educational attainment,
who were employed full-time in 2010. As the figure makes clear,
young adults with postsecondary credentials fare much better in the
labor market than do those with only a high school diploma or less.
The difference between outcomes for those with bachelor's degrees
and those with less than a high school diploma is more than 30 percent
(73 percent versus 41 percent). The advantage enjoyed by holders of
associate degrees over their less educated peers is also striking.

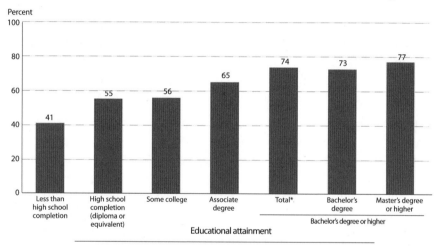

*Percentage of young adults with bachelor's degrees or higher who were employed full time

**Figure 4. Percentage of Adults Ages 25–34 Who Were Employed
Full Time, by Educational Attainment, 2010 (Source: Aud et al.,
The Condition of Education 2011, Indicator 18)**

Figure 5 shows the percentage of adults ages 25–34, by race and
educational attainment, who were *un*employed in 2010. Using three
general levels of educational attainment (less than high school completion, high school completion [diploma or equivalent], and bachelor's
degree or higher), the figure shows that employment outcomes among
all racial and ethnic groups improve dramatically with attainment of
postsecondary credentials.

---

16 Carnevale and Rose, *The Undereducated American.*

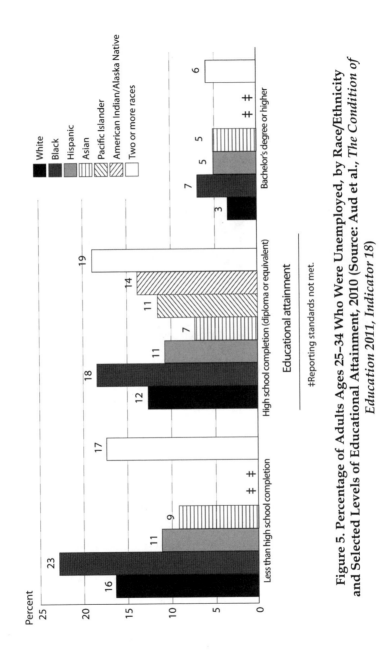

Figure 5. Percentage of Adults Ages 25–34 Who Were Unemployed, by Race/Ethnicity and Selected Levels of Educational Attainment, 2010 (Source: Aud et al., *The Condition of Education 2011, Indicator 18*)

Whether a person has a postsecondary credential or not signifi-cantly affects earning potential. Figure 6 shows the earnings gap between a high school diploma and a bachelor's degree.

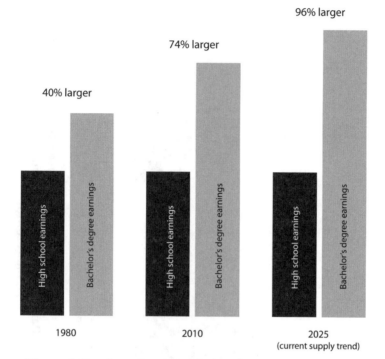

Figure 6. Earnings Gap Between a High School Diploma and a Bachelor's Degree (Source: Carnevale and Rose, *The Undereducated American*)

So the mission is clear — increasing the number of American workers with the right postsecondary skill sets and credentials. Augmenting the American workforce by several million postsecondary educated workers over the next 15 years is not out of the question. It will raise our educational attainment to a level that is comparable to that of other developed nations, help us meet the economy's need for high-level skills, and close the growing gap in incomes.[17] But even opti-

---

17 Carnevale and Rose, *The Undereducated American*. See also *The Credential Differential: The Public Return to Increasing Postsecondary Credential Attainment*, Center for Postsecondary and Economic Success (CLASP) (http://www.clasp.org/admin/site/publications/files/Full-Paper-The-Credential-Differential.pdf).

mists would concede that this is a huge challenge, considering the increasing cost of a college education, soaring levels of student debt, and recent declines in median family income. So meeting the challenge will clearly require innovative responses, from both policymakers and institutions.

One Size Does Not Fit All

One reason the current U.S. education system is falling short of its potential in the preparation of young adults for careers is that it continues to take a one-size-fits-all approach. "The whole system is geared to [transitioning from high school to a four-year degree]," writes Anthony Carnevale. "You need to have more than a one-size-fits-all. Everyone assumes education is very linear—you get a high school degree, you go to college and you go to work. The truth is, the issue for most people is what are they going to do next? A lot of those kids who come out of high school and don't go to college end up wandering around."[18] And as the wave of recent media stories has made clear, even many four-year graduates are uncertain about their place in the economy and unable to find a job that requires a four-year degree.

While much emphasis is placed in high school on going to four-year colleges, only a third of the jobs created in the coming years are expected to require bachelor's degrees or higher. Roughly the same number will require only associate degrees or occupational credentials.[19] Moreover, these degrees and credentials typically cost far less than a four-year degree, meaning students have to take on less debt.

According to Symonds et al., our education system "has not evolved to serve young adults in this radically different world. Behaving as though four-year college is the only acceptable route to success clearly still works well for many young adults, especially students fortunate enough to attend highly selective colleges and universities. It also works well for affluent students, who can often draw on family and

---

18 Karen Farkas, "Is a College Education Worth the Price?" September 2011, *Cleveland Plain Dealer* (http://blog.cleveland.com/metro/2011/09/is_a_college_education_worth_t.html).
19 Carnevale et al., *Help Wanted*.

social connections to find their way in the adult world. But it clearly does not work well for many."[20]

Within the U.S. economy, there is growing evidence of a "skills gap" in which many young adults lack the skills and work ethic needed for many jobs that pay middle-class wages. The skills required are not merely "hard" (technical) skills but "soft" skills—the ability to work in teams, communicate, and demonstrate a strong work ethic, for example—skills that are more likely to be learned in postsecondary settings than in high school. The realities of our economy demand both types of skills. Many of the nation's most prominent companies are increasingly reluctant to hire young people with only a high school diploma. When hiring begins to resume its normal pace after the current recession has run its course, businesses may face skill shortages across a wide range of occupations, from non-residential construction and energy to information technology, health care, and the STEM fields (Science, Technology, Engineering, and Mathematics)—almost all of which require at least some postsecondary education, *but not necessarily bachelor's degrees.*[21]

In 21st-century America, education beyond the high school diploma is the still the surest passport to the "American Dream." But this raises the question: "How much and what kind of postsecondary does the new American economy really require?" According to some projections, 14 million job openings—nearly half of those that will be filled by workers with postsecondary credentials—will go to people with associate degrees or occupational certificates.[22]

In his February 2009 address to Congress, President Obama laid out a path to restoring America's international leadership in postsecondary attainment.

> Tonight I ask every American to commit to at least one year or more of higher education or career training. This can be community college, a four-year school, vocational training, or an apprenticeship. But whatever the training may be, every American will need to get more than a high school diploma.

---

20 Symonds et al., *Pathways to Prosperity*, p. 13.

21 Symonds et al., *Pathways to Prosperity*.

22 Symonds et al., *Pathways to Prosperity*.

What is most noteworthy about the President's statement is the implicit recognition that if the United States is going to make dramatic progress in reclaiming its historic leadership position in postsecondary attainment, it must focus much more attention and resources on programs and pathways that prepare young people for middle-skill jobs (i.e., jobs requiring more than a high school diploma but less than a bachelor's degree). By calling attention to the central role that community colleges, Career Technical Education programs, and apprenticeships can play in moving us toward the goal of greater postsecondary attainment, the President is acknowledging that the "college for all" rhetoric that has been so much a part of the current education reform movement should be significantly broadened to become a "post high school credential for all."

The Rising Demand for Employability and STEM Skills

Today's advanced economies, innovation-driven industries and firms, and high-growth jobs require more highly educated workers with the ability to respond quickly to complex problems, communicate clearly, manage information effectively, work in teams, and produce knowledge. Companies are hiring workers with a higher skill set, particularly expert thinking and complex communication skills.[23]

All Americans, not just an elite few, need 21st-century skills that will increase their marketability, employability, and readiness for citizenship. These skills include:

- Thinking critically and making judgments about the barrage of information that workers receive every day
- Solving complex, multidisciplinary, open-ended problems that all workers, in every kind of workplace, encounter routinely
- Creativity and entrepreneurial thinking—a skill set that is highly associated with job creation
- Communicating and collaborating with teams of people across cultural, geographic, and language boundaries

---

23 *21st Century Skills, Education & Competitiveness: A Resource and Policy Guide*, 2008, Partnership for 21st Century Skills (http://www.p21.org/storage/documents/21st_century_skills_education_and_competitiveness_guide.pdf).

- Making innovative use of knowledge, information, and opportunities to create new services, processes, and products

- Taking charge of financial, health, and civic responsibilities and making wise choices[24]

Skills in STEM fields are critical to America's economic competitiveness because they directly impact innovation, productivity, and economic growth.[25] Even though in the coming decade jobs in STEM fields will account for only about 5 percent of all U.S. jobs, STEM skills are in demand across a wide range of Career Clusters™. STEM-skilled technicians are needed in advanced manufacturing, utilities and transportation, mining, health care, and other technology-driven industries — throughout the U.S. economy. While the number of U.S. workers with STEM skills is growing, the demand is growing faster. Even in Career Clusters™ that are reducing their overall employment (e.g., utilities and transportation), the demand for STEM competencies is rising. Thus, the current U.S. education system is not producing enough graduates with strong STEM skills. The resulting shortage impacts both employers, who struggle to find qualified workers, and potential employees, who miss out on the significantly higher earnings that STEM skills provide. Occupations that require STEM competencies are among the highest paid in the U.S. economy.

One cause of the current shortage of STEM talent is *diversion*, "a process through which both students and workers steer away from STEM degrees and STEM careers for numerous reasons. Diversion, which affects more than 75 percent of the students whose abilities qualify them to pursue STEM careers, is both voluntary and involuntary and students and workers divert at various points throughout K-12 and postsecondary education as well as in the workforce."[26] Nearly 40 percent of students who enter the STEM pipeline in college divert to other fields while in college, and a comparable percentage of STEM graduates choose not to work in STEM fields. Diversion

---

24 *21st Century Skills, Education & Competitiveness.*

25 The remarks in this section are based on Anthony Carnevale, Nicole Smith, and Michelle Melton, *STEM: Science, Technology, Engineering, Mathematics,* October 2011, Georgetown University Center on Education and the Workforce (http://cew.georgetown.edu/stem).

26 Carnevale et al., *STEM.*

is a major cause of American employers' increasing reliance on foreign-born STEM talent.

STEM competencies are valued partly because they are widely applicable. As Carnevale et al. point out,

> The core work interests associated with STEM occupations are Realistic and Investigative interests. People with these work interests enjoy practical, hands-on problem-solving (Realistic) and working with ideas and solving problems (Investigative), but there are other work interests that compete for STEM talent, including Artistic interests (focused on self-expression); Social interests (focused on the well-being of others); Enterprising interests (associated with selling and leading); and Conventional interests (associated with highly ordered work environments).
>
> Similarly, the work values associated with STEM are Achievement, Independence, and Recognition, but there are other work values that compete for STEM talent such as Relationships (valuing friendly, noncompetitive work environments), Support (valuing supportive management), and Working Conditions (valuing job security and good working conditions). (p. 4)

Other key aspects of the current demand for STEM skills include the following:

1. Traditional STEM jobs have grown faster than job growth overall for decades, and the future promises more of the same.

2. By 2018, roughly 35 percent of the STEM workforce will be composed of those with sub-baccalaureate training, including 1 million associate degrees, 745,000 certificates, and 760,000 industry-based certifications.

3. STEM wages are high and have kept up with wages as a whole over the last 30 years. STEM workers have earnings advantages at nearly every level of educational attainment.

4. Women and minorities (excepting Asians) continue to be underrepresented in STEM occupations, and are paid less than white males, relative to their positions in the labor market as a whole. Women are strong in educational programs that lead to careers in health care but are less strongly represented in engineering and physical sciences occupations.

5. In recent years, STEM positions in the United States have been disproportionately filled by foreign-born workers.

6. Going forward, the U.S. labor market will require more workers with STEM competencies, though not necessarily traditional STEM workers in traditional STEM jobs.

7. The STEM jobs of the future will not be just for the elite few at the top of the educational ladder. The rising demand for STEM competencies outside traditional STEM occupations calls for a broader-reaching strategy in the U.S. K-16 education system.

8. A significant proportion of the STEM jobs of the future will continue to require postsecondary education but not necessarily bachelor's degrees. The role of secondary and sub-baccalaureate education in strengthening the STEM pipeline is critical. Going forward, our CTE system will need a stronger STEM curriculum at the high school and sub-baccalaureate levels that is more closely linked to the competencies required for STEM jobs.

The STEM workforce will remain essential to U.S. economic vitality in the coming years, contributing to innovation, technological advancement, and economic development. From K-12 through the postgraduate level, the pipeline will require capable STEM students for careers that use STEM competencies and increase our capacity for innovation. The United States cannot win the future without recognizing the growing need for STEM competencies throughout the economy. The need for STEM talent is great, not only in traditional STEM occupations but across the entire spectrum of occupations.

Achieving Our Educational and Economic Goals Through Career Pathways

This chapter gives the reader a picture of current conditions in education and the labor market in the United States. The following goals for educators stand out:

1. To increase the number of holders of postsecondary credentials, not only bachelor's degrees and beyond but associate degrees and occupational certifications.

2. To strengthen the secondary-to-postsecondary pipeline, specifically by enabling more high school graduates to begin postsecondary education ready for true college-level courses, rather than remedial instruction.

3. To increase emphasis on STEM competencies, bearing in mind that the skills required are broad and apply to many more fields than traditional STEM fields.

4. To increase opportunities for historically underrepresented and lower-paid minorities and women.

5. To establish partnerships that enable educators to respond quickly to changes in the labor market so that graduates at every level can be prepared for the challenges of the workplace.

6. To increase the college and career readiness of every American student.

The current national attention being given to College and Career Readiness and to the Common Core Standards, discussed in later chapters, gives us hope that we can reach these goals.

Comparative International Approaches

William C. Symonds

All across the United States, there is widespread agreement that we have lost our global leadership in preparing young people to lead successful lives as adults. No wonder. As observed in the 2011 report of Harvard's *Pathways to Prosperity* Project, the evidence of our comparative decline is as incontrovertible as it is alarming.[1] U.S. Secretary of Education Arne Duncan recently warned, "Our nation faces urgent educational problems. . . . In international comparisons, our performance is mediocre at best. It's telling that the only thing our students lead the world in is self-esteem. The hard truth is that many nations are out-performing and out-educating us."[2]

The decline in American educational leadership has been coupled with another worrisome development: the growing difficulty teens and young adults are having in successfully transitioning to the labor market. As economists Paul Harrington and Neeta Fogg documented in a recent article, unemployment among 16- to 24-year-olds has doubled over the past decade. "The nation's teen unemployment rate rose from 13 percent in 2000 to 26 percent in 2010," they write. "Among young adults between the ages of 20 and 24, the unemployment rate increased from 7 percent in 2000 to over 15 percent in 2010."

---

1 William C. Symonds, Robert B. Schwartz, and Ronald Ferguson, *Pathways to Prosperity: Meeting the Challenge of Preparing Young Americans for the 21st Century,* Pathways to Prosperity Project, February 2011, Harvard Graduate School of Education (http://www.gse.harvard.edu/news_events/features/2011/Pathways_to_Prosperity_Feb2011.pdf).

2 From remarks delivered by Education Secretary Arne Duncan at the Harvard Graduate School of Education on February 7, 2012 (http://www.ed.gov/blog/2012/02/in-boston-arne-says-we-must-invest-in-education/).

Moreover, many young adults have simply dropped out of the labor market entirely (meaning they don't show up in the unemployment numbers). That's illustrated by a sharp drop in the labor force participation rate among both teens and young adults.[3]

To be sure, the Great Recession contributed to this spike in unemployment. But the trend was apparent well before the Recession began in 2008. And coupled with the decline in our educational performance, it has ominous implications for the future of the U.S. economy. The teen and young adult years are critically important in acquiring the skills needed to lead a successful life as an adult. The fact that so many of our young adults are not learning and developing the skills they need to prosper in the 21st century—either in school or in the workplace—suggests we are in danger of creating a "wasted generation" of millions of young people who will never realize their full potential. And that would be both a human and an economic tragedy.

Many reasons have been offered for the comparative U.S. decline, including the fact that some nations do a much better job of recruiting, training, and rewarding high-quality teachers. But the most important reason we've lost ground is arguably that some other leading nations have developed superior systems of vocational education—what we in the United States call Career Technical Education (CTE). These systems offer an attractive and highly effective alternative to academic programs of study designed for those who want to attend universities. In effect, these nations—including many of the most prosperous nations in central and northern Europe, as well as Australia and New Zealand—are offering teens multiple pathways to success.

Take Finland, which has often been celebrated as "number one" in education, thanks in part to its superior performance on the Programme for International Student Assessment (PISA). In his compelling 2011 documentary—*The Finland Phenomenon: Inside the World's Most Surprising School System*—Dr. Tony Wagner noted that virtually half of Finnish teens choose the vocational track when they arrive at "upper secondary" school (which most students enter around age 16). Vocational education prepares them for skilled jobs

---

3 Neeta Fogg and Paul Harrington, "The Collapse of the Labor Market for 16- to 24-Year-Olds," Fall 2011, Federal Reserve Bank of Philadelphia (http://www.philadelphiafed.org/community-development/publications/cascade/78/04_collapse-of-16-to-24-labor-market.cfm).

in the highly advanced Finnish economy—which is home to Nokia, one of the early leaders in cell phones—but also for further study, including university, if they wish. Wagner was deeply impressed with how Finnish vocational education engages high school students. "I have to wonder if we gave every American high school student a choice of enrolling in high-caliber vocational education, might we not significantly reduce our epidemic dropout rate?" Wagner concluded.[4]

Finland is not unique in its recognition of the importance of vocational education. There's growing evidence from many places that high-quality vocational education is more effective than a strictly academic approach in increasing educational performance and attainment, as well as in helping young adults make a successful transition to the workforce. And yet the idea that vocational education is a key reason other countries are surpassing us comes as a surprise—if not a shock—to many Americans. In recent years, the United States has taken an increasingly academic approach to high school, with the goal of preparing students to attend four-year colleges—widely seen as the preferred pathway to success.

The work of the *Pathways to Prosperity* Project has challenged this thinking. We argue that the nation must adopt a broader, more holistic approach to education and youth development. Perhaps the strongest argument in favor of this is that many other leading countries have already built successful multiple-pathway systems. The Pathways report was informed by a growing body of research on these systems. Most notably, in late 2010, the Organisation for Economic Co-operation and Development (OECD) published *Learning for Jobs*, perhaps the most extensive study ever done of vocational education.[5] Then, in late 2011 (after the Pathways report was published), Dr. Nancy Hoffman—a vice president at Jobs for the Future who was involved in the OECD study—published a book that helps translate the OECD findings for an American audience. This chapter draws heavily on her book—*Schooling in the Workplace: How Six of the World's Best Vocational Education Systems Prepare Young People for Jobs and Life*

---

4 *The Finland Phenomenon: Inside the World's Most Surprising School System* was produced by Robert Compton and released by New School Films in 2011.

5 ISBN 9789264087460, http://www.oecd.org/edu/highereducationandadultlearning/oecdreviewsofvocationaleducationandtraining-learningforjobs.htm

(Harvard Education Press, 2011) — as well as on OECD's *Learning for Jobs.*

The bottom line is that the United States is increasingly an outlier in its approach to education and youth development. While we continue to overemphasize the academic, four-year-college pathway, other nations are increasingly embracing high-quality vocational education. If we hope to regain our leadership in education, we must adopt a broader approach, one that puts far more emphasis on development of a world-class, rigorous system of multiple pathways. A central component of this system must be high-quality CTE that is widely available to students across the country, rather than just in islands of excellence, as is the case today.

This chapter offers a closer look at some of the best foreign systems of vocational education. We'll examine how they're structured and how they work to prepare students to lead successful lives as adults. We'll then examine the key principles and practices embodied in these high-quality systems, as well as the evidence for their effectiveness. Finally, we'll consider what all this means for the United States.

When Vocational Education Is Intended for Most Students: Inside the Best Foreign Systems

Most of the world's advanced nations place far more emphasis on vocational education than we do. In the prosperous nations of central and northern Europe, as well as in Australia and New Zealand, vocational education is seen as a mainstream system that is best able to prepare many if not most teens to lead successful lives as adults. From Finland, the Netherlands, and Denmark to Germany, Switzerland, and Austria, 40 to 70 percent of the students in "upper secondary" school (which begins around what we call 10th grade) are involved in what is known as vocational education and training (VET). And in Switzerland, which has arguably the world's best system of vocational education, two-thirds of students opt for this more real-world approach, while just a third take a more academic route to university.[6]

This is a world apart from the United States, where CTE is often disparaged and demeaned. In recent years, we Americans have increasingly come to believe that by far the best pathway to success

---

6 OECD, *Learning for Jobs,* pp. 31–34.

is to attend a four-year college. In turn, that implies that high school should be devoted to taking an academic, college-prep curriculum that leaves little room for CTE. For most students, this means that CTE courses are crowded into the small amount of the schedule allotted to "electives." In an excellent new book on the U.S. system — *College and Career Ready in the 21st Century: Making High School Matter* (Teachers College Press, 2012) – authors James R. Stone, former director of the National Research Center for Career and Technical Education, and Morgan V. Lewis report that 97 percent of all high school graduates in 2005 took at least one CTE course. "The average graduate earned a half credit in family and consumer sciences, a second half credit in general labor market preparation, and three credits in occupational courses," they write. But just 21 percent of graduates qualified as CTE concentrators — meaning that they earned three or more credits in a sequence of related courses within a defined occupational area. In effect, most U.S. high school students are dipping their toes into career education, even as their counterparts in countries like Germany and Switzerland are experiencing total immersion.[7]

Foreign systems of vocational education are not all cut from the same cloth. Germany and Switzerland are the best-known examples of the "dual apprenticeship" model, in which students typically spend three days a week at the place of employment, the other day or two being devoted to academic work in the classroom. These intense programs often last for three to four years and are carefully designed to prepare students to succeed not just in narrow jobs but in careers and adult life. Students are given an immense number of choices. In Germany, more than 1.6 million students are enrolled in training programs for some 360 occupations. And in Switzerland, students can choose from among 230 careers. The options extend far beyond the "trades" and include many apprenticeships in what we Americans would consider "white collar" professions, such as banking and telecommunications.[8]

Indeed, Hoffman notes that in Switzerland one of the most popular apprenticeship programs is offered by Swisscom, the country's leading telecom provider. In 2010, Swisscom chose 813 apprentices from more

---

7 Stone and Lewis, *College and Career Ready*.

8 Nancy Hoffman, *Schooling in the Workplace: How Six of the World's Best Vocational Education Systems Prepare Young People for Jobs and Life* (Harvard Education Press, 2011), pp. 76–77.

than 7,000 applicants—a degree of selectivity that rivals that of the most elite U.S. colleges. These apprentices choose from among five lines of work within Swisscom, ranging from IT specialist to technician and client-relations specialist. Each apprentice is assigned a "coach." Apprentices undertake projects that can last from two months to a year, and that expose them to the kind of issues they would confront as full-time employees. At Swisscom, some apprentices work in the company's phone stores, where they help customers find the phones and plans that will best suit their needs. Similarly, in an apprenticeship offered by a Swiss regional bank, some apprentices are asked to evaluate requests for home improvement loans and to then tell the applicants if the loans have been approved.[9]

Other countries structure their systems of vocational education quite differently, and often put more emphasis on school-based instruction. Norway offers what is known as a "two-plus-two" system, in which students spend the first two years in school studying a mixture of academic subjects (including English, Norwegian, math, and economics) and their vocational majors. The next two years are devoted to working as apprentices, during which students are paid a portion of the regular wages associated with jobs for which they are training. The Norwegian VET program ends with a final exam that leads to a recognized qualification, typically a craftsman or journeyman certificate. And the training is good enough that virtually all students pass the exam.[10]

In the Netherlands, some 70 percent of students in upper-secondary are involved in vocational education, but most of these are in school-based programs, while just a third are in apprenticeships. Similarly, vocational education has been booming in Australia, where 60 percent of 11th- and 12th-grade students are involved. Most get much of their education in school and then leave school to work at sponsoring companies for blocks of time.[11]

Americans often dismiss foreign vocational education on the grounds that some countries track students into vocational programs based on their test scores. The best-known example of tracking is the German system, which sorts students into different types of middle

---

9 Hoffman, *Schooling in the Workplace,* p. 133.

10 Hoffman, *Schooling in the Workplace,* pp. 87–88.

11 Hoffman, *Schooling in the Workplace.*

schools after 4th grade. The academically strongest students go to a *Gymnasium,* which can ultimately lead to universities. The middle group attends *Realschule,* which at age 16 can lead to vocational education or, for those who have done best, back to a *gymnasium.* And the weakest students are sent to the *Hauptschule,* which culminates in a separate school-leaving certificate that is seen as inferior. At the Pathways to Prosperity Project, we vigorously condemn such rigid tracking systems and argue they have no place in America. Instead, we contend that individual students, along with their parents, should make decisions about which pathways they wish to pursue. It's also important to note that the German system is hardly universal, and that many other countries have more flexible systems. Finland and Denmark, for instance, keep all students in a common, untracked comprehensive school up through grade 9 or 10, after which the students and their families decide which kind of upper secondary education to pursue.[12]

The controversy over tracking practices has unfortunately obscured many other commendable features of the best foreign VET systems. While many Americans sometimes still denigrate vocational education as narrow training for "dead-end" jobs, the German system is designed to equip students with a comprehensive set of competencies that will enable them to prosper as adults—including personal traits such as reliability and self-confidence and social competencies such as the ability to form good relationships, along with technical and critical thinking skills. The curriculum is not "dumbed down." Those who complete high-quality programs have qualifications roughly equivalent to Americans who have earned technical degrees at community or technical colleges.[13]

While Americans worry that vocational education will deprive students of a "liberal" education, the best VET systems incorporate a strong dose of more general subjects in their curricula. In Switzerland, for example, most VET students study two or three languages, as well as economics, history, and math. In short, these systems fully recognize that they cannot hope to prepare youth for "one job for life." That kind of career path is as extinct in Europe as it is in the U.S. But unlike many Americans, these foreign educators believe that the *best* way to

---

12 Hoffman, *Schooling in the Workplace,* pp. 99–107.
13 Hoffman, *Schooling in the Workplace,* pp. 99–107.

prepare most young people for the 21st century is through a system that includes extensive exposure to working adults, real workplaces, and authentic work experience.[14]

Compared to the United States, the best VET systems also provide far clearer and more extensive "pathways" leading from school and/ or vocational training to employment in the careers of the students' choice. Most VET culminates with students earning qualifications that have real value in the labor market. In contrast, the U.S. has taken a scattershot approach to developing industry-recognized qualifications. Meanwhile, the European Union has embarked on a very ambitious effort to develop a "European Qualifications Network" that aims to standardize qualifications across Europe. One goal is to make it far easier for the more than 400 million people who live in the EU to move across borders to seek work—creating a kind of "common market" for labor.[15]

One final point is that VET also increasingly provides a pathway to postsecondary study. Switzerland, for instance, offers some 400 "professional education and training" programs (PET), which are tertiary-level programs for students who have completed VET. And in the Netherlands, about a quarter of VET students continue into tertiary-level programs after graduation. In short, students who choose the vocational route are not foreclosing the option of "going to college."

Learning for Jobs found that across the advanced industrialized world, there is an increasing emphasis on high-quality vocational education. Countries that already offer strong VET systems are working to improve them by expanding pathways to postsecondary education, adding apprenticeship opportunities and upgrading curriculum. And countries that have not been part of this tradition are now racing to create more high-quality pathways for young adults. New Zealand, for instance, has adopted an ambitious "youth guarantee" program that aims to increase the percentage of young people earning a "level 2 certificate" (the equivalent of a high school diploma) by expanding choices for students, including more trades academies and other vocational pathways. These pathways identify and describe the skills, knowledge, and competencies valued by a broad sector of industry,

---

14 OECD, *Learning for Jobs*, p. 2.
15 Hoffman, *Schooling in the Workplace*, pp. 37–43.

as well as important curriculum objectives, and include career maps to help students plan the way forward.[16]

And in an effort to increase its high school graduation rate, the Canadian province of Ontario has adopted a Student Success Strategy that aims to promote four pathways leading from high school: apprenticeship, polytechnical college, university, and actual work. A decade ago—when the effort got underway—research revealed that while Ontario high schools provided good pathways for students heading to university (what Americans call four-year colleges), only about a third of students were actually on the university pathway. Meanwhile, pathways for the majority of students were not as well developed. In response, Ontario developed the "Specialist High Skills Major," which allows students in 11th and 12th grade to pursue programs of study organized around any of 18 economic sectors, ranging from arts and culture to manufacturing and sports and transportation. These majors must incorporate five components. First, students must earn 8 to 10 course credits, including 4 credits in their "career majors," and two cooperative education credits designed to provide authentic workplace experience. The majors must also include industry-recognized certifications, experiential learning and career exploration, and documentation of the development of skills mastered using the Ontario Skills Passport.

This program has enjoyed enormous growth. By early 2011, there were some 28,000 students participating in 540 high schools. Even more encouraging, 94 percent of the students involved in the high-skills major are successfully completing their courses, which is well above the course completion rate for students on the university pathway. As a result, Ontario's graduation rate has risen sharply, from 68 percent to 79 percent.[17]

The clear conclusion is that the United States is increasingly out of the mainstream in the way it educates high school students. While other nations increasingly recognize the value of vocational education, many Americans continue to minimize its importance. Instead we've chosen to increase academic rigor, in the hope that this will produce the results we seek. Stone and Lewis note that by 2005 the

---

16 Materials prepared by the New Zealand Ministry of Education, summer 2011.

17 Ontario Ministry of Education.

average high school graduate earned a total of 17.4 academic credits, up from just 12.9 in 1982. "The average student in 2005 had, in effect, experienced one full year more academic courses," they write. And yet there's been no real improvement of 17-year-old students on the National Assessment of Education Progress (NAEP) reading, math, and science tests, known as the Nation's Report Card. Nor has there been a significant increase in the percentage of young adults who earn bachelor's degrees by their mid-20s. As we wrote in the Pathways report: "College for All might be the mantra, but the hard reality is that fewer than one in three young people achieve the dream." These disappointing results make a compelling case for carefully studying the best foreign systems of vocational education. We turn now to what these systems can teach us about the elements that are critical to creating effective career education.

The Most Important Features of the Best Foreign Systems

Though the best foreign systems vary considerably, they tend to embrace several key principles that help explain their success. The most important is extensive engagement of employers in every-thing from developing qualifications and assessments to providing ample opportunities for apprenticeships and other forms of work-based learning. For students, the most notable feature of VET is that they spend much of their time "learning for jobs," often right at an employer's place of work. Because students must choose from among many options, extensive career counseling is essential. Also essential are high-quality teachers to train students in the skills they need to succeed in their chosen vocations. Finally, the best foreign systems are increasingly adopting comprehensive "youth policies" that aim to serve all young people, including those most at risk of falling behind. Let's take a closer look at these five critical principles found in successful foreign vocational systems.

1. **Extensive employer engagement:** High-quality vocational education cannot succeed without the extensive involve-ment of employers. In Switzerland, for instance, trade asso-ciations and professional organizations help define the curric-ulum as well as the qualifications needed to enter jobs. And

about 30 percent of Swiss companies are directly involved in providing apprenticeships.[18] In Germany, which has by far the largest VET system, "economic chambers" that are organized by occupational sector assume responsibility for quality control by monitoring the quality of training in companies, assessing the qualifications of trainers, and even conducting final exams. They also make a huge financial investment, contributing about half the overall cost of providing VET training.[19] Similarly, employers in Australia, Denmark, and the Netherlands are also deeply involved in their systems.

Americans naturally wonder why these foreign employers are willing to make such a huge commitment to the education and training of young people. One reason is that they often receive financial incentives for participating. In addition, many countries allow firms to pay "training wages" to apprentices, which range from 30 to 80 percent of what qualified full-time workers would be paid initially. Though the training wage typically rises as the apprentice gains experience, studies suggest that the value of the work done by apprentices often exceeds the labor costs. Meanwhile, because most apprentices are under 20 and often live at home, the reduced wage can still be a powerful incentive. But the most important reason may be that many foreign employers believe this is the best way to identify and train a high-quality workforce. Not only can they ensure that apprentices are getting high-quality training, they also have a prolonged opportunity to observe them at work and are thus able to select the most capable for regular employment.[20]

2. **Ample apprenticeships and other opportunities for work-based learning:** *Learning for Jobs* identifies four types of work-based learning, two of which are typically unpaid (job shadowing and service learning) and two of which are based at the workplace (internships and apprenticeships). Ironically,

18 *Vocational and Professional Education and Training in Switzerland 2012: Facts and Figures,* Federal Office for Professional Education and Technology (http://www.bbt.admin.ch/themen/berufsbildung/index.html?lang=en).
19 Hoffman, *Schooling in the Workplace,* pp. 99–107.
20 Hoffman, *Schooling in the Workplace.*

the U.S. has recognized the value of such workplace training for some of the highest-paid, most prestigious professions. Beginning lawyers often serve as "associates" with major law firms, and new doctors are expected to complete internships and residencies. But the best foreign systems make far more extensive use of apprenticeships for a much wider range of careers. While they have long been used to train people for the "trades," increasingly apprenticeships are expanding into such "modern" fields as laboratory and hospital technicians, as well many IT occupations.[21]

Learning for Jobs identifies four major advantages of training young people at workplaces, rather than in schools. First, it allows students to learn and practice skills on state-of-the-art equipment under the supervision of trainers who are completely familiar with current work practices. (U.S. CTE teachers are all too aware that this is often not the case in our school-based programs.) Second, students can develop essential "soft" skills — such as learning to work in teams and dealing with customers — in real-world environments. Third, workplace learning facilitates the transition to more permanent employment by allowing both the apprentice and the employer to learn more about each other. And finally, while they are learning, apprentices are also making positive contributions to the businesses for which they work.

Of course, these benefits all hinge on the quality of workplace training. The danger is that unscrupulous companies will take advantage of "cheap labor" or offer training that is so narrow that it won't prepare the apprentice for the broader labor market. To guard against this, apprentices often sign contracts that help guarantee their rights, and industry organizations oversee and inspect companies that offer apprenticeship training. But done well, apprenticeship training offers enormous benefits to both students and employers.[22]

3. **Comprehensive career counseling:** Career counseling is essential to help students choose careers that will be both personally

---

21 OECD, *Learning for Jobs.*
22 OECD, *Learning for Jobs.*

rewarding and in-demand in the labor market. The best foreign systems make this a high priority. In Japan, Norway, and Finland, for instance, nearly 100 percent of schools schedule career guidance into the school day. Comprehensive career guidance educates students about the broad labor market and then helps students make informed choices about the careers for which they are best suited. In addition, to ensure that students are being trained for jobs that will actually exist, these countries regulate openings for apprenticeships so that they correspond to expected labor market demand.

Americans are well aware of the problems that can undermine career counseling. In many other countries, as in the United States, "counselors" often spend much of their time dealing with the psychological and social challenges faced by teens, rather than career guidance. Many of these counselors don't have a comprehensive understanding of labor market opportunities and consequently steer students toward only a limited range of options—like four-year colleges in the United States. *Learning for Jobs* argues that, given these challenges, career guidance should be its own profession, separate from psychological and social counseling. And these professionals should be well trained *and* have access to a wide range of up-to-date materials on labor market opportunities. Without such guidance, students often make critically important career decisions on the basis of advice from well-meaning but poorly informed friends and family members. And this approach—which is all too common in the United States—tends to perpetuate inequalities, since low-income parents are less likely to know how to direct their children to higher-status occupations.[23]

The Swiss have one of the world's best systems. Career guidance counselors must complete a rigorous training program that includes a year-long internship and culminates in a specialized diploma. For students, career education and career guidance are mandatory beginning in middle school. This begins at a student's school but often continues at so-called BIZ centers, which are separate institutions designed

---

23 OECD, *Learning for Jobs.*

to provide career information and guidance. In addition, middle-school students may take part in short "work placements" that give them a real taste of what an apprenticeship is like. Most students take part in these before making a final choice. Similarly, to help ensure quality and availability, New Zealand has created a government agency—Careers New Zealand—that provides career information, guidance, and support to both students and adults. Careers NZ works closely with business and industry to stay abreast of emerging opportunities, as well as with counselors in schools to help them offer high-quality career programs.[24]

4. **High-quality teachers:** The quality of teachers and trainers, both in vocational schools and at the workplace, is an essential ingredient in building an excellent system. The "meisters" who oversee German apprentices are legendary for their expertise in their fields, as well as for the exacting standards they typically set for students. But *Learning for Jobs* found that many countries are struggling to build a high-quality corps of teachers and trainers. And this challenge is compounded by the fact that many vocational teachers are nearing the end of their teaching careers.

   One critical issue is ensuring that trainers are current with the latest industry practices and procedures. Teachers and trainers who work in school-based settings can easily lose touch with evolving practices. One Australian study, for instance, found that nearly three out of four full-time trainers felt that their technical knowledge was not up to date.[25] That's why the OECD report endorsed the practice of employing trainers who spend part of their time working in industry. Of course, this is easier if the students are trained directly at the place of employment, as they are in the dual-apprenticeship model.

   To help ensure the quality of teachers and trainers, the Swiss have created a Federal Institute for Vocational Education and Training (SFIVET), which provides programs for those who

---

24 OECD, *Learning for Jobs;* interview conducted by the author with Careers New Zealand.

25 OECD, *Learning for Jobs.*

want to teach in vocational schools and professional colleges, as well as continuing education for existing teachers and trainers. It also conducts research and evaluations of current teaching. In addition, companies must meet certain quality standards before they are allowed to take on apprentices. And the Swiss cantons employ inspectors who interview apprentices and employees in participating companies to ensure the quality of training.[26]

5. **Comprehensive youth policies:** Countries with the most successful vocational education programs have usually adopted financial policies and practices that strongly encourage young people to continue and complete their education. The practice of paying apprentices—even if they receive only a "training wage"—gives students a strong financial incentive and some measure of financial independence. And because their work is intimately tied to their studies, they don't face the kind of juggling act that so many American students do. In the U.S., many college students must work to help pay for their education, and yet that work is often disconnected from their programs of study. In sharp contrast, students enrolled in foreign apprenticeship programs don't have to pay for their education. Their countries tend to view education as a public investment in the nation's future rather than (as in the U.S.) solely a private good.

Some countries go even further, providing "guarantees" aimed at youth who are most at-risk of dropping out. Australia, for instance, has adopted a policy that provides that youth aged 15 to 24 are entitled to education and/or employment training. That's the carrot. The stick is that young people who refuse to take part risk losing government-provided support. This is a powerful incentive for students to remain engaged and enrolled in their programs. Similarly, to help ensure that all young people earn the equivalent of a high-school diploma, New Zealand has embraced a youth guarantee policy that includes creating more "free" opportunities for youth to get training and education, alternative pathways, and expanded

---

26 OECD, *Learning for Jobs.*

career education and counseling. The bottom line is that these countries recognize the huge long-term benefit of ensuring that young people are prepared for success. In contrast, in the U.S., we are effectively tolerating a situation in which millions of young Americans are entering their 20s without the skills and education they need to prosper in the 21st century economy.[27]

The Superior Outcomes of the Best Foreign Systems

The most persuasive argument in support of the best foreign systems is that they are clearly doing a much better job of helping their young people successfully transition from adolescence to productive lives as adults. It is not surprising that high-quality vocational education is more effective than a more academic approach in helping young people enter the workforce. But there are three other benefits that might not be as obvious. First, there is persuasive evidence that most teens actually learn more in high-quality vocational education. Second, this pedagogical effectiveness—combined with the fact that students in vocational education tend to be more engaged—helps produce higher rates of attainment. And third, work-based learning— and especially apprenticeships—are especially effective in helping teens navigate the transition to adulthood. Let's take a closer look at these four benefits of high-quality vocational education:

1. **The pedagogical benefits:** *Learning for Jobs* presents impressive evidence that from late adolescence on, most teens learn best in structured programs that combine work and learning. It's not just that, as the report argues, "workplaces provide a good place to learn both hard skills on modern equipment and soft skills in terms of working with people in a real-world context."[28] Learning in a real-world environment also helps mathematical principles and the need for literacy skills and other academic concepts and objectives come alive in a way that they simply don't (at least for many students) in a classroom. That's borne out by the PISA assessments. In 2009, U.S. 15-year-olds ranked well below their counterparts in

---

27 Presentation prepared by the New Zealand Ministry of Education; Hoffman, *Schooling in the Workplace.*
28 OECD, *Learning for Jobs.*

many countries that place far more emphasis on vocational education, including Finland, Switzerland, Australia, and New Zealand. The same trend was observed in science literacy.[29] The performance of U.S. teens was disappointing. They ranked just 17th on science achievement, and 25th on math achievement. At a time when so many educators and business leaders are arguing we need to devote more attention to the STEM subjects, this should be a wake-up call.

Ironically, the United States has long embraced work-based learning for some of our most prestigious professions. Surgeons, for example, are trained in rigorous residency programs in which they must spend hours in the operating room, working under the guidance of master surgeons. Similarly, many of our most promising law-school graduates become associates in large law firms, where they work alongside experienced partners. But when it comes to high school students—and especially those who are struggling academically—we somehow think the best way for them to learn is to force them to sit in a classroom all day. Such struggling students are often told they cannot take CTE classes until they master the academics. Yet in many of the countries that are surpassing us, educators believe that a better way to develop academic skills is to embed them in high-quality vocational programs that include work-based learning.[30]

2. **Higher attainment:** Every recent U.S. president has bemoaned the comparative decline in U.S. educational attainment, and then vowed to reverse this troubling trend, often by redoubling our efforts to improve academic education. Yet many of the countries that are surpassing us are those that place greater priority on vocational education. Moreover, many countries with strong vocational systems have made greater strides in increasing attainment in recent years. One powerful reason for this is that students in high-quality vocational education are

29 *Highlights from PISA 2009: Performance of U.S. 15-Year-Old Students in Reading, Mathematics, and Science Literacy in an International Context, National Center for Education Statistics,* December 2010, U.S. Department of Education (http://nces.ed.gov/pubs2011/2011004.pdf).
30 Hoffman, *Schooling in the Workplace,* pp. 99–107.

often more engaged than those in academic education. Indeed, studies of why U.S. students drop out of high school show that boredom and a feeling that the education is irrelevant to their future are often key drivers. But students in vocational education don't wonder if their education is relevant — it clearly is, even if they ultimately decide they don't want to pursue those particular vocations.

The effectiveness of vocational education in increasing attainment is apparent in the leading systems. Consider Switzerland, where two-thirds of upper secondary students choose to enroll in vocational education. That's helped Switzerland achieve a 90 percent upper-secondary graduation rate (and students with this qualification are often ahead of U.S. high school graduates). Increasingly, these graduates are going on to postsecondary education. Similarly, in Germany, most students earn "VET qualifications" at the conclusion of their apprenticeship, which certifies that they have completed the training and education needed to enter a field. The standards for these VET qualifications are quite rigorous, and certainly equivalent to what Americans must learn to earn some postsecondary degrees, such as many AA degrees. In effect, perhaps 75 percent of German students earn what we Americans would consider a postsecondary certificate, well above our own rate of around 50 percent.[31]

3. **The impact on youth employment and the transition to the labor market:** As you would expect, high-quality vocational education is excellent preparation for entering the workforce, especially since students are often required to earn certificates with real value in the labor market. Another factor is that employers in countries with strong apprenticeship systems are already committed to helping young people find their way in the labor market. In the strongest economies, the payoff has been dramatic. In mid-2010 — despite a sluggish recovery from the Great Recession — unemployment among youth under age 25 was less than 10 percent in Germany. And in Switzerland it was under 5 percent. In contrast, youth unemployment is around 50 percent in the southern European countries of

---

31 Hoffman, *Schooling in the Workplace,* pp. 99–107.

Greece and Spain, where the economies are much weaker and apprenticeship programs are nowhere near as strong.[32]

But even though the U.S. economy is significantly outperforming Europe, the unemployment rate among youth 16 to 24 has more than doubled over the past decade, and for teens it reached 24 percent in early 2012 — nearly three times the national unemployment rate of 8.3 percent. Bad as they are, these figures understate the problem. For in recent years the percentage of teens and young adults who have "dropped out" of the labor market has risen sharply. In 2011 the percentage of teens who were employed fell to just 26 percent, down from over 45 percent in 2000. Similarly, the percentage of young adults who are employed fell to 61 percent, from 72 percent in 2000. "These are the lowest employment/population ratios for both teens and young adults ever recorded in the U.S. since the end of World War II," writes Andrew Sum, director of the Center for Labor Market Studies at Northeastern University.[33]

4. **Impact on youth development and transition to adulthood:** There is also impressive evidence that the most intensive forms of workplace learning — apprenticeships and sustained internships — are especially effective in meeting the developmental needs of young people. They provide a structure for supporting the tricky transition from adolescence to adulthood. "Apprenticeship has always done more than teach a specific trade," argues Stephen Hamilton in his seminal book, *Apprenticeship for Adulthood.* "Being a productive worker calls for many of the same qualities as being an active citizen and a nurturant family member. Fostering young people's growth in one of these adult roles improves their ability to fill the others." Indeed, Hamilton notes that after completing a three-year apprenticeship, German youth typically assume "adult"

---

32 Hoffman, *Schooling in the Workplace.*

33 Andrew Sum et al., *The Great Recession of 2007–2009, the Lagging Jobs Recovery, and the Missing 5–6 Million National Labor Force Participants in 2011: Why We Should Care,* January 2012, Center for Labor Market Studies, Northeastern University (http://www.northeastern.edu/clms/wp-content/uploads/Lagging-Jobs-Recovery-Report-jan-2012.pdf).

jobs around the age of 18. In contrast, many American youth end up floundering until their mid-20s.[34]

The Implications for the United States

This review of the best foreign systems of vocational education will hopefully serve as a wake-up call to Americans concerned about the future of our youth and, ultimately, our economy. It's not just that these systems are surpassing us in educational excellence. They are also doing a much better job of preparing their young people to succeed in the 21st-century economy. And because they have embraced a broader, more holistic approach to education, they are also reaching a larger portion of the young population than we do with our system, which is so heavily focused on an academic approach to education.

As readers of the *Pathways to Prosperity* report cited at the beginning of this chapter know, these findings led us to call for a systemic change in the American approach to educating our youth in high school and beyond. We did not argue that America should try to import any foreign model. Rather, we suggested we could use the key principles of the best foreign systems to help shape a uniquely American answer to the challenge we face. Our vision is built around three elements: multiple pathways; an expanded role for employers; and a new "social compact" with our youth, in which we assume more collective responsibility for the education and training of our youth. The Career Pathways movement is broadly consistent with this vision.

Many Americans despair that we can ever achieve this vision. Our dominant educational culture—which all too often demeans CTE—is deeply entrenched. Even so, we already have some outstanding examples of models that open up multiple pathways to success. They include the Massachusetts network of regional vocational-technical high schools,[35] Oklahoma's technology centers,[36] and Tennessee's technology centers.[37] Our challenge now is to move from such islands of excellence to a more comprehensive system of pathways to prosperity.

---

34 Stephen F. Hamilton, *Apprenticeship for Adulthood: Preparing Youth for the Future* (New York: Free Press, 1990).

35 http://www.masshome.com/votech.html

36 http://www.okcareertech.org/technology-centers

37 http://www.tbr.edu/offices/tennesseetechnologycenters.aspx?id=322

SECTION I CHECK-UP

After reading the **LEAD** section chapters, complete this initial formative assessment to determine where your schools, colleges, and region stand regarding the organization and structures needed to support career pathways implementation, evolution, and sustainability. How you rate your readiness may indicate the need for a deeper analysis, including a comprehensive self-evaluation and external evaluation.

LEAD Checklist	NA	Disagree		0	Agree	
		−2	−1	0	1	2
(1) There is an understanding among all stakeholders that CTE and Career Pathways are critical to ensuring that the United States leads in global competitiveness and that CTE and Career Pathways prepare students to succeed in further education and careers.						
(2) CTE is delivered through comprehensive programs of study aligned to the National Career Clusters™ Framework.						
(3) The silos of academics versus CTE are eliminated.						
(4) Secondary education, postsecondary education, and business/industry/labor are working together for the design and implementation of Career Pathways.						

Section II. Succeed

CTE prepares students to succeed in further education and careers.

The benchmarks of success can change. Across the country, we have high school graduates who have passed state course examinations and then test remedial in mathematics and communications upon entering college. Therefore, the question is raised—What is success?

Attention has turned toward college and career readiness standards to better delineate success in further education and success in careers. As the competitive global economy places pressure on the desire to maintain or increase individuals' living standards, the nation and its states are considering the impact and role of legislation and policy. Aligning policy at all levels—national, state, and local—has implications for what should be success for our students. The section considers how CTE, together with good policy, can prepare students to succeed in their education and careers.

The section includes chapters on national policy trends and on their implementation at the state and local levels. The chapter on national policy discusses initiatives such as the Common Core Standards, Rigorous Programs of Study (RPOS), and movements designed to ensure or influence the development of a skilled workforce. The chapter on using legislation and policies to drive change treats those policies pertaining to CTE and education in general, including examples of the spectrum of approaches across the states.

POS Framework Component Supported
Legislation and Policies

National Policy Trends

Jan Bray, Nancy Conneely, Kimberly Green, and Kara Herbertson

Should There Be a U.S. Department of Education?

While those of us in education might assume that the undisputed answer to this question is *yes*, recent political debates have once again called this into question. In an era of tight fiscal restraints, politicians are looking for ways to save resources. And while education remains among the top priorities in public opinion polls, opponents suggest that the Federal Government is overstepping its authority, noting that education is a matter for the states and local communities to govern. Their position is rationalized by the fact that there is no provision in the U.S. Constitution authorizing a federal role in education.

According to a brief published by the Center on Education Policy in 1995, "the law establishing the U.S. Department of Education in 1979 stated that '. . . the establishment of a Department of Education is in the public interest, will promote the general welfare of the United States, will help ensure that education issues receive proper treatment at the federal level, and will enable the Federal Government to coordinate its education activities more effectively.' The constitutionality of a federal role in education is based on the 'general welfare' clause of the Constitution which the U.S. Supreme Court has interpreted as authorizing federal aid to education and to other areas not explicitly outlined as a federal power in the Constitution."[1]

---

1 Center on Education Policy, "Information Bulletin #4: Should There Be a U.S. Department of Education?"January 1, 1995 (http://www.cep-dc.org/publications/index.cfm?selectedYear=1995).

The creation of a cabinet-level position for education symbolized the priority the United States was placing on education as a legitimate national interest "since it [education] directly impacts the nation's ability to compete internationally and to defend itself in a time of war."[2] This national interest and rationale for a federal role in education persists today, and bears even more importance and meaning given the current economic and education realities of global competition.

Critics of the U.S. Department of Education at the time of its creation have much in common with today's critics, noting the danger of an intrusive Federal Government that puts in place burdensome requirements and regulations. While these debates will continue to arise periodically, it is clear that the rationale used to justify the creation of a U.S. Department of Education acknowledges and underscores the critical intersection between education and our nation's economic prosperity, as well as our national security. And with the public's continued support for prioritizing education, we are likely to see a strong federal presence in education for years to come.

The leadership of Congress and the Administration dictates the tenor and focus of federal policy debates and priorities. When elections result in shifts among the political parties, so too do the areas of focus. There is, however, a degree of predictability in national policy discussions, regardless of the outcomes of elections. This chapter considers trends that transcend political parties and lines and will likely remain in the national spotlight during the coming years:

- Focus on innovation
- Common standards and assessments
- College and Career Readiness
- Aligned academic and technical content
- Focus on postsecondary attainment
- Accountability, data quality and use
- Closing the skills gap
- Competition for resources

---

2 Center on Education Policy, "Should There Be a U.S. Department of Education?"

A Focus on Innovation

Beginning with the Smith-Hughes Act in 1917, the Federal Government became more involved in secondary education by increasing access to "vocational education," for the purpose of addressing the lack of skilled workers in agriculture and manufacturing, and preparing the workforce for the increasing industrialization of the economy.[3] Since then, the Federal Government has used legislation such as the Elementary and Secondary Education Act and the Higher Education Act to target its resources toward innovation, reform, and program improvement in education.

The federal investment in education accounts for about 10 percent of funding[4]; state and local funds make up the rest. While relatively small, the federal investment serves the U.S. Department of Education's mission of promoting student achievement and preparation for global competitiveness by fostering educational excellence and ensuring equal access.[5]

Innovation in CTE

The purpose of the federal investment in Career Technical Education (CTE) has always been to drive innovation and programmatic improvement, ensuring that CTE can meet the needs of the nation's economy. As the Smith-Hughes Act evolved into the Perkins Act, Tech Prep was included in federal CTE legislation in 1990 (Perkins II)[6] to address some of the same issues facing the country in 1917—increasing the number of skilled workers and preparing students for the changing economy—but also to improve secondary students' academic achievement and to meet the needs of the "neglected majority."[7]

---

3 Neville B. Smith, "A Tribute to the Visionaries, Prime Movers and Pioneers of Vocational Education, 1892 to 1917," *Journal of Vocational and Technical Education*, Fall 1999 (http://scholar.lib.vt.edu/ejournals/JVTE/v16n1/smith.html).

4 U.S. Dept. of Ed., "Federal Role in Education," 2012 (http://www2.ed.gov/about/overview/fed/role.html).

5 U.S. Dept. of Ed., "About ED" (http://www2.ed.gov/about/landing.jhtml).

6 The Carl D. Perkins Vocational and Applied Technology Education Act of 1990, Public Law 101-392.

7 U.S. Dept. of Ed., Office of the Under Secretary, Policy and Program Studies Service, *National Assessment of Vocational Education*, 2004 (http://www2.ed.gov/rschstat/eval/sectech/nave/navefinal.pdf).

Tech Prep was legislated to spur local innovation to help more students transition from high school to postsecondary and the workplace, with the most promising strategies to be scaled up to reach more students through CTE programs. However, because of the lack of consistent implementation and mainstreaming of the tenets of Tech Prep into CTE, the Carl D. Perkins Career and Technical Education Act of 2006 (Perkins IV)[8] gave states the option of consolidating Tech Prep into the Basic State Grant and also introduced the concept of *Programs of Study* (POS). POS reflects earlier research which found that implementing Tech Prep as a structured program of study "appears more likely to improve student outcomes than emphasizing individual elements in isolation, and better promotes transitions to postsecondary education."[9] But by then it was too late. In 2011, in response to a proposal from President Obama, Congress defunded Tech Prep, citing inconsistency and lack of data. While funding for Tech Prep was lost, the requirement that all Perkins-eligible recipients, at both the secondary and postsecondary levels, had to implement at least one POS persisted. We can build on the lessons learned from Tech Prep and usher in the era of POS.

Recent Innovations in Federal Education Policy: Race to the Top

Current federal reform efforts have included competitive grants such as Race to the Top (RTTT), Investing in Innovation, and School Improvement grants. Initially funded through the American Recovery and Reinvestment Act of 2009, RTTT is a competitive grant program that has awarded $4 billion over three years to 19 states. RTTT rewards states that implement plans for reform in four key areas:

1. Enhancing standards and assessments
2. Improving the collection and use of data
3. Improving teacher effectiveness and achieving equity in teacher distribution
4. Turning around struggling schools

---

8 Public Law 109-270.

9 Mathematica Policy Research, Inc., *Focus for the Future: The Final Report of the National Tech-Prep Evaluation*, 1998 (http://www.mathematica-mpr.com/PDFs/Tech.pdf).

This multi-billion-dollar investment in education is the Obama Administration's attempt to move states in the direction they believe to be most beneficial to students. As a result, many states, not just those that were awarded grants, have adopted common standards, made changes to their charter school laws, and implemented new teacher evaluation systems.

In addition, some states have made changes that involve CTE, such as an increased emphasis on STEM education (Science, Technology, Engineering, and Mathematics). For example, Florida developed an Aerospace Technology Career Academy at First Coast High School in Jacksonville that allows students who complete required coursework and take part in dual enrollment classes to obtain associate degrees in air operations within the first year after graduation.[10] North Carolina's plan for education reform, *Career and College: Ready, Set, Go!*, is built around the four RTTT goal areas and strives to ensure that every student graduates from high school prepared for success in postsecondary education, a technical training program, or a career.[11] As a part of this effort, North Carolina is developing more college-level CTE courses that will be available online to high school students. In addition to grant awards to states, the Obama Administration is offering RTTT funding to districts that use individualized classroom instruction to help close achievement gaps and prepare all students for college and careers. While political parties leading Congress and the Federal Government may be deeply divided on many issues, this isn't one of them. A focus on innovation and using federal funds and bully pulpit to drive innovation, improvement, and reform is here to stay.

Adoption of common standards may have been encouraged through RTTT but the Federal Government wasn't the driver. It was the states. And because of this state ownership, the movement toward common standards and assessments is a national trend we believe will have longevity.

---

10 U.S. Department of Education, "Race to the Top: Florida Report," January 2012 (http://www2.ed.gov/programs/racetothetop/performance/florida-year-1.pdf).

11 U.S. Department of Education, "Race to the Top: North Carolina Report," January 2012 (http://www2.ed.gov/programs/racetothetop/performance/north-carolina-year-1.pdf).

Common Standards and Assessments

Chapter 9 provides a comprehensive history of the path that led to common standards and assessments. The following remarks address the *national* trend toward common standards and assessments. The work around common standards and assessments is perhaps the most influential policy trend in recent history. And since the deadlines for implementation of the Common Core State Standards (CCSS) are rapidly approaching, the reality and efficacy of this work will soon become known.

The CCSS are K-12 standards for English Language Arts and mathematics that specify what students who graduate from high school should know and be able to do in order to "succeed in entry-level, credit-bearing academic college courses and in workforce training programs." Building on a decade of Career Cluster™ work to define what students need to know and be able to do in the 16 Career Clusters™ and 79 Career Pathways, in June 2012 the National Association of State Directors of Career Technical Education Consortium (NASDCTEc) unveiled the Common Career Technical Core (CCTC). The initiative, which engaged 42 states, DC, and Palau, defines what students should be able to know and do after completing instruction in a POS. More details on the CCTC can be found in Chapter 9. The CCSS and the CCTC together reflect a prominent national trend for states to band together to build resources and define performance expectations. A recent poll by Gallup/PDK found that 75 percent of Americans believe that "Common core standards will make the U.S. more competitive, improve schools in our communities, and provide more consistency between districts within a state and between states."[12]

Global competition, efficiency in resource allocation, equity/ equitable access, or simply higher quality standards—whatever the chosen rationale—common standards and assessments will be at the forefront of national policy discussions.

---

12 Gallup/PDK, *2012 Annual PDK/Gallup Poll of the Public's Attitudes Toward the Public Schools* (http://www.pdkintl.org/poll/index.htm).

College and Career Readiness

The advent of the CCSS heightened a national conversation about expectations for high school graduates. And the CCSS framework of "college and career readiness" (CCR) served as the springboard for CCR to enter into the mainstream of education policy discussions. The upside of this focus is that people are saying the right words — *college and career readiness*. The CTE community saw this as an exciting opportunity to break down the college and work silos and shift the discussion from *college OR work* to *college AND work*.

Unfortunately, policy discussions often still focus only on college readiness. College readiness has an academic focus, the primary goal being for students to graduate high school with diplomas, ready to pursue postsecondary education or training without need for remediation. Career readiness includes, but extends beyond, college readiness. But what is career readiness? There are many definitions. Some people believe that the CCSS are all that is necessary to be fully college and career ready. Others believe that CCR is a set of "employability skills," or soft skills, such as critical thinking and problem solving that students need for the workplace. The Association for Career and Technical Education (ACTE) defines career readiness as having three components — academic, technical, and employability skills.[13] The Career Readiness Partner Council[14] was formed in January 2012 to bring together national policy organizations, leading foundations and businesses to agree on a common definition for career readiness and to promote national policies and supports to realize its successful implementation. This work is slated for completion in fall 2012.

POS are a perfect vehicle for preparing students for both college and careers. POS seamlessly link students' educational experiences through coherent course sequences between the secondary and post-secondary levels. They also link academic and technical content, which is our next enduring national policy trend.

---

13 ACTE, *What Is Career Ready?*, April 13, 2010 (https://www.acteonline. org/uploadedFiles/Publications_and_Online_Media/files/Career_ Readiness_Paper.pdf).

14 http://www.careertech.org/legislation/crpc/.

Aligned Academic and Technical Content

The United States' focus on global competitiveness has drawn attention to the nation's high secondary dropout rates and low postsecondary completion rates. Increased student motivation and engagement are necessary to address these national education challenges, and many people are recognizing that increased rigor in standards is only part of the solution. Relevancy of instructional content is the other. Contextualizing learning through academic and technical instruction is a hallmark of CTE.[15] Education decision makers have come to recognize that "real world" jobs require the integration of both academic and technical skills, and secondary and postsecondary curriculum should reflect this reality. Researchers from the National Research Center for Career and Technical Education have concluded that POS can enhance the effectiveness of CTE, especially by aligning technical instruction with rigorous academic standards. Using federal policy to break down silos among areas such as education and labor, as well as academic and technical content, will be necessary. While POS is reflected in Perkins IV, changes to general education and workforce legislation such as the Elementary and Secondary Education Act and the Workforce Investment Act will be necessary to fully break down these silos and provide more relevant instruction to students.

It is important to note that the inclusion of POS in Perkins IV was an intentional lever designed to more systemically address academic and technical integration, along with improved alignment across learner levels, resulting in more students attaining postsecondary degrees or industry-recognized certificates or credentials. The goal of preparing students for postsecondary education was a departure from previous versions of the law that focused on providing school-to-work transitions for students,[16] but this new priority foreshadowed the substantial national and federal interest in postsecondary attainment.

---

15 http://136.165.122.102/UserFiles/File/Snapshots/Snapshots_Impact_of_POS_3.pdf.

16 S. 250, Carl D. Perkins Career and Technical Education Improvement Act of 2006 (http://www.gpo.gov/fdsys/pkg/BILLS-109s250enr/pdf/BILLS-109s250enr.pdf).

Focus on Postsecondary Attainment

In his 2010 State of the Union address, President Obama challenged each American to earn a college degree by 2020 and return the United States to its former position as the largest producer of college graduates in the world.[17] This position comes as no surprise. Recent data shows that most jobs through the year 2020 will require at least some postsecondary education.[18] Therefore, earning postsecondary degrees, credentials, or certificates increases the marketability of graduates in an ever-competitive global economy. Because they are designed to encourage deliberate links between secondary and postsecondary education and the workforce to facilitate learning that leads to postsecondary degree attainment, POS are essential to achieving the completion goal and meeting the forecasted needs of our labor market. College and career readiness standards, assessments, and performance metrics will reinforce the focus on postsecondary attainment and keep it in the national spotlight.

Accountability, Data Quality and Use

Since standards-based education reform began in the 1980s, data has played an increasingly important role in the U.S. education system. Decades ago, education data was primarily collected to account for the number of students being served by the allotted federal funding. Today, the uses of education data are much more varied and dynamic to correspond to the changing needs of the country's education system.

Over the last three decades, data collection and usage in education have improved dramatically. Standards-based education reform began in the 1980s with the goal of improving education by requiring all students to meet the same expectations through academic standards. These outcomes were intended to be measurable, and enrollment information on students was collected to assess the equitability

---

17 Barack Obama: "Inaugural Address," January 20, 2009.

18 William C. Symonds, Robert B. Schwartz, and Ronald Ferguson, *Pathways to Prosperity: Meeting the Challenge of Preparing Young Americans for the 21st Century*, Pathways to Prosperity Project, February 2011, Harvard Graduate School of Education (http://www.gse.harvard.edu/news_events/features/2011/Pathways_to_Prosperity_Feb2011.pdf).

of the distribution of funds. Perkins II refocused vocational education to increase global competitiveness and workforce preparedness in the United States through the integration of academic and technical education. Perkins II required states to report on student performance, but it was not until the Carl D. Perkins Vocational-Technical Education Act Amendments of 1998 (Perkins III)[19] that a full state performance accountability system was enacted. Taking the lead of the Goals 2000: Educate America Act,[20] Perkins III set a precedent for other legislation in requiring states to negotiate performance standards in an effort to improve student outcomes.[21] Perkins III set out to establish performance accountability for CTE programs by measuring performance through several core indicators, including rates of placement in employment and secondary diploma attainment.

In 2001, No Child Left Behind (NCLB) took data collection and usage to a new level by assessing state education systems based on their students' outcomes on standardized tests. The legislation also required the collection and monitoring of special populations data to improve equity in education. When Perkins IV was reauthorized in 2006, CTE indicators were further refined to reflect the goals of the new law, including the requirement that states negotiate annual performance targets with local eligible recipients and entities, the requirement of the academic performance measures to be aligned to NLCB, and the inclusion of a technical skills assessment measure.

As the education community rethinks academic and technical standards and assessments through the CCSS and the CCTC, the issue of data quality and usage has become increasingly important. Through the efforts of various organizations and stakeholders, more states are building their capacity to launch state data warehouses, link data across education systems, and use longitudinal data to improve student performance.[22] With the basic infrastructure in place, many states have been able to develop systems where data are more acces-

---

19 The Carl D. Perkins Vocational–Technical Education Act Amendments of 1998 (Public Law 105–332).

20 The Goals 2000: Educate America Act (P.L. 103-227).

21 U.S. Department of Education, "Carl D. Perkins Vocational and Technical Act of 1998" (http://www2.ed.gov/offices/OVAE/CTE/legis.html).

22 Data Quality Campaign, "Data for Action 2011: State Analysis by Action" (http://www.dataqualitycampaign.org/stateanalysis/actions/).

sible and usable to stakeholders who need this information. As states' data capacity continues to expand, so will their ability to provide essential feedback and strategies to improve their state education systems.

Accountability is here to stay—the public is demanding it, and federal programs require it. As technology is employed to gather more accurate data, and deliver this data in real-time, more and more decisions will be driven by data. This trend will impact what gets funded and how funds are allocated among programs, and hopefully it will also drive marked gains in student achievement and close the skills gap.

Closing the Skills Gap

Unfortunately our nation's Sisyphean efforts to dig our way out of the Great Recession make discussions and debates about the economy and the skills gap a persistent national policy priority. Policymakers talk every day about the United States' high unemployment rate. It may seem logical to assume that Americans face unemployment because employers are not hiring, but the "jobless recovery" is somewhat of a misnomer. On the contrary, there are numerous employment opportunities available for workers with the right skills. In recent years, the idea of a "skills gap" between the available workforce and the jobs that are and will be available in the future has begun to dominate policy debates, particularly the debates related to workforce and economic development.

This skills gap, which has contributed to the long-term unemployment trend, stems from a widespread mismatch between employer needs and worker skills. As the workplace of the 21st-century continues to evolve, so too must the skills needed for successful employment. Unfortunately, many individuals lack the knowledge and skills needed in industries where jobs are available.

In some cases, this reflects a lack of education and training on the part of workers, a trend that is expected to continue. With 63 percent of jobs expected to require some form of postsecondary education by 2018, those with a high school diploma or less will find it increasingly difficult to find and keep full-time employment that pays family-sustaining wages and offers opportunities for advancement. At the same time, America's relative position in the global economy and its rate of educational attainment have dropped. Data from the World Economic Forum shows the United States slipping to fifth in the rankings in global competitiveness. The March 2012 issue of the *Harvard Business Report,* which focuses on rethinking education, points out that the latest set of comparative international exams administered by the Organisation for Economic Co-operation and Development ranked American 15-year-olds 25th in math, 17th in reading, and 22nd in science among its 34 member nations.[23]

In other cases, the mismatch reflects the downsizing of some industries and the growth of others, such as those offering careers in advanced manufacturing; science, technology, engineering, and math (STEM); and health care. New jobs may require skills that unemployed workers don't possess or have not developed because they were not required for previous positions.

However, closing the skills gap is both necessary and possible through high-quality education and training, and great strides have already been made through CTE programs. Throughout these programs, one critical strategy in closing the skills gap is ensuring career readiness for all students through high-quality POS. The concepts of career readiness and POS can help to close the future skills gap, but policymakers also must address the needs of adults who have already exited the educational system but still don't have the skills necessary for available careers. The nation's community and technical colleges and area CTE centers are an important source for many Americans to train and re-train for high-skill, high-wage, high-demand jobs. As a major creator of associate degree and certificate holders, these institutions are poised to have a tremendous impact on the future workforce, in which workers at the middle-skill level will be in high demand. The Bureau of Labor Statistics (BLS) projects that middle-skill jobs (jobs that generally require some significant education and training beyond high school but less than a bachelor's degree) will account for about 45 percent of all job openings projected through 2014. In addition, jobs requiring an associate degree are projected to grow the fastest of all jobs requiring postsecondary education.

Community and technical colleges often offer accelerated learning options, support services for students, and industry engagement

---

23 http://www3.weforum.org/docs/WEF_GCR_CompetitivenessIndexRanking_ 2011-12.pdf; http://hbr.org/2012/03/rethinking-school/ar/1

that make a difference for students. And the importance of industry involvement in preparing the workforce and addressing the skills gap cannot be overstated. Policymakers often stress the importance of public-private partnerships to address the country's workforce issues, including through programs such as the Trade Adjustment Assistance Community College and Career Training (TAACCCT) Grant Program. This focus on partnership and business involvement is a key part of the success of Gateway Technical College's (WI) Horizon Center, which provides NATEF-certified automotive programs, an auto diagnostics certification program, and aeronautics-pilot training to high school, college and adult learners. The Advanced Propulsion Lab allows students to train with diesel and related "green" technologies such as hybrid biodiesel. The Horizon Center was designed with the help of Snap-on Corporation, which provided not only cash donations, equipment cost reductions, and scholarship funds, but also expertise and curriculum support. Snap-on designated the Horizon Center as its first location in the world for delivery of its Diagnostic Coursework and Certification program.[24]

The U.S. economy depends on a highly skilled, adaptable, and competitive workforce. With celebrity advocates such as Mike Rowe, who promotes the value of the technical trades, speaking up in public and on Capitol Hill, it is apparent that work is back in vogue.[25] But this is not enough. The nation must ensure the availability of high-quality CTE education and training programs through investments in programs such as the Perkins IV Act that build the capacity of education institutions to offer training for high-wage, high-skill, and high-demand jobs.

Through policies that support and enhance the increasing diversity in the sources for education and training and the creation of systemic solutions, like POS, America is staged to defeat the skills gap. But will the nation invest its resources where it needs to so that we can close the skills gap?

---

24 http://www.gtc.edu/page.asp?q=267; http://www.gtc.edu/page.asp?q=289

25 http://www.mikeroweworks.com/2011/05/mike-rowes-oral-testimony-to-the-senate-commerce-committee/

Competition for Resources

Putting It in Context

Despite increased demand (CTE program enrollments exceed 14 million participants[26]), CTE funding from the Federal Government has been on the decline. While federal education funding has seen a substantial increase in recent years, Perkins funding has been cut, and now reflects a smaller percentage of the overall federal education funding. From Fiscal Years (FY) 2002 to 2010, Perkins Act funding remained flat. However, in FY 2011 Perkins was cut by $140 million, completely eliminating funding for Tech Prep and cutting Basic State Grants by $37 million.

> **CTE PROGRAMS** at the secondary, postsecondary and adult levels receive federal funds via the Carl D. Perkins Career and Technical Education Act (Perkins). Perkins funding is the largest programmatic federal investment in high schools (not including American Reinvestment and Recovery funds or Race to the Top grants), as well as one of the largest federal sources of institutional support for community colleges.

As federal dollars overall become more scarce, Congress and the Administration are focusing their spending on programs that can demonstrate monetary value and social benefits. Public outcry at perceived overspending by the Federal Government has also resulted in a desire for greater accountability. For years the CTE community has been asked to show a positive return on investment to justify federal funding for Perkins. More recently, the Office of Management and Budget (OMB), which plays an influential role in establishing budgetary priorities, has indicated that they plan to use a cost-benefit analysis approach to future budget proposals.[27]

Unfortunately, doing a return on investment (ROI) study of Perkins at the national level is extremely difficult because many states are not able to meet the conditions necessary to conduct a true ROI

---

26 U.S. Department of Education, Office of Vocational and Adult Education, *Report to Congress on State Performance, Program Year 2007-2008* (http://cte.ed.gov/docs/Rpt_to_Congress/Report_to_Congress_07-08.pdf).

27 Office of Management and Budget, *Analytical Perspectives: Budget of the U.S. Government*, Fiscal Year 2011 (http://www.gpoaccess.gov/usbudget/fy11/pdf/spec.pdf).

analysis. For example, such an analysis would require all states to have robust longitudinal data systems capable of tracking individuals from secondary to postsecondary and into the workforce. Also, not all states collect data on individuals' earnings, so that critical data point could not be measured at a national level.

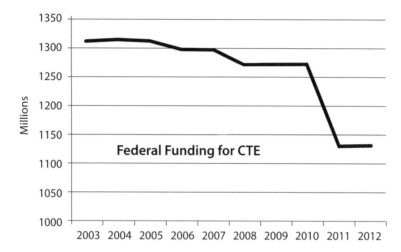

However, some states have undertaken such studies with positive results. In fact, the studies provide a clear indication that funding provided for CTE has a broad and positive impact on individuals, businesses, and our economy and government. The effects include increased wages, reduction in government spending on public assistance, and increased tax revenues. For example, Tennessee found that for every dollar spent on secondary and postsecondary CTE, $5.37 is returned to the state economy in direct earnings, increased productivity, and additional labor income and taxes.[28]

Given the current fiscal climate, OMB is increasingly concerned with making investments that "achieve the maximum benefit to society and do not impose unjustified or excessive costs."[29] To date,

---

28 University of Memphis, *The Economic Impact of Secondary and Post-Secondary Career and Technical Education in Tennessee*, December 2006 (http://www.tn.gov/education/cte_council/doc/econimpact.pdf).

29 Office of Management and Budget, *Analytical Perspectives: Budget of the U.S. Government*, Fiscal Year 2011 (http://www.gpoaccess.gov/usbudget/fy11/pdf/spec.pdf).

OMB has used this approach to propose increased funding for pre-K programs and Nurse-Family Partnership programs.

After evaluating programs using cost-benefit analysis, OMB recommends the expansion of programs that result in net benefits, and the reassessment or discontinuation of programs that underperform. Unless Perkins can clearly demonstrate that its benefits to students, institutions, states, and the Federal Government outweigh the federal investment, it remains at risk of having its funding cut in future budgets.

Focusing on Efficiency

Along the same lines as positive ROI and greater accountability for federal expenditures is the call for greater efficiency in how federal funds are spent. During a debt ceiling debate in 2010, Senator Tom Coburn (OK) included an amendment in the bill requiring the Government Accountability Office (GAO) to conduct a three-year study of duplicative programs in the Federal Government.[30] These reports by GAO have found duplication and overlap in programs spanning the Federal Government, including job training and employment programs, STEM education, and teacher quality programs.[31] These reports have spurred legislative proposals from members of Congress on both sides of the aisle to cut duplicative programs and streamline systems.

Perkins IV was implicated in a 2011 GAO report that found overlap among 47 federally funded employment and training programs.[32] Despite protests from the U.S. Department of Education to remove Perkins from the report because of the primary focus of CTE programs on education, GAO maintained that Perkins programs met their defi-

---

30 CONG. REC. 8 S156, (daily ed. January 22, 2010) (amendment of Sen. Coburn) (http://www.gpo.gov/fdsys/pkg/CREC-2010-01-22/pdf/CREC-2010-01-22-pt1-PgS156-2.pdf#page=1).

31 Senator Tom Coburn, *GAO Duplication Report – Highlights* (http://www.coburn.senate.gov/public/index.cfm?a=Files.Serve&File_id=73039811-667b-4620-811a-69f7690e2360).

32 Government Accountability Office, *Multiple Employment and Training Programs: Providing Information on Colocating Services and Consolidating Administrative Structures Could Promote Efficiencies*, January 2011 (http://www.gao.gov/new.items/d1192.pdf).

nition of an employment and training program. As a result, Rep. Virginia Foxx (NC) introduced a Workforce Investment Act reauthorization bill that allows Governors to use Perkins Act funds for workforce-related activities as part of a unified state plan. While national policy organizations were successful in removing Perkins from this proposal, it is likely that we haven't seen the last of proposals that could block grant programs, allow for consolidation of programs, or give states authority to merge funding streams. And because Perkins straddles the education and workforce worlds, it is often a target.

Programs of Study: A Pathway to Success

How can we progress on the path toward meeting the nation's economic, educational, and workforce needs, and how can national policy help facilitate this progress? As discussed throughout this chapter, creating pathways from secondary through postsecondary education and into successful careers is an important part of the solution. Federal policy initiated the focus on POS through Perkins IV. The next round of federal CTE legislation should expand this focus and strengthen the requirements for all federally funded CTE to be delivered through POS to guide students to success through education and into the workplace.[33]

POS hold much potential to address the enduring national trends discussed in this chapter. POS built upon college and career readiness standards will align academic and technical content and learner levels, thus increasing the efficiency of the educational enterprise. POS are also responsive to the needs of the labor market and are an innovation, built upon years of precursor initiatives, that has the potential to close the skills gap. Research verifies the effectiveness of the POS model, which embraces the use of data-driven decision-making. All of these aspects, together, will produce the evidence base and validation needed to position CTE in an advantageous way for continued, if not increased, federal support.

---

33 http://136.165.122.102/UserFiles/File/Snapshots/Snapshots_Impact_ of_POS_3.pdf

Legislation and Policies: Levers to Drive Change

Scott Hess, Libby Livings-Eassa, and Kimberly Green

L egislation and policies can serve as a barrier to transformation and success or they can spark, support, leverage, scale up, and systematize successful models. This chapter explores federal and state legislation and policies that have been used to move the needle and bring Career Pathways and Programs of Study (POS) into the spotlight and mainstream of our nation's education and workforce systems.

Evolution of a Concept

The concepts that underlie Career Clusters™ and Career Pathways aren't new, but they have been relatively slow to be adopted because, as with all innovations, recipients will not adopt them until they see value in them. Recent and ongoing changes, especially in technology, are creating an environment that is favorable to widespread adoption. Today the educational expectations of the nation reflect a changed landscape in which postsecondary education is increasingly recognized as a necessity in preparing for the modern workplace.

Federal legislation beginning with the Goals 2000: Educate America Act[1] and continuing through the School-to-Work Opportunities Act,[2] the reauthorization of the Carl D. Perkins Vocational and Technical

---

1 Public Law 103-227.
2 Public Law 103-239.

Education Act of 1998 (including Tech Prep),[3] and the Workforce Investment Act[4] created a national focus on increasing student achievement and improving transitions into postsecondary education and the workplace. While the federal legislation gently supported the movement toward Career Pathways, the U.S. Department of Education's Office of Vocational and Adult Education (OVAE) made investments in several key initiatives that built resources and momentum for the transformation of vocational education to Career Technical Education (CTE). The chart below spells out elements of transformation needed.

Vocational Technical Education	Career Technical Education
For a few students	For all students
For a few jobs	For all careers
6 to 7 program areas	16 Career Clusters™ and 79 Career Pathways
In lieu of academics	Aligns/Supports Academics
Limited articulation	Portable, transferable credit
Secondary versus postsecondary	Secondary and postsecondary

Chapter 8 provides a history of the Career Clusters™ initiative, which laid the foundation for the transformation of CTE and the building blocks for several additional OVAE initiatives, noted below, that contributed to progress in advancing Career Pathways.

The College and Career Transitions Initiative

In November 2002, the College and Career Transitions Initiative (CCTI) of the League for Innovation in the Community College received a federal grant to select 15 community colleges, in partnership with employers and secondary education, to design model strategies for implementation of Career Pathways and to conduct research and develop case studies to determine the effectiveness of Career Pathways. CCTI implemented Career Pathways in five of the

---

3 The Carl D. Perkins Vocational and Applied Technology Education Act of 1990 (Public Law 101-392) to Carl D. Perkins Vocational-Technical Education Act of 1998 (Public Law 105-332) to Carl D. Perkins Career and Technical Education Act of 2006 (Public Law 109-270).

4 Public Law 105-220.

16 Career Clusters™: Health Science; Law, Public Safety, Corrections, and Security; Education and Training; Information Technology; and Science, Technology, Engineering, and Mathematics (STEM).

CCTI formulated the following definition of the term *career pathway:*

A career pathway is a coherent, articulated, rigorous sequence of academic and career courses, commencing in the 9th grade and leading to an associate degree, and/or industry recognized certificate or licensure, and/or a baccalaureate degree and beyond. A career pathway is developed, implemented, and maintained in partnership among secondary and postsecondary education, business, and employers. Career pathways are available to all students, including adult learners, and are designed to lead to rewarding careers.[5]

CCTI, which was created in the era of No Child Left Behind had three goals:

1. close the achievement gap;
2. create meaningful educational options that help students with diverse backgrounds and needs reach uniformly high standards; and
3. ensure that students attain these high standards at each level of their educational careers.[6]

These goals underscored the breadth of the possible impact Career Pathways could have. CCTI was further influenced by the policy environment, and grantees were required to measure and report performance in the following areas:

*   decreased need for remediation at postsecondary level;
*   increased enrollment and persistence in postsecondary education;
*   increased academic and skill achievement at secondary and postsecondary levels;

---

5 League for Innovation in the Community College, *Pathways to Student Success: Case Studies from The College and Career Transitions Initiative,* 2006 (http://www.league.org/league/projects/ccti/files/CCTI_Pathway_Book.pdf), p. 8.

6 http://www.league.org/league/projects/ccti/index.html

- increased attainment of postsecondary degrees, certificates, or other recognized credentials; and

- increased entry into employment or further education.

CCTI, built upon Career Clusters™ and Tech Prep, contributed many positive elements to the progress of Career Pathways: It created a structured, replicable model and a clear definition of the term *career pathway*. It highlighted the opportunity for Career Pathways to align, and underscore the importance of aligning, systems (education and workforce) and to serve the full spectrum of learners — youth to adult. And it highlighted the importance of building an evidentiary and data-driven case that the model works.[7]

Federal Legislation: Bringing POS into the Spotlight

One of the purposes of the Carl D. Perkins Career and Technical Education Act of 2006 (Perkins IV)[8] was to call for "providing individuals with opportunities throughout their lifetimes to develop, in conjunction with other education and training programs, the knowledge and skills to keep the United States competitive."[9] One way to achieve this goal was to incorporate the notion of Career Pathways into the Act. Perkins IV introduced a new term — CTE *Program of Study (POS)* — instead of calling it a "career pathway," despite the similarities in definition. This new label was the result of a contingent in Congress which felt that the term *Career Pathway* connoted job training or tracking and opted for the term *Program of Study*, which has its roots in higher education community, as a better indication of their intentions.

The introduction of POS and the allowance for states to choose to merge Tech Prep funding into the Basic State Grant reflect Congress's intention to bring the concepts underlying Tech Prep, Career Pathways, and POS into the mainstream of CTE. The requirements of Perkins IV, however, were timid with regard to the implementation

---

7 League for Innovation in the Community College, *Pathways to Student Success.*

8 The Carl D. Perkins Career and Technical Education Act of 2006, Public Law 109-270.

9 Section (2)(7), The Carl D. Perkins Career and Technical Education Act of 2006, Public Law 109-270.

of POS: Eligibility for funding required implementation of only one POS. Some state and community leaders saw that POS could serve as a vehicle for the implementation of aspects of the federal legislation that the CTE community had struggled with, for example, connecting learner levels with workplace expectations and seamlessly integrating academic and technical instruction. The same leaders also saw the potential for Perkins IV to be a key tool in achieving the goal of transforming vocational education from preparation for *jobs* to preparation for *careers* in an ever-changing global economy.

Unfortunately, the Perkins IV definition for a POS was vague. The legislative language states that, at a minimum, a POS must:

- Incorporate and align secondary and postsecondary education elements,

- Include academic and CTE content in a coordinated, non duplicative progression of courses,

- Offer the opportunity, where appropriate, for secondary students to acquire postsecondary credits, and

- Lead to an industry-recognized credential or certificate at the postsecondary level, or an associate or baccalaureate degree.[10]

The four statutory requirements for POS did not fully explain what was unique about a POS, compared to Tech Prep or any CTE program. Some people interpreted this as Perkins IV's way of perpetuating "business as usual."

As the federal legislation's reauthorization was about to be finalized, there was a call from national and state leaders for tools to help the CTE community see how they could align their programs to industry sectors or Career Clusters™. OVAE funded NASDCTEc, through the League for Innovation's CCTI grant, to develop sample plans of study for each of the 81 (now 79) Career Pathways. This "CCTI template"[11] has been modified for both state and local use. It outlines a six-year educational plan showing academic and technical courses, courses offered for dual high school and college credit, and postsecondary courses. The sample plans of study were intended to show

---

10 Section 122 (c)(1)(a) of the Carl D. Perkins Career and Technical Education Act of 2006 (Public Law 109-270).

11 http://www.league.org/league/projects/ccti/files/Career_Pathways_Template.xls

how to construct non-duplicative instructional sequences, inclusive of academic and technical requirements, across learner levels. Built using the National Career Cluster™ knowledge and skills statements, the plans of study, unveiled in the summer of 2007, became the visual for what many think of as a POS today.

SAMPLE

Health Science

Career Cluster Plan of Study for ▶ Learners ▶ Parents ▶ Counselors ▶ Teachers/Faculty

This Career Cluster Plan of Study (based on the Health Science Career Cluster) can serve as a guide, along with other career planning materials, as learners continue on a career path. Courses listed within this plan are only recommended coursework and should be individualized to meet each learner's educational and career goals. This Plan of Study, used for learners at an educational institution, should be customized with course titles and appropriate high school graduation requirements as well as college entrance requirements.

GRADE / EDUCATION LEVELS	English/Language Arts	Math	Science	Social Studies/Sciences	Other Required Courses/Other Electives/Recommended Electives/Learner Activities	*Career and Technical Courses and/or Degree Major Courses for Health Science	SAMPLE Occupations Relating to This Career Cluster
	Interest Inventory Administered and Plan of Study Initiated for all Learners				All plans of study should meet local and state high school graduation requirements and college entrance requirements. Certain local student organization activities are also important including public speaking, record keeping and work-based experiences. A foreign language is recommended.		**Occupations Requiring Less than Baccalaureate Degree** ▲ Dental Assistant/Hygienist ▲ EMT/Paramedic ▲ Health Information Coder ▲ Home Health Aide ▲ Lab Technician ▲ Phlebotomist ▲ Radiographer ▲ Registered Nurse
9 (SECONDARY)	English/Language Arts I	Algebra I	Dependent on chosen pathway	State History Civics		**Health Science I: Introduction to Health Science** / *Information Technology Applications*	
10	English/Language Arts II	Dependent on chosen pathway	Dependent on chosen pathway	U.S. History		**Health Science II: Health, Safety and Ethics in the Health Environment**	**Occupations Requiring Baccalaureate Degree** ▲ Athletic Trainer ▲ Biochemist ▲ Biostatistician ▲ Geneticist
11	English/Language Arts III	Dependent on chosen pathway	Dependent on chosen pathway	World History Sociology		**Health Science III: Employment in Health Occupations**	▲ Industrial Hygienist ▲ Nutritionist ▲ Occupational Therapist ▲ Physician (MD/DO) ▲ Physician's Assistant ▲ Psychologist ▲ Radiologist ▲ Research Scientist ▲ Speech/Language Pathologist ▲ Toxicologist ▲ Veterinarian
	College Placement Assessments-Academic/Career Advisement Provided						
12	English/Language Arts IV	Dependent on chosen pathway	Dependent on chosen pathway	Psychology Economics		Continue courses pertinent to the pathway selected.	
	Articulation/Dual Credit Transcripted-Postsecondary courses may be taken/moved to the secondary level for articulation/dual credit purposes.						
Year 13 (POSTSECONDARY)	English Composition	Dependent on chosen pathway	Dependent on chosen pathway	American Govt. Psychology	All plans of study need to meet learners' career goals with regard to required degrees, licenses, certifications or journey worker status. Certain local student organization activities may also be important to include. Work-based learning is an integral part of this Career Cluster.	Continue courses pertinent to the pathway selected.	
Year 14	Speech/Oral Communication/Technical Writing	Dependent on chosen pathway	Dependent on chosen pathway	American History Sociology			
Year 15		Continue courses in the area of specialization.					
Year 16							

** See course descriptions on page 2.

http://www.careertech.org/career-clusters/resources/plans.html.

SAMPLE

First Steps Toward a Common Approach

With Perkins IV having just passed and the Federal Government having made the decision not to enact regulations, states and communities found that they had tremendous flexibility in interpreting the requirements of the new law. Leaders from the Career Clusters™ work and the Tech Prep movement recognized that successful programs are driven by the same core principles. Further, there was a growing call from researchers for consistency in programs within states, or even among states. The final evaluation of Tech Prep, conducted by Mathematica in 1998, called for federal and state leadership to strengthen Tech Prep by placing greater emphasis on comprehensive Programs of Study. The evaluation found that by implementing individual and often unconnected elements of Tech Prep, most consortia have foregone the chance to change students' experiences substantially and have put only modest emphasis on promoting the anticipated seamless transition from the secondary to the postsecondary stage of Tech Prep. Further, the report suggested that a more structured program approach has a better chance of improving student learning and postsecondary transitions. Federal and state leadership could encourage local consortia to adopt a more structured, comprehensive program as the model for Tech-Prep implementation.[12]

One response to this call for consistency was NASDCTEc's 15 critical components[13] for effective implementation of Career Clusters™.

15 Critical Components for Career Cluster™ Implementation

• Administrative Support	• Parent and Community Support	• Flexible Schedules
• Shared Planning Time	• Education Partnerships	• Integrated Curriculum
• Career Development	• Business and Industry Partnerships	• Creative and Innovative Teaching Strategies
• Professional Development	• Multi-Measure Assessment	• Workplace Learning
• Standards-Based Curriculum	• Interdisciplinary Teams	• Student-Centered Learning

---

12 Mathematica, *Focus on the Future: The Final Report of the National Tech-Prep Evaluation*, 1998 (http://www.mathematica-mpr.com/PDFs/Tech.pdf).

13 http://www.careertech.org/career-clusters/ccresources/index.html

These components, built (along with the accompanying rubric) from research conducted by the National Consortium on Health Science Education, [14] outline the steps to be taken by states and communities in implementing Career Clusters ™. While this resource existed, there was no requirement or policy or legislation requiring its use and so its impact was somewhat limited. It did, however, begin the movement toward a common policy framework for implementation.

The First National Models

In 2008, OVAE initiated a grant competition to promote the development of common POS models within states. Each of six states received a grant to create a statewide articulation agreement in one of the 16 Career Clusters™:

- Florida — Health Science and Manufacturing focusing on Biotechnology
- Hawaii — Marketing
- Indiana — Transportation, Distribution and Logistics
- Nebraska — Transportation, Distribution and Logistics
- New Hampshire — Finance and Health Science
- South Carolina — Science, Technology, Engineering and Mathematics

The intent of the initiative, titled "Promoting Rigorous Programs of Study Through Statewide Articulation Agreements" (RPOS 1),[15] was to create a system in which students throughout the state would receive the same rigor of instruction, verified by a common state-approved assessment, and could transfer cluster credits to any postsecondary institution offering the same Career Cluster-related programs. OVAE believed that working through the process of creating statewide agreements would require states to implement certain steps that could define what a high-quality POS looks like.

RPOS 1 was designed with the awareness that implementation of statewide articulation agreements is difficult and has sometimes been thought impossible. But as states began working together to develop

---

14 http://www.healthscienceconsortium.org/healthcare_standards.php
15 http://cte.ed.gov/nationalinitiatives/rposgrants.cfm

a common interpretation of the definition of POS, secondary and postsecondary education began collaborating at the local level and aligning with other local partnerships, creating an environment in which statewide articulation agreements became possible. The most difficult issues the RPOS 1 grantees had to work through were these:

- Statewide partnerships — bringing all the players to the table

- State and local secondary and postsecondary validation and agreement on POS standards based on industry standards (Career Cluster™ standards were recommended because they are the only nationally validated set of standards organized with a broad-to-narrow focus.)

- Common sequences of courses organized around the validated standards

- Adapting the broad-to-narrow approach in lieu of traditionally narrow, job-specific training

- Common, validated technical skills assessments, including state-approved assessments resulting in high school credit, postsecondary credit, and (where appropriate) industry certifications

- Common teacher certification requirements

RPOS 1 achieved its goals, with most of the participating states achieving their goal of creating statewide agreements.

Getting to More Consistency

As states and local recipients began to work through the early stages of Perkins IV implementation, OVAE held a series of regional summits designed to showcase POS as a transformative tool for CTE. It became increasingly evident that states and locals were seeking more guidance, more specificity in how to define and implement high-quality POS. In summer 2010 OVAE convened CTE leaders, national associations, states, participants from OVAE-funded projects, representatives from secondary and postsecondary education, and employers. Drawing from lessons learned from Tech Prep, the 15 Critical Components, and the National Research Centers for CTE's Technical Assistance Academy, OVAE formulated a "career and technical programs of study design framework," which this book refers to as the *POS design framework*. The POS design framework serves as a quality-assurance marker for states seeking to promote local development of consistent POS that comply with Congressional intent and promote continuous improvement of Perkins-funded programs.

The POS design framework consists of *10 POS components*:

1. Legislation and Policies
2. Partnerships
3. Professional Development
4. Accountability and Evaluation Systems
5. College and Career Readiness Standards
6. Course Sequences
7. Credit Transfer Agreements
8. Guidance Counseling and Academic Advisement
9. Teaching and Learning Strategies
10. Technical Skills Assessments

The POS design framework provides clarity in defining the core elements of a POS and articulates the supporting subcomponents necessary for a POS to succeed. The following figure shows how the 10 POS components function in relation to one another and to secondary and postsecondary education.

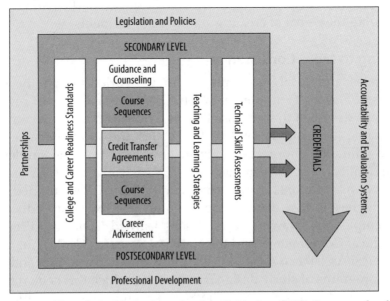

(Adapted from http://cte.ed.gov/nationalinitiatives/POS_Framework.pdf)

The 10 POS components can be viewed as a scaffold for strengthening the four Perkins IV statutory requirements. Each component can be associated with a particular requirement, as is shown in the following table.

Perkins POS Requirements	POS Framework Components
A. Incorporate and align secondary and postsecondary education elements	*1. Legislation and policies* *2. Partnerships*
B. Include academic and CTE content in a coordinated, non-duplicative progression of courses	*5. College and career readiness standards* *6. Course sequences* *8. Guidance counseling and academic advisement* *9. Teaching and learning strategies*
C. Offer the opportunity, where appropriate, for secondary students to acquire postsecondary credits	*3. Professional development* *7. Credit transfer agreements*
D. Lead to industry-recognized credential or certificate at the postsecondary level, or an associate or baccalaureate degree	*4. Accountability and evaluation systems* *10. Technical skill assessments*

The four statutory requirements of the Perkins legislation focus on secondary-postsecondary alignment, course sequencing, dual credit, and attainment of degrees and other credentials. The 10 POS components of the POS design framework compliment and go beyond the Perkins requirements and, in so doing, more thoroughly assist students in achieving the "college and career readiness" that today's educational and business climate demand. A POS is the sum of multiple parts, each of which must be present in order for a Career Pathways system to achieve the rigor that the POS definition requires. "Each of the (POS framework) elements has a pivotal role to play with POS development and implementation. They are not independent of each other nor are they of equal priority."[16]

---

16 MPR Associates, Inc., *Programs of Study: Local Implementation Readiness and Capacity Self Assessment: A Tool for Local College and Career Readiness* (http://cte.ed.gov/docs/POSLocalImplementationTool-9-14-10.pdf), p. 6.

Each of the 10 POS components has two or more subcomponents, as is shown below.[17]

POS Components and Subcomponents

1. Legislation and Policies
State and local legislation, rules and regulations, or administrative policies that promote POS development and implementation, such as–

- The allocation of state or local funding (and other non-federal resources) designed to promote POS development and long-term sustainability;
- The use of established, formal procedures for the design, implementation, and continuous improvement of POS;
- Adherence to policies that ensure opportunities for any interested secondary student to participate in a POS; and
- The use of individual graduation or career plans for participating students.

2. Partnerships
Ongoing relationships among education, business, and other community stakeholders that support POS design, implementation, and maintenance, such as by—

- Using written memoranda that specify the roles and responsibilities of partnership members;
- Conducting ongoing analyses of economic and workforce trends to identify POS that should be created, expanded, or discontinued;
- Linking POS development to existing initiatives that promote workforce and economic development; and
- Identifying, validating, and updating technical and workforce readiness skills to be taught within POS.

3. Professional Development
Sustained, intensive, and focused professional development opportunities for administrators, teachers, and faculty that foster POS design, implementation, and maintenance, and that—

- Support the alignment of academic and technical curriculum within the POS from grade to grade (within grades 9 through 12) and from secondary to postsecondary education;
- Support the development of integrated academic and CTE curriculum and instruction within the POS;

---

17 See also the list at the website of the Perkins Collaborative Resource Network (PCRN) (http://cte.ed.gov/nationalinitiatives/rpos.cfm).

- Ensure that teachers and faculty have the necessary content knowledge to align and integrate curriculum and instruction within the POS;
- Foster innovative teaching and learning strategies within the POS; and
- Assist administrators, teachers, and faculty in using assessment data for POS program and instructional improvement.

4. Accountability and Evaluation Systems

Systems and strategies that gather quantitative and qualitative data on all 10 POS design framework components as well as on student outcomes to inform ongoing efforts to develop and implement POS and to determine their effectiveness, and that—

- Yield valid and reliable data on key student outcomes (indicators of performance) referenced in the Perkins act and other relevant federal and state legislation; and
- Provide timely data to inform ongoing efforts to develop, implement, evaluate, and improve the effectiveness of POS.

5. College and Career Readiness Standards

POS content standards that define what students are expected to know and be able to do to enter and advance in college, their careers, or both, and that include aligned academic and technical content, and that—

- Are developed and continually validated in collaboration with secondary, postsecondary, and industry partners;
- Incorporate essential knowledge and skills that students must master regardless of their chosen career area or POS;
- Provide the same rigorous knowledge and skills in reading or language arts and in mathematics that employers and colleges expect of high school graduates; and
- To the extent practicable, are internationally benchmarked so that students are prepared to succeed in a global economy.

6. Course Sequences

Course sequences within a POS that help students transition to postsecondary education without the need to duplicate classes or enroll in remedial courses, as evidenced by—

- Course sequence plans that map out recommended academic and career and technical courses for the POS;
- Course sequence plans that begin with introductory courses that provide broad foundational knowledge and skills common across all POS and then progress to more occupationally specific courses that provide the knowledge and skills required for entry into and advancement in

the selected POS; and

- Opportunities for students to earn postsecondary credit for coursework taken during high school.

7. Credit Transfer Agreements

Formal credit transfer agreements among secondary schools and postsecondary institutions that—

- Provide a systematic, seamless process for students to earn college credit for postsecondary courses taken in high school, transfer high school credit to any two- or four-year institution in the state that offers the POS, and transfer credit earned at a two-year college to any other two- or four-year institution in the state that offers the POS;

- Record college credit earned by high school students on their high school transcripts at the time the credit is earned so that they can transfer seamlessly into the college portion of the POS without the need for additional paperwork or petitioning for credit; and

- Describe the expectations and requirements for teacher and faculty qualifications, course prerequisites, postsecondary entry requirements, locations of courses, tuition reimbursement, and the credit transfer process.

8. Guidance Counseling and Academic Advisement

Systems that provide career counseling and academic advisory services to help students make informed decisions about which POS to pursue and that—

- Are based on state or local guidance and counseling standards, such as the National Career Development Guidelines;

- Ensure that guidance counselors and academic advisors have access to up-to-date information about POS offerings to aid students in their decision-making;

- Offer information and tools to help students learn about postsecondary education and career options, including about the prerequisites for particular POS;

- Provide resources for students to identify career interests and aptitudes and to select an appropriate POS;

- Provide information and resources for parents, including workshops on college and financial aid applications, on helping their children prepare for college and careers; and

- Provide web-based resources and tools for obtaining student financial assistance.

9. Teaching and Learning Strategies

Innovative and creative instructional approaches that enable teachers to integrate academic and technical instruction and also enable students to apply academic and technical learning in their POS coursework, as evidenced by —

- Interdisciplinary teaching teams of academic and career and technical secondary teachers or postsecondary faculty;
- The use of contextualized work-based, project-based, and problem-based learning approaches; and
- The use of teaching strategies that foster team-building, critical thinking, problem-solving, and communication skills.

10. Technical Skills Assessments

Existing valid and reliable technical skills assessments that provide ongoing information on the extent to which students are attaining the necessary knowledge and skills for entry into and advancement in postsecondary education and careers in their chosen POS and that —

- Are either third-party assessments recognized by industry or are technical skills assessments developed or approved by the state that are based on industry standards;
- Measure student attainment of technical skill proficiencies at multiple points during a POS;
- Incorporate, to the greatest extent possible, performance-based assessment items through which students must demonstrate the application of their knowledge and skills; and
- Result in the awarding of secondary credit, postsecondary credit, or special designation on a student's high school diploma.

The components represent:

- all aspects of what POS are: college and career readiness standards, course sequences, credit transfer agreements, technical skills assessments, and innovative teaching and learning;
- the partnerships and conditions that should be in place to support POS: legislation and policies, partnerships;
- the supports needed to implement POS: professional development, guidance counseling and academic advisement); and
- reinforcement of the importance of measuring progress and data-driven decision-making (accountability and evaluation systems).

The subcomponents sometimes indicate multiple means of implementation. (See *credit transfer agreements*.). In other instances they provide definitions. (See *college and career readiness standards* and *course sequences*.) The POS design framework put the stake in the ground in clearly defining high-quality CTE delivered through POS.

The POS design framework was further validated in 2010 through NASDCTEc's fourth principle — *Reflect, Transform, Lead: A Vision for CTE*[18] — which calls for all of CTE to be delivered through "comprehensive programs of study (footnoted as being defined by the POS design framework) aligned to The National Career Clusters™ Framework." This national and state support, coupled with growing community-level calls for guidance, provided fertile ground for the growth and expansion of systemic approaches to Career Pathways and POS.

Rigorous Programs of Study
National Activity 2 (RPOS 2)

In the fall of 2010, through a project titled "Promoting Rigorous Career and Technical Education Programs of Study" (RPOS 2), OVAE awarded grants to six states to "promote and improve state and local development and implementation of rigorous programs of study."[19] RPOS 2 is similar to RPOS 1, but the RPOS 2 grantees were asked to create POS that are organized around the 10 POS components and their subcomponents. Each participating state was required to select three local education agencies (LEA) to implement a POS based on the POS design framework and then collect data on how well participating students are prepared for college and careers, compared with similar sets of students from the general education track. The six states selected to put the POS design framework to the test are Arizona, Kansas, Maryland, Montana, Utah, and Wisconsin.

Initially the RPOS 2 states struggled to align with the POS design framework. The most difficult of the subcomponents to implement are the same as in RPOS 1. RPOS 2 differs from RPOS 1 mainly in that it requires the following:

---

18 MPR Associates, Inc., *Programs of Study*.

19 http://www2.ed.gov/news/newsletters/ovaeconnection/2010/10072010.html

- Selection of general education students for the comparison group and collection of data for the required performance indicators

- Ensuring common technical skills assessments for non-industry certification standards and setting the level for success aligned with college and career readiness standards

- Implementing a common POS in all three LEAs

The Six States in RPOS 2

RPOS 2 states have established formal procedures for the design, implementation, and continuous improvement of POS. The following provides a snapshot of each.

The first two examples, Montana and Wisconsin, provide excellent snapshots of how policy is established in locally controlled states.

Montana

Because Montana is a locally controlled state, the state board of education provides formula-based funding to support the Big Sky Pathways Consortium (2010–2011). LEAs develop local policies supported by memoranda of understanding (MOU) inclusive of all stakeholders to execute development and implementation of POS.

The Office of Postsecondary Instruction and the Office for Continuing Higher Education partnered with the Montana Department of Labor to include the Big Sky Pathways Consortium and the capacity to develop individual Big Sky Pathway MAPs (Montana Achievement Plans) in Montana's Career Information System (MCIS). The completion of POS at each high school that can be formatted as MAPs in MCIS is viewed as essential to the ultimate effectiveness of that career and curriculum-advising tool.

Wisconsin

Wisconsin's "Promoting and Supporting High School to College Transitions for CTE Students" provides flexible funds via the Wisconsin Technical College System's Grant Category #150-242 with requirements for development of POS.

Because Wisconsin is a locally controlled state, LEAs drive development of POS with MOUs via advisory boards that include representatives of local manufacturing businesses and postsecondary institutions, K-12 district personnel and faculty members, school board members, and parents. Local economic development associations drive studies and data collection relating to local employment trends, changes in the economy, and employment demand. This advisory board reviews quarterly employment data.

Arizona

Arizona State Statute ARS 15-391 provides for the formation of joint technical education districts and allocates funding to:

- Meet the standards of a CTE preparatory POS that, as determined by the CTE division of the department of education, must meet requirements of the POS design framework.
- Have a defined pathway to career and postsecondary education.
- Require an assessment that demonstrates a level of skill or competency in a vocation or industry or that leads to certification in and acceptance by that vocation or industry.
- Require work-based learning components, CTE student organization participation, and laboratory experience as determined by the CTE division of the department of education.

Kansas

In 2010 the Kansas State Board of Education approved actions designed to promote "comprehensive redesign with integration and partnerships" and "redefine the delivery model by integrating career/technical and academic standards." The initiative will:

- Create and approve gold standard assessments (industry-recognized credentials and certifications) for each of the Career Clusters™ that support high expectations.
- Integrate core content standards with technical program standards utilizing the 16 Career Clusters™ as the organizing principle.
- Support implementation of personal plans of study for all students in 8th grade and above.
- Improve access to CTE by removing barriers and promoting partnerships.

- Support alignment of guidance counseling initiatives with the Career Ready Kansas website (http://crk.ksde.org/) to disseminate POS implementation.

Maryland

The Maryland State Board of Education's "Policies and Procedures for the Development and Continuous Improvement of Career and Technology Education Programs" were formulated to organize and develop CTE POS within ten broad career clusters for the purpose of providing multiple career pathways to employment and further education, rather than narrow job training. The state department of education's ten career cluster frameworks are described in "Maryland Career Clusters: Restructuring Learning for Student Achievement in a Technologically Advanced, Global Society."[20] The frameworks were developed by career cluster teams comprising over 350 business and industry partners in collaboration with secondary and postsecondary educators.

Utah

The Utah legislature provides separate funding for CTE. Utah State Board of Education (USBE) policy requires a unique program approval process for high schools to be eligible for these funds. The policy requires that each high school have at least one POS to qualify for the funds.[21]

For over 25 years, Utah has had a strong concurrent enrollment program, established through a secondary-postsecondary partnership. The program is guided by state board of regents policy R165-1, state board of education policy R277-713, and state legislative statute 53A-15-101. Last year over 27,444 secondary and postsecondary students participated in CTE concurrent enrollment, earning over 73,485 credit hours. Utah's POS initiative utilizes well-established

---

20 http://www.marylandpublicschools.org/NR/rdonlyres/ C46A5E1C-C622-4EBB-89F9-B29ABD3EB0A7/16644/ INTRODUCTION31309.doc

21 The policies can be found at http://www.rules.utah.gov/publicat/ code/r277/r277-911.htm#T3.

legislation, funding, and policies as the backbone of articulation agreements.[22]

Building Capacity to Implement Programs of Study

Not every state would be a recipient of an RPOS grant, nor would every community benefit from these grants. To help expedite the adoption of POS that meet the expectations of the POS design framework, in 2010 OVAE contracted MPR Associates (http://www.mprinc.com) to produce a self-assessment tool based on the POS design framework. The purpose of the tool, titled *Programs of Study: Local Implementation Readiness and Capacity Self-Assessment: A Tool for Local College and Career Readiness,* was to provide clarity and offer criteria for assessing whether the four statutory requirements *and* the 10 POS components of the POS design framework are being satisfied. The tool provides self-assessment templates for the 10 POS components and suggests readiness and capacity guidance to which states can refer when providing technical assistance to local POS developers and reviewing state CTE program approval processes.[23]

The POS design framework is the foundation for self-assessment of local capacity for POS implementation. Consideration of each component of the POS design framework fosters stakeholder conversation and reflection. In the assessment tool, the "implementation characteristics" described on the template for each of the 10 POS components serve as quality indicators that enable the user to gauge POS implementation readiness and capacity, at both the state and local levels. Some of the quality indicators may be better suited to either a state application or a local application, but all can be adapted for use at either level. Each component has a pivotal role to play. They are not independent of each other, nor are they equal in priority. In carrying out their self-assessments, state and local POS developers and implementers must determine which of the components are the most critical and thus should be given highest priority.

The self-assessment tool provides a template for assessing the extent to which each of the 10 POS components is being met, or has the potential to be met. The process of self-assessment is helpful in

---

22 http://www.rules.utah.gov/publicat/code/r277/r277-713.htm

23 http://cte.ed.gov/docs/POSLocalImplementationTool-9-14-10.pdf

determining capacity for local POS implementation and readiness for state POS approval as well as for statewide systems and local programs. Consideration of each of the 10 POS components can foster stakeholder conversation and reflection on the status of local and/or state readiness and capacity for full POS implementation. The process of analysis that the tool makes possible is necessary to determine which components require policy support and to provide seamless delivery of career technical education. States use different methods of policy implementation, ranging from state-led to site-based. These differences are illustrated in the implementation examples provided at the end of this chapter.

State and Local Sustainability of Career Pathways Through Legislation and Policies

Sustainability is not possible without sound legislation and policies — the first of the 10 POS components. Legislation and policies at the federal, state, and local levels should mandate, support, and foster practices that encourage and help to sustain POS. The early part of this chapter lays out how the federal legislation (Perkins IV) and policies (Career Clusters™, CCTI, RPOS, RPOS 2 and the POS design framework) have paved a solid pathway for building and sustaining a national interest and support for Career Pathways and POS. We now turn to the role state and local legislation and policies can have in sustaining and supporting Career Pathways.

To be effective, legislation and policies should:

- Provide for state and/or local funding and other resources for POS development (e.g., professional development and dedicated staff time).
- Establish formal procedures for the design, implementation, and continuous improvement of POS.
- Ensure that all learners have the same opportunities to participate in POS.
- Require that secondary students develop individual graduation or career plans.
- Provide resources for long-term sustainability.

A first step might be to use the *Programs of Study: Local Implementation Readiness and Capacity Self-Assessment* tool, pages 16 and 17, to see how your state or local community rates itself on the current status and importance of the elements of legislation and policies.

Legislation and Policies
Self-Assessment Ranking of Current Implementation Status and Importance to Your Implementation

Rank your development and appropriate implementation progress for Legislation and Policy using the measurement criteria listed. Determine the level that most closely aligns with the progress made toward addressing appropriate Legislation and Policy implementation. The self-assessment is intended to be an authentic gauge of actual implementation. Results from the self-assessment can be used to target areas for technical assistance and professional development. An analysis of the level of importance can assist in establishing the priority and possible timeline for implementing technical assistance and scheduling professional development.

Implementation Characteristics	Current Status	Importance
State plans lay out provision for funding initial development of POS including formation of advisory teams and analysis of demand.	☐ None ☐ In Progress ☐ Operational	☐ Low ☐ Important ☐ Critical
Instructors of both academic and technical courses have access to both relevant professional development and paid release time to collaborate on curriculum integration.	☐ None ☐ In Progress ☐ Operational	☐ Low ☐ Important ☐ Critical
Advisory committees consisting of secondary, postsecondary, business and instructor representatives convene regularly to assess quality and need for current POS.	☐ None ☐ In Progress ☐ Operational	☐ Low ☐ Important ☐ Critical
States have statewide graduation requirements and policies that support the creation of individual graduation plans. All students have access to information regarding career planning and POS courses.	☐ None ☐ In Progress ☐ Operational	☐ Low ☐ Important ☐ Critical
Overall Status Summary	**Current Status**	**Importance**
After considering each of the implementation characteristics, please rank: 1) your current status of POS Legislation and Policy implementation; and 2) the level of importance this element has to your POS implementation. Transfer these rankings to the Self-Assessment Summary to compare the status and importance of this element to the other POS framework elements.	❶ None ❷ In Progress ❸ Operational	❶ Low ❷ Important ❸ Critical

Legislation and Policies—Implementation Capacity Analysis
Self-Assessment Reflection and Action Planning

In the section below, identify your current capacity assets in the area of **Legislation and Policy** by responding to the question prompts. Give equal analysis to local capacity barriers, items of critical importance, and steps needed to remedy these capacity concerns.

State or Local Self-Assessment	Items of Critical Importance/Action Steps
• What's working well that is worth keeping? • What goals do you have to sustain and enhance the level of collaboration among the partners? • What strategies will you use to sustain the engagement of partnership members? • How will you know if your partnership is being successful?	• What will be new or needs to be revised? • What strategies will you use to address items identified as being of critical importance? • What are the indicators you will use to measure your improvement? • How will you know if you are successful? And when?
Notes	Notes

Much can be learned from others who have led in the area of legislation and policies. Consider the following examples from South Carolina, California, and Maryland.

In 2005, **South Carolina** enacted the Education and Economic Development Act. The EEDA established the Personal Pathways to Success system to help South Carolina students be prepared for good jobs and help businesses find good workers.

Combining high academic standards with enhanced opportunities to explore career options and build real-life working skills, Personal Pathways to Success gives students the guidance and experience they need to take full advantage of real opportunities in the South Carolina economy. . . . The Personal Pathways system maintains the state's established high school graduation requirements — 17 required academic core courses plus seven electives — but requires that all students declare a career major in one of a number of different clusters of study. . . .

Schools partner with businesses and other local institutions to provide students with the chance to get hands-on, real-world working experience in the field of their choice. . . .

Beginning in the elementary grades, Personal Pathways to Success provides programs of career awareness and exploration. Skilled counseling is a linchpin of the program. In the eighth grade, students and their parents or guardians sit down with counselors and create individual graduation plans (IGPs) that lay out their personal education and career strategies. IGPs specify students' choices of cluster, major, postsecondary goals, high school course work, out-of-class learning experiences, and more. Students and their parents revisit these choices at least once a year to make adjustments in their plans or change course altogether if that is required.

In today's economy, postsecondary education and training is a prerequisite for success. For nearly every student, career preparation continues after high school — at two-year or four-year colleges, in the military, in on-the-job training, or in state-approved apprenticeships. Personal Pathways will set up seamless transitions to postsecondary education by establishing articulation agreements among the state's high schools, two-year colleges, and four-year colleges.

To effectively implement Personal Pathways to Success the EEDA mandates a variety of supporting initiatives, including:

- *Individual Attention for Students:* High schools are mandated to hire more guidance counselors to achieve a ratio of one counselor for every 300 students, and counselors specializing in career guidance will help students plan their educations. Students at risk for dropping out will be identified early and models will be developed to help these students graduate.

- *Protection Against Tracking:* EEDA includes provisions that protect students against being steered into pathways that do not fit their best interests. Parents or guardians review their children's IGPs at least once a year and can designate someone to represent them if they cannot participate. An appeals process will be created to resolve disagreements and ensure that every student has equal access to educational opportunities.[24]

California has enacted a Model Curriculum Standards and Framework that includes skills and standards for each CTE program in each Career Cluster. California also showed specific examples of how CTE and academic content could be integrated to qualify as part of the state's A-G Curriculum, which would help students transfer their credits into the University of California and California State University systems.[25]

Maryland's Department of Education has supported the Career Pathways concept since 1989, when the state's Commission on Vocational-Technical Education instated a new model to prepare students for jobs and postsecondary education.[26] The Commission put into place POS to sequence coursework based on the needs of industry. By 1992, CTE POS were one of three elective choices that

---

24 Excerpted from the Executive Summary of the Education and Economic Development Act of 2005 (http://www.che.sc.gov/AcademicAffairs/EEDA/2-ExecutiveSummary.pdf). For more, see also http://www2.scpathways.org/aboutUs.html.

25 Achieve, Inc., "The Perkins Act of 2006: Connecting Career and Technical Education with the College and Career Readiness Agenda," January 2008 (http://www.achieve.org/files/Achieve-CTEPolicyBrief-02-07-08.pdf).

26 Jobs for the Future, *Remaking Career and Technical Education for the 21st Century: What Role for High School Programs?* April 2005 (http://www.jff.org/sites/default/files/RemakingCTE.pdf).

students could choose to fulfill high school graduation requirements. Currently, over half of Maryland high school students are enrolled in CTE programs and many complete CTE POS. Districts have the option of using localized POS or fast-track, state-regulated POS.

The self- assessment tool also provides links to other state resources linked to legislation and policies:

- Illinois Curriculum Development: http://www.ilcte.org/content-areas/industrial-technology

- New York State Program Approval Process: http://www.emsc.nysed.gov/cte/ctepolicy/documents/Implementation-guide2010.doc

- New Jersey Perkins State Plan: http://cte.ed.gov/Docs/CARNarrative/NJ_narrative_2006-2007.pdf

- Georgia Student Graduation Plan: http://www.doe.k12.ga.us/_documents/doe/legalservices/160-4-2-.48.pdf

Policies and Legislation: The Vehicle for Full Systemic Implementation

Continuous attentiveness and oversight in the establishment of and adherence to policy and legislation is critical to the success of POS implementation. U.S. Secretary of Education Arne Duncan endorsed the POS design framework in an April 2011 speech titled "Rigor, Relevance, and the Future of CTE." In that speech he stated,

> Career pathways now spelled out in the Rigorous Programs of Study initiative would span secondary and postsecondary education by design, and concentrate much more on high-demand, high-wage occupations. . . . These courses combine the rigor of a college-prep curriculum with real-life experiences. . . . They offer a springboard to higher education and postsecondary training—not a dead-end. Let's all work together to make this happen.[27]

The "working together" to which Secretary Duncan refers requires sound policies at all levels. Policies provide for the development and sustainability of POS while driving the delivery of instruction and the

---

[27] http://www.edweek.org/media/ovaeconferencespeech_april_2011_final_small.pdf

development and implementation of strategic plans. Basing their decisions on information gained via the POS assessment tool (*Programs of Study: Readiness and Capacity Self-Assessment*), policymakers and practitioners should move toward full systemic implementation.

Recommendations

The following recommendations are intended for all stakeholders and can be implemented at state, district, and local levels.

Recommendation 1: Articulate a Clear Vision

Policymakers can provide effective leadership by articulating a clear vision for how resources can be best allocated to support a systemic approach to knowledge and skill development for all youth, both in and out of school. Policymakers should acknowledge the key role CTE programs can play in meeting the needs of young people. Education policymakers, along with parents, employers, and the public, must engage in a dialogue around the full range of skills that are needed to be successful in today's global economy.

Recommendation 2: Break Down Silos

Educational bureaucracies at the federal, state, and local levels are organized around discrete divisions of instruction, pedagogy, and services, such as academic instruction, special education, CTE, and student support services. Because policy has traditionally been developed by people who are responsible for academically oriented education, this structure often prevents the development of holistic and integrated policies.

State and local policy leaders must break down silos between academic, general, career technical, and special education so that all perspectives and stakeholders are involved in policy development. When all perspectives are integrated and involved, more comprehensive policies and programs that draw upon all instructional resources, pedagogies, and supports can be developed. Policy leaders must ensure that CTE is "at the table" when developing and implementing high school reform strategies.

Recommendation 3: Support Research and Disseminate Research-Based Information

Studies and research receive little attention by national policymakers, other researchers, educators, and the public. Moreover, despite the well-publicized efforts of campaigns such as the National Association of Manufacturers' *Dream It, Do It* to change public perception, teachers, parents, and guidance counselors are still slow to encourage students to pursue high-skilled manufacturing and other technical career tracks, despite the availability of high-wage, career ladder jobs.

Policymakers should use this research to inform the development of high school reform policies and programs. More high-quality research about the value of CTE should be supported, particularly longitudinal research that examines student outcomes in postsecondary education and careers.

Recommendation 4: Provide Funding

Policy leaders should develop and provide funding for a clearly defined high school reform framework that serves all students, supports multiple pathways to graduation, and includes a well-defined role for academically rigorous CTE. Policymakers should fund innovative, replicable approaches to the development of multiple pathways based on CTE and career clusters. At the local level, community colleges and CTE programs should collaborate to develop agreements supporting the academic and financial support systems necessary for success.[28]

Recommendation 5: Support Connections

Policies should support stronger connections between secondary and postsecondary education to enable more high school students to earn college credit and progress to postsecondary education more easily. States should conduct system-wide reviews of articulation agreements to clarify which college credits earned by high school students are accepted by postsecondary education institutions in the state.

---

28 *Funding Career Pathways and Career Pathway Bridges: A Federal Policy Toolkit for States,* Oct. 2012, Center for Law and Social Policy (CLASP) Center on Postsecondary and Economic Success (http://www.clasp.org/admin/site/publications/files/FundingCareerPathwaysFederalPolicyToolkitforStates.pdf).

Recommendation 6: Provide Student Guidance and Advisement

All stakeholders should encourage and support guidance and advisement via administrative policy. Most counselors require professional development to be well informed about the value of CTE and its role in preparing students for careers in the 16 Career Clusters™. Professional development for teachers should include information about the Career Clusters™ and strategies for building career awareness into instruction. States can require students to develop four- or five-year college and career plans, or to designate career majors during high school, as a way to help connect their academic studies to future plans. The recommendations of section 118 of the Perkins Act, which discusses funding to support career guidance and academic counseling programs and promote improved career and education decision-making, should be followed.

Recommendation 7: Align Funding and Focus

Professional development should help CTE teachers learn more about the academic content they can supplement, reinforce, enhance, and apply in their classrooms, and help academic teachers learn how academic knowledge and concepts can be applied in technical settings.

Recommendation 8: Gauge Quality and Success

Appropriate measurements should be in place so that students, parents, postsecondary educators, and employers can gauge the quality and success of CTE programs. Quality assessments should be developed with strong industry input to ensure relevance to the labor market. States should support efforts to build the capacity of administrators and teachers (both regular and CTE) that is essential to creating and sustaining high-quality CTE programs.

Recommendation 9: Establish Policy for Data Collection

As states develop longitudinal student record data systems and student identifiers, they should identify and track students who participate in CTE to determine their long-term outcomes. States should develop the capacity to track labor market participation of all students, and incorporate external industry certifications in any data collection system, to the extent possible.

The Bottom Line

All educational systems rely on sound federal, state, and local policy. Success is not possible without solid policy—whether legislative, administrative, or both. State and local entities must consistently examine and reexamine delivery structures and adjust strategic plans to facilitate systemic Career Pathways implementation. Such policies see greater success when they are adopted at state and local levels and emphasize integration and alignment of all stakeholders.

SECTION II CHECK-UP

After reading the **SUCCEED** section chapters, complete this initial formative assessment to determine where your schools, colleges, and region stand regarding the organization and structures needed to support career pathways implementation, evolution, and sustainability. How you rate your readiness may indicate the need for a deeper analysis, including a comprehensive self-evaluation and external evaluation.

SUCCEED Checklist		Disagree			Agree	
	NA	−2	−1	0	1	2
(1) Formal procedures have been established for the design, implementation, and continuous improvement of Career Pathways.						
(2) Funding (federal, state, or local) and other resources (*professional development or dedicated staff time*) have been provided for the development of Career Pathways.						
(3) A process and resources have been outlined for long-term sustainability of Career Pathways.						

Section III. Partner

CTE actively partners with employers to design and provide high-quality, dynamic programs.

The American education system does not function in a vacuum. Outside the classroom our teachers are also parents, spouses of businesspersons, taxpayers and voters, and members of volunteer groups. All community stakeholders are part of a complex mix that makes up the fabric of a community, a state, and the nation. Why do we often ignore this and treat our schools and its teachers and faculty as a separate function within the greater community?

Businesses have found that partnering with other businesses has been a key to improving the return on investment for both parties. Joint ventures are commonplace in every industry sector. When education partners effectively with business, with other levels of education, and with other stakeholder groups, it too creates a win-win opportunity for all concerned.

This section includes chapters on leadership roles and responsibilities and partnerships. It considers the types of stakeholders, mainly at the local level, required for effective Programs of Study, and provides information on organization, strategies for influencing people, and maintaining momentum. It also makes a case for the importance of partnerships among business, education, and community stakeholders in effecting change and sustaining initiatives that tie education to local economic development. Specific "how to" suggestions are offered.

POS Framework Component Supported
Partnerships

Leadership Roles and Responsibilities

Richard Hinckley and Tony Iacono

If your actions inspire others to dream more, learn more, do more and become more, you are a leader. – John Quincy Adams

Career Technical Education (CTE) and all of education need the best possible leaders and leadership skills; however, those leaders must represent the broadest possible range of community stakeholders: students, teachers, and parent groups; business/industry; faith-based and nonprofit organizations; and government, to name only a few.

A tremendous amount of material has been written on the topic of leadership, and studies continue to consider what skill sets separate leadership roles from managerial roles. In the world of education, we're always seeking change agents who can lead the way in raising lagging student and school performance, and we worry about how we're going to replace the growing number of retirees, so the topic is always current. The need for Career Pathways leaders is great. This chapter considers the topic of leadership among Career Pathways stakeholders, mainly at the local level.

What Is Leadership?

Social scientists, business writers, and other professionals are always striving to define the essence of leadership. Many colleges and universities boast of centers of leadership study and research, and many publish journals on the topic, such as the *Journal of Leadership Studies* of the School of Advanced Studies of the University of Phoenix. The standard approach is to study the actions and beliefs of those who are considered successful leaders. Langdon Morris, in his book *Permanent Innovation* (Innovation Academy, 2006), states that leaders must be innovators, not just managers: "Leaders define and create the organizational culture in which innovation blossoms, ensuring that the right set of tools helps everyone organize their thoughts and their actions to support and enhance innovation. Thus, innovation begins at the top of every organization" (p. 93). Other writers concentrate on managing from the middle or bottom of the organization, recognizing that influence and change can be initiated from points throughout organizations and that we do not always have to wait to be led from the top. Business sections of bookstores are full of books on the topic. In education, when "promising practices" and "best practices" monographs are written, they almost always speak to the vision and innovation of leaders as a key ingredient. The education field has also been keen on creating leaders through college, credentialing, and mentoring programs.

In searching for models of leadership in the education community, we should begin by considering familiar people with proven records of excellence. Consider the following three examples.

Example 1—Dr. Vernon O. Crawley, retiring 21-year president of Moraine Valley Community College (Illinois), was recently asked how he defines leadership. His answer was this: "I don't. You could go to 100 different sources and each would have their own definition. I talk about its characteristics. Like vision, trust, and expectations. What are your responsibilities? Did you get people on board? Did you get them to understand? Did you get them to follow?" Over his years in leadership, Dr. Crawley has honed eight steps that leaders should consider and work toward with their employees.

1. Always do the right thing.
2. Never say, "It can't be done."
3. Never make the same mistake twice.
4. Remember that the process is as important as the result.
5. Strive to communicate effectively. Communication is critical.
6. Remember that timing and the art of compromise are essential.
7. Give your opinion but remain positive.

8. Don't just do your job. Do it well.[1]

As Dr. Crawley suggests, leadership is about doing things for the benefit of others. Effective leadership helps people grow as individuals and professionals while simultaneously creating systems that can positively impact large populations. Leadership is never about a title. It's about ability — the ability to value people, even when their potential is difficult to understand; the ability to understand the past; and the ability to shape the future. When these three factors are combined with the courage to do the "right thing" and the honesty to own up to individual shortcomings and appraise situations accurately, we see the making of a great leader.

Example 2 — At Indian River State College (IRSC) in Florida, leadership is most often demonstrated through the following characteristics:[2]

1. Honesty: Appraise yourself as an individual and as a leader in an honest and forthright manner, even when it's less than flattering.

2. Responsibility: To whom much is given much is expected.

3. Desire to communicate effectively: Communication is a work in progress — work at it and lead by example.

4. Awareness of historical context: Visit the past but live in the future while staying grounded in the now.

5. Leadership by example: People are inspired by great words but they follow great actions. Dr. King's "I Have Dream Speech" would have been forgotten if he hadn't pursued the dream so vigorously.

6. Energy: You can't lead if you're sitting in the grandstand — get on the field.

7. Generosity, patience, a spirit of forgiveness, and desire to find the best in others.

8. Willingness to compromise: Leadership is not about getting your way. It is about compromising to find the best possible outcome in the midst of complex variables and situations.

---

1 Adapted from Moraine Valley Community College's publication *Valley View* April 5, 2012.

2 This section is based on the experiences of coauthor Iacono, who serves as IRSC's Vice President of Academic Affairs.

9. Enthusiasm: Love what you do and let others see your passion — help them find theirs.

10. Enjoyment: Have fun with your leadership — every day!

11. Vision: If you're going to dream, dream BIG! President Kennedy never talked about putting monkeys in orbit. He talked about putting men on the moon!

IRSC has enjoyed a strong reputation as a leader in STEM education (Science, Technology, Engineering, and Mathematics), Career Pathways, and Adult Education Career Pathways and serves as a best practices model in many publications.

Example 3 — Dr. Belle Wheelan, Ph.D., President of the Southern Association of Colleges and Schools Commission on Colleges, defined effective leadership qualities in her article "10 Qualities of a Strong Community College Leader." She listed them as the following:

- Laughter
- Decision-Making
- Support
- Excellence
- Ethics
- Honesty
- Ambiguity
- Respect
- Influence
- Patience[3]

In relating those qualities to her own experiences, she made it clear that leadership traits are often situational and that CTE and education in general require the engagement of many stakeholders who bring a broad range of skills to the table.

Throughout the nation, as Tech Prep consortia were being developed, superintendents, principals, CTE directors, and others from the secondary level assumed leadership with intergovernmental agreements to link heretofore independent and autonomous operations toward the common goal of increasing high-quality opportunities

---

3 *Community College Journal,* April/May 2012.

for more of their students. While the names Paul Vallas (Chicago and Philadelphia), Arne Duncan (Chicago), and Michelle Rhee (Washington, D.C.) were often cited for their bold leadership in efforts to improve failing school districts, thousands of other leaders have emerged at the secondary and postsecondary levels to provide the essential ingredients that motivate others into positive action.

Many examples can be referenced, and all of us can point to exceptional leaders and the institutions that they influenced. They help us answer the question, "What is leadership?" by the outcomes, and often we find a common focus on those being led.

Other Traits of Leaders

The late Peter Drucker, a prolific writer on management and business, stated that leaders must work in three areas of basic competency:

As the first such basic competence I would put the willingness, ability, and self-discipline to listen.

The second essential competence is the willingness to communicate, to make yourself understood.

The last basic competence is the willingness to realize how unimportant you are compared to the task.[4]

In discussions of leadership, people often inquire as to the difference between a leader and a manager. Kenneth Preiss and his coauthors state that "the difference between a leader and a manager can be summed up in a phrase: Leaders do the right things; managers do things right." Preiss et al. go on to say that "People work *with* a leader, but work *for* a manager. The skill sets of leaders and managers diverge when one starts to consider that organizations need to be led with vision, direction, and energy toward goals that are larger than the organization itself."[5]

In the educational world it is sometimes assumed that certain key figures should be both leaders and managers. This may be due to the fact that in many school districts, superintendents and principals — who

---

4 *Managing the Nonprofit Organization* (Harper Collins, 1990), p. 20.
5 Kenneth Preiss, Steven L. Goldman, and Roger N. Nagel, *Cooperate to Compete* (Van Norstrand Reinhold, 1996).

both lead and manage — are the primary administrators. Even when it possible to distinguish management from leadership conceptually, the two roles often coexist in the same person. Principals, for example, are usually responsible for both school vision (leadership) and taking the steps necessary to attain the vision (management). Leadership roles in teaching can also "coexist" in the same person. Traditional leadership roles for teachers, such as heads of departments and chairpersons of textbook adoption committees, have been filled by teachers who were also responsible for providing leadership.[6]

Warren Bennis and Patricia Ward Biedermann describe how groups, not individuals, provide breakthroughs that leaders, working on their own, could not have achieved. They discuss the characteristics of "great groups" in which each person has the right job and in which collective action enables them to achieve more than could be achieved through the individual efforts of their members.[7]

At this point, however, we must begin to consider what this means within the CTE arena and for educators in general.

Stakeholders Should Provide Leadership

Development of successful Career Pathways programs requires more than educators. It requires the involvement and leadership of many segments of the community working in partnership toward common goals. It also requires the support and involvement of state-level leadership. Key Career Pathway leadership categories include the following:

- *Business and Industry* — Business and industry involvement in Career Pathways programs is vital. Without it, the connection to real-world experiences and employment opportunities is lost. Further, each and every business person is a member of one more other stakeholder groups — parents, members of faith-based organizations, affiliates of nonprofits, volunteer or elected government officials, members of workforce boards, and so on. Those people represent the fabric of the community. Career Pathway programs provide multiple points at which business persons can be placed into leadership positions.

---

6 SEDL, "Leadership Characteristics That Facilitate School Change" (http://www.sedl.org/change/leadership/character.html).
7 *Organizing Genies: The Secrets of Creative Collaboration* (Addison-Wesley, 1997).

- *Counselors*—School counselors are the main source of school-based career guidance for most high school students. With voluminous caseloads and other assigned duties such as testing, they are usually overcommitted already. Yet their involvement and input in Career Pathways are essential, and they should be involved as both members and leaders across the entire spectrum of programs and services.

- *Faith-Based and Nonprofit Organizations*—Faith-based and nonprofit organizations have access to both human and financial resources that can make the difference in the success or failure of students in Career Pathways programs. Examples of their support are almost limitless. They provide, for example, transportation assistance; financial assistance for books, materials, and tuition; help with part-time employment; access to mentorships and internships; occupational and personal counseling; and tutoring services. Career Pathways programs should reach out to representatives of faith-based and nonprofit organizations, whether for sustained or periodic student support, and include them in leadership positions.

- *Government*—Governmental offices and office-holders are a source of public support and access to policymakers. They have the ability and connections to convene other stakeholders and entities. At a minimum, they should be made aware of Career Pathways programs and services and be engaged in leadership opportunities.

- *Parent Groups*—As individuals, parents can have a tremendous influence on their children's selection of courses, majors, and Career Pathways. In groups such as the Parent-Teacher Association (PTA) and academic booster clubs, parents' involvement can mean the difference between success and failure. To build the grassroots support that parents are specially qualified to provide, leaders should involve parent groups in all phases of Career Pathway program planning.

- *Students*—Because Career Pathways provide vision and a roadmap for the future, students are perhaps the most important stakeholders of all. Leaders should involve students in program development and give them leadership roles. How better to build support for program change and improvement than by involving one of the main end-use customers?

- *Teachers*—Teachers are the primary delivery agents of Career Pathways programs and a chief determinant of the quality ultimately achieved by these programs. They are fundamentally involved in delivering critical components such as integrated curriculum, dual credit, and contextual teaching. Leaders should involve teachers at all points along the continuum of Career Pathways program development and give them leadership roles at every opportunity.

- *Workforce*—Workforce boards are direct pipelines to collaborative opportunities involving grants and Career Pathways-related initiatives. Their interests are vitally served by the primary outcomes of Career Pathways programs, that of placement of qualified workers into suitable jobs. Because they are populated with business persons, workforce boards take a lively interest in any education and training program that can improve workers' ability to meet the skill needs of local businesses and industries. Leaders should ensure that workforce boards are involved in all aspects of program delivery and should provide a broad range of opportunities for workforce professionals to take on leadership roles.

Leadership Roles and Opportunities That Support Career Pathways

OVAE's 10 components for successful POS implementation provide leadership opportunities for every stakeholder. The chart on the next page indicates areas in which stakeholder groups can be involved.

To be effective, leaders should provide the following:

- Vision, direction, and purpose
- Awareness of ability to implement promising and best practices
- Ability to galvanize others into action toward common goals
- A plan to raise support, including financial support
- The will to lead by example and advocate for programs and services

Leadership Opportunities for Stakeholders

10 Components	Business & Industry	Counselors	Faith-based & Nonprofit	Government	Parents	Students	Teachers	Workforce
Legislation/Policy	◆			◆				
Partnerships	◆	◆	◆	◆				◆
Professional Development	◆	◆					◆	
Accountability and Evaluation					◆		◆	◆
College and Career Readiness	◆	◆			◆	◆	◆	◆
Course Sequences	◆	◆					◆	
Credit Transfer Agreements		◆		◆			◆	
Guidance and Advisement	◆	◆	◆	◆	◆	◆	◆	◆
Teaching and Learning	◆	◆			◆	◆	◆	
Technical Skills Assessments	◆	◆				◆	◆	◆

Leadership must include the establishment of pilot programs for proof of concept and the willingness to take measured risks. Leaders must be ready to collaborate in the give and take involved in gaining community support. Sometimes that means taking charge. Sometimes it means letting others take charge and acting as a supporter.

Who Should Take the Lead?

A. The Case for Educators

While leadership is needed and can be exercised at every level of an organization, secondary superintendents and college presidents are best positioned to provide the most effective leadership. Their offices enable them to act as the 5 C's—Conveners, Compromisers, Collectors, Consensus Builders, and Collaborators. Whether working individually or jointly in alliances of secondary and postsecondary, superintendents and college presidents are in positions that enable them to mobilize people and build support structures. Deans, student services program directors, and curriculum directors are also in positions of influence that enable them to mobilize others in education and communities at large. Educators have strong motivations to take the lead. The college and career readiness of students (a fundamental goal of Career Pathways) lies at the heart of their mission. Among educators' motivations are the following:

- Reduction of postsecondary remediation rates and high school dropouts
- Improved academic performance
- Students who are well-prepared for the workforce and for higher education
- Improved instructional delivery through contextual teaching
- Increased emphasis on attainment in math, science, and technology
- Increased attention to economically disadvantaged students in the community[8]

B. The Case for Business and the Community

Business sectors are integral parts of every Career Pathways initiative. One of the reasons they can provide excellent leadership is that they naturally form alliances. Moreover, entities such as industry associations and trade groups have the potential to influence educators.

---

8 Adapted from *Career Pathways: Education with a Purpose* (CORD Communications, 2005), p. 259.

Change in education is possible when business and industry representatives bring to educators a strong case for change. Business and industry representatives have many motivations to take the lead, including access to a more highly qualified workforce, a reduction in their training and retraining costs, and a desire to improve the communities in which they live. Specifically, as discussed in Chapter 7, taking the lead can help to address the following issues:

- Rising costs, especially in training, retraining, and staff turnover
- Increased productivity to address the pressure to lower prices
- Shortage of qualified hires (especially in high-skills jobs) with proper employability skills[9]

C. The Case for Education, Business, and Community Collaboration

Collaboration involving education, business, and community stakeholders will yield quicker and more lasting results than will the efforts of entities acting alone. Whether the objective is to start a new Career Pathways program or to embed an established program deeper into the fabric of the community, richer and more permanent results will be obtained through the involvement of a coalition of stakeholders. (For more on partnerships, see chapter 7.)

How to Get Organized

Whether your goal is to begin with a holistic approach in which multiple Career Pathways programs will be designed simultaneously or to focus on only one or two program areas, a well-conceived plan is essential. The plan will generally call for transforming existing programs and services and reorienting them within a new structure. Like any strategic plan, it must consider strategies, tactics, opportunities, and threats; involve all stakeholders; and provide for management and resolution of conflict. It must consider the variety of organizations and organizational models within the stakeholder and partnership groups and exclude no one from the implementation process.

---

9 Adapted from Richard Hinckley, Debra Mills, and Hope Cotner, *Adult Career Pathways: Providing a Second Chance in Public Education, 2nd Edition* (CORD Communications, 2011), p. 39.

Most importantly, the plan should consider the professional development necessary to bring the entire Career Pathways community up to levels of understanding that will enable participants to implement programs effectively. Subjects for professional development include the following:

- Understanding the global economy
- Perkins IV requirements
- Partnership development
- Programs of Study (POS)
- Developing standards-based curriculum
- Course and program articulation
- Teaching and learning strategies
- Career planning and guidance
- Work-based learning
- Labor markets
- Accountability and evaluation
- Where to find resources (i.e., adoptable POS models)

Planners should be able to make the case for the buy-in of each stakeholder group, which involves (a) showing stakeholders how they will realize a reasonable return on investment and (b) determining what factors will be deemed indicators of success. To achieve swifter implementation, planners should study the excellent models already in place across the country (see following section). Learning from the promising and best practices that are already being used will ultimately save time and resources.

A Case Study in Leadership: Indian River State College

Indian River State College (IRSC) in Fort Pierce, Florida, provides an excellent model. IRSC is well-respected for its years of leadership in a wide range of programs and services and has positively impacted not only its service area but the state of Florida and the nation. Florida recently embraced Career Pathways as part of a massive revamping of its approach to adult education. Leadership of a significant portion of the statewide planning and implementation was assigned to IRSC.

The College

IRSC is a comprehensive institution that serves more than 32,000 degree- and certificate-seeking students each year. More than 3000 additional students are enrolled in the college's Adult Education Career Pathways (AECP) program. In 2011, the U.S. Department of Education listed IRSC as the third-most affordable college in the country. In 2012, *U.S. News and World Report* ranked IRSC as the twelfth top public regional college in the south for its retention and graduation rates. According to *Community College Week*, IRSC ranks number 48 in the nation in the production of associate degrees. IRSC is also the only school in the southern United States to receive the coveted national Metlife/Jobs for the Future Award (2006) for supporting underserved students in the earning of postsecondary degrees and certificates. On an annual basis, approximately 25 percent of the college's associate degrees are awarded to people who began their educational careers at IRSC in the college's AECP program. Located in a region of Florida that does not have a state university, the college began offering baccalaureate degrees in 2008 to support employer demand. To date, more than 700 students have earned bachelor's degrees in programs designed to strengthen the region's workforce. IRSC's job placement rate of 91.5 percent is a testament to the college's partnership with area employers.

IRSC's Leadership Reach

An important part of IRSC's culture can be found in the college's willingness to assume local, statewide, and national leadership on a multitude of projects and initiatives. Innovation and progress are at the heart of IRSC, a factor that can be observed from the college's president, Edwin R. Massey, all the way through the ranks of the administration, faculty, and staff. For IRSC, the return on investment is measured by the fulfillment of the college's mission, which is rooted in helping individuals achieve their academic and career goals while supporting community and economic growth. For this reason, IRSC employees provide leadership for numerous local, state, national, and international initiatives and programs. Strong examples of the college's impact on large-scale initiatives can be found in IRSC's development of three Employ Florida Banner Centers that focus on energy, homeland security, and life sciences. IRSC's Banner Centers foster economic growth not only in Florida, but also for the nation and, in the case of the Banner Center for Homeland Security, internationally. The more than 400 businesses, schools, public agencies, and hospitals that partner with IRSC help to ensure the success and sustainability of what the college considers three of the most important areas of focus in building a better future for its service area and the nation as a whole.

Examples of how IRSC lives out its mission can be seen at every level of its activity. In 2003, the college's Adult Education program refocused its vision by developing a unique Career Pathways model designed to meet the needs of Adult Education students. Administrators, faculty, and staff members developed a system that applies the proven effectiveness of Career Pathways to the special circumstances of Adult Education students, thereby helping them to reclaim their right to the American dream of economic independence rather than continued reliance on government assistance. IRSC has since helped thousands of GED, English as a Second Language, and adult high school students find their way into postsecondary programs and ultimately into the workforce as middle- and high-skilled workers. By developing career academies, redeveloping curriculum to meet postsecondary and industry standards, and energizing an entire college to embrace the idea that even the most at-risk students can succeed, IRSC's AECP program has become a state and national model. Recognizing IRSC's AECP model as a success, the Florida Department of Education (FLDOE) partnered with a dedicated team at IRSC to develop the Institute for the Professional Development of Adult Education (IPDAE) in 2007.

The joint efforts of the FLDOE and IPDAE have been instrumental in repurposing adult education in Florida. What was once a traditional program with the goal of helping people improve their literacy skills and earn a GED now helps people earn the credentials they need to become productive members of Florida's workforce (especially at the middle-skill level). Because more than 1,000,000 adults in Florida lack a high school diploma and, consequently, are either unemployed or underemployed, IRSC's IPDAE team is passionate about finding ways to help these individuals play a part in creating a better Florida. IPDAE works closely with FLDOE officials and program leaders across the state to develop strategic plans and to provide professional development workshops and e-courses to the more than 5000 individuals who work in schools across Florida to support more than 300,000 enrolled students. Eager to make Florida not only the nation's first AECP state but the best AECP state, IPDAE and the FLDOE have partnered to develop a comprehensive AECP website designed to support the specific needs of Florida's AECP programs.

Since 2010, IPDAE's leadership team has played a key role in helping more than a dozen other states create AECP programs while working closely with the U.S. Department of Education, the U.S. Department of Labor, and numerous research and development organizations interested in advancing AECP across the nation. The need is great. More than 43 million adult Americans lack high school diplomas and, consequently, put a strain on the U.S. economy. The need for STEM skills (Science, Technology, Engineering, and Mathematics) in the U.S. workforce is rapidly growing. That need will not be met if we leave 43 million adults behind. IRSC personnel throughout the college are exercising leadership, motivated by the belief that there is no greater return on investment than improving the lives of others.

Maintaining Momentum of Leaders

At IRSC a commitment to high-quality leadership has been a key success factor that has spread throughout the institution. Over the years, the names of the leaders have changed but the commitment endures.

Leaders may leave or be replaced for any number of reasons — the desire to "move on," for example, or the feeling that all of one's professional goals have been met. As a Career Pathways program develops, its leadership requirements will inevitably change and there will be new opportunities for new people. While many of the Career Pathways leaders will be from education, many others will be volunteers from other parts of the community. Nurturing volunteer leaders, indeed, all community volunteers will require maintaining clear role expectations, good communication, follow-up with agendas and initiatives, and periodic celebrations of success.

121

Partnerships

Bryan Albrecht and Richard Hinckley

The days of turf battles, the star system, and the Lone Ranger are over. The day of the partnership is upon us. Leaders who learn to work with other corporations, government agencies, and social sector organizations will find new energy, new impact, and new significance in their organization's work. (The Organization of the Future, *Frances Hesselbein, Marshall Goldsmith, Richard Beckhard, Editors; Jossey-Bass 1997, p. 83, The Peter F. Drucker Foundation for Nonprofit Management*)

We Know Partnerships Are Valuable

Is it really necessary to convince educators, businesspersons, and community groups of the importance of working together? Have we not learned through many excellent examples that we can better accomplish our common goals when we leverage our resources? Perhaps if the importance and power of partnerships were better understood and more effectively utilized, Career Technical Education (CTE) — indeed, all of education — would be producing better results. Partnerships with business and industry have been well understood and utilized by many schools and colleges as components of their CTE courses and programs. Some have also used partnering to support their general education programs. In each case partnerships have enhanced the readiness of the future workforce and enriched the educational experience. They have created success stories and data elements that are worthy of consideration. A strong example is that of career academies (see chapter 11). The success of career academies, as demonstrated in metrics such as high school graduation rates, is due in part to the exceptionally strong partnerships they have with local business communities. According to the National Academy Foundation (NAF), in 2011, 97 percent of NAF academy seniors graduated from high school, compared to a 50 percent graduation rate among non-academy participants in the cities where most NAF academies are located; 52 percent of NAF graduates earn bachelor's degrees in four years, compared with 32 percent nationally; and career academy graduates earned $16,704 more over the eight years following high school than non-academy students who were also studied.[1]

Many people in business have long recognized the value of partnerships, not only business-to-business but partnerships that team businesses with educational institutions. Research-supported best practices for "high-impact corporate philanthropy" include the following:

1. Develop a comprehensive theory of change.
2. Consider the corporate context.
3. Use information, research, and data to make decisions and assess outcomes.
4. Support partnerships, collaboration, and advocacy to magnify impact.
5. Align K-12 investments with school district improvement efforts to maximize impact.[2]

Later in the chapter we will examine how Snap-on Incorporated and Gateway Technical College have collaborated within this framework.

Perkins IV on Partnerships

The Carl D. Perkins Career and Technical Education Act of 2006 (Perkins IV) calls upon states to offer "career and technical programs of study and to include partnerships among the key components."[3] Specifically, the Act states in Section 2, Purpose, that

---

1 From the statistics and research page of the NAF website, http://naf.org/statistics-and-research.

2 Kirstin McCarthy et al., "Corporate Investments in Education During an Economic Downturn," *International Journal of Educational Advancement*, Vol. 9, 4, pp. 251–265.

3 For a PDF of the complete text of the Act, go to http://www.gpo.gov/fdsys/pkg/BILLS-109s250enr/pdf/BILLS-109s250enr.pdf.

the purpose of this Act is to develop more fully the academic and career and technical skills of secondary education students and postsecondary education students who elect to enroll in career and technical education programs, by . . . (6) supporting partnerships among secondary schools, postsecondary institutions, baccalaureate degree granting institutions, area career and technical education schools, local workforce boards, business and industry, and intermediaries.

The Act calls for ongoing relationships among education, business, and other community stakeholders to assist in both the implementation and maintenance of programs of study. Specifically, in Subsection (b)(6) of Section 134, State Leadership Activities, it requires state leadership in

supporting partnerships among local educational agencies, institutions of higher education, adult education providers, and, as appropriate, other entities, such as employers, labor organizations, intermediaries, parents, and local partnerships, to enable students to achieve State academic standards, and career and technical skills, or complete career and technical programs of study.

The Act goes on to describe the appropriate use of funds for activities and structures that support partnerships, such as articulation agreements.

This chapter looks beyond the requirements of Perkins to make a case for partnerships among business, education, and community stakeholders as a means of effecting change and sustaining initiatives that tie education to local economic development and the social fabric of our communities, states, and the nation.

Advantages of Partnerships Among Educators and Other Stakeholders in the Community

Publicly supported educational entities must continually consider their budgets and use of limited resources when making decisions concerning services. Funding factors are generally dictated by state and local policy, methods of taxation, and other influencers of income. Whether schools or colleges seek bond referendums for operations or building funds or support from their foundations, standing

125

partnerships within their communities can assist when it is time to solicit votes or donations. Partnerships broaden the support base, providing friends through both good and challenging times.

Partnerships allow the education community to leverage and enhance programs and services. Almost any community has a mixture of federal and state programs with their own sources of funding. Through collaboration (to avoid duplication of effort) and alignment of programs with one another, results can be magnified. The fabric of every community is made of many stakeholder groups, each with its own focus and financial and/or physical support. Identifying and working with these groups in areas of common interest extends the classroom and the impact of school programs and services.

Advantages for Teaching and Learning

Partnerships can provide student experiences that schools might otherwise not be able to provide—from guest speakers to workplace visits, job shadowing, internships, and apprenticeships, to name a few. These real-world opportunities enable students to plan better for their further education and career choices. Through business and industry scenarios and problem-based learning, among other means, these opportunities bring the world of work into the classroom. Chapter 11, *Teaching and Learning,* provides examples of work-based learning and further treats the role and impact of partnerships in creating real-world contexts in instruction.

Partnerships provide additional resources for teachers. Problem-based case learning (PBCL) is a strong example of how partnerships can assist teachers. According to Johnson and Loring, "the PBCL approach enables educators to design learning based on problem-solving, critical thinking, and current authentic problematic situations encountered in business and industry. By bringing real-time, real-world problems to their students, instructors can significantly minimize the barriers that typically separate the classroom from the real world."[4] Such approaches help students develop the skills needed to be college and career ready, including teamwork, communication, and systems thinking. Another example of how partnerships can directly assist teachers involves businesses providing teachers

---

4 http://www.makinglearningreal.org/basics.html

with work-based learning experiences. Summer externships, in which teachers work in business and industry settings for weeks or months, provide first-hand immersion into the workplace that can greatly enhance the effectiveness of instruction.

Natural Partners Are in the Community

Looking around any community, one finds entities representing education (Pre-K through postgraduate), business/industry, labor, community and faith-based organizations, government, workforce entities, parent groups, and non-profit organizations. Those groups typically represent many organizational types, as, for example, when business and industry representatives serve on the boards of chambers of commerce, industrial coalitions, and economic development foundations.

Groups may have been formed around specific goals and/or for the purpose of providing services such as Adult Education or instruction in English as a Second Language. Specialized groups may focus on and/or represent Adult Education, customized training, financial aid services, business/industry sectors, labor associations, social service providers, faith-based organizations, workforce boards, and one-stop centers. Some groups are high-profile and easy to find while others may not be so easily recognized.

In determining which stakeholder group to partner with, education should consider the return on investment (ROI), i.e., the costs and benefits impacting the parties involved. ROI for the education community may be easily gauged through metrics such as increases in retention and graduation rates and scholarship and internship opportunities. Gauging ROI for businesses and other organizations may be more difficult. For example, calculating increases in business revenue that might result from partnering with education is problematic because it may take a few years to be realized. It is important that educators can build understandable models whose application to business is readily discerned. Typical ROI data points for business include the following:

- Increase in the size and quality of the workforce pool
- Increase in the availability of graduates with technical skills specified by industry

- Increase in the availability of graduates with soft skills specified by industry
- Decrease in company retraining costs
- Decrease in company employee turnover

Businesspersons will be able to pinpoint their ROI data points; educators should be ready to assist them in building their models.

When considering likely partners, it is good to reflect on the roles that various organizations play in the community and how those roles support the implementation tools referenced in Perkins IV.

For example,

- *Adult Education* addresses program design, curriculum development, bridge programs, techniques for teaching lower-skill adults, basic literacy, math and computer skills, ESL, and assessment tools.

  Partnering with Adult Education providers can result in greater coordination along the education pipeline, improved articulation from one education level to the next, decreased duplication of effort, increased efficiency of services, and the identification of where services and programs are lacking.

- *Community and technical colleges* provide linkages between credit and non-credit instruction, chunking and modularization of programs, articulation agreements, support services, and financial aid.

  Partnering with community colleges can result in greater coordination along the education pipeline, improved articulation from high school to postsecondary, opportunities for advanced placement and dual credit, improved career path transitions, reduced cost of duplicate services, and opportunities for students to begin their career paths earlier.

- *Employers* help by identifying in-demand and emerging occupations and skill sets (essential, workplace, foundational, employability); advising in curriculum development; and providing internships and project-based learning, mentors, employment opportunities, career ladder[5] information, and funding in various forms such as tuition reimbursement.

Partnering with employers can provide experiences that extend beyond the classroom, responsive and relevant curriculum and career opportunity information for teachers and counselors, human and financial support, and job placements.

- *Community-based organizations* provide referrals and recruitment, support services, marketing, case management, and financial assistance (food support, dependent care, transportation).

Partnering with community-based organizations can add considerable breadth to services not readily available to educators, can provide volunteers for in-class and out-of-class experiences, can provide financial support for goods and services outside the education budget, and can provide a basis for support for education initiatives.

- *Workforce entities* provide labor market information and economic and workforce condition analysis, identify high-growth industries, advise in resource development and allocation, ensure employer engagement, assist in skills assessment and job searches, provide job placement services, and advise in policy development.

Partnering with workforce entities can provide supportive data for education initiatives, enhanced access to business, tie-in to policymakers, and direct links for students within their Career Pathways.[6]

Other groups and entities that may fall into the categories described above, but are often overlooked, include local and state governmental agencies, employer coalitions, labor and trade groups, faith-based organizations, proprietary and private schools, and professional organizations and societies.

---

5 Richard Hinckley, Debra Mills, and Hope Cotner, *Adult Career Pathways: Providing a Second Chance in Public Education* (CORD Communications, 2011) defines the term *career ladder* as "a series of steps or occupational levels within a given company or occupation"(p. 132).

6 Debra Mills, *Florida Adult Education Career Pathways Toolkit* (CORD, 2012), p. 44.

All of the above partner groups can provide quick-connect part-nerships and points of asset leverage as educators respond to state, federal, and foundation grant opportunities.

Partnerships already exist in most communities. Directories of non-profit organizations provide a good place to start in identifying groups that have common or complimentary goals that would form the basis of a partnership. "If career and technical education program advisory committees already exist in your area, consider inviting them to join the partnership. At the very least, cross-representation for existing secondary and/or postsecondary program advisory committees should be explored."[7] It should be readily apparent that this would ease course and program articulation, promote dual and concurrent credit options, provide improved business and industry curricular input at the secondary level, and promote the sharing of resources.

Partnering Education to Education and with Business and Industry

The most logical partnerships for the education community are with other education providers and with business and industry. Education partnerships that target dual and concurrent credit opportunities and other methods of facilitating transitions from secondary to post-secondary can produce significant results. Cost savings of time and dollars for students and parents are easily realized when duplica-tion of effort is reduced. Partnering with business and industry often requires that business and industry clearly understand how the part-nership can benefit them. Partnerships with business and industry are best approached when the education community grasps the chal-lenges facing American employers. Partnering with education can help employers address problems they face in today's challenging competitive environment, including the following:

- Rising costs
- Pressure to lower prices
- Increasing cost of health care
- Shortage of qualified hires

---

7 Mills, *Florida Adult Education Career Pathways Toolkit*, p. 39.

- A lack of experience and skilled workers
- A labor pool with poor employability skills
- A labor pool in need of basic skills remediation
- Reduced worker productivity[8]

An education-to-education partnership example:

The South Metropolitan Regional Higher Education Consortium (SMRHEC), which comprises Chicago area community colleges, public and private universities, and other education providers and is housed at Governor State University, was "organized to foster new and enhanced educational services and programs to citizens, businesses, and other institutions in the region. Through institutional collaboration, the Consortium emphasizes the development of instructional models and delivery systems that will give students and employers access to higher education and training opportunities in the most effective means possible." In fall 2009, SMRHEC began work on the South Metro College Compact. The Compact will *guarantee* that beginning students from the six SMRHEC community colleges who meet institutional requirements can transfer *without loss of credit* to any of the six SMRHEC universities. These common articulation agreements will be developed in 12 majors. Agreements in Elementary Education, Engineering, and Business were in place for freshmen students in fall 2010. (http://www.southmetroed.org/mission.php)

Effective partnerships between education and business/industry can help employers by improving the quality and quantity of graduates needed for specific workforce opportunities. According to Rick Stephens, Senior Vice President for Human Resources at the Boeing Company, educators should consider how to approach business and industry leaders and should create and document "a clear understanding of the motivation of each of the partners (why they are involved and what they hope to gain) from the partnerships." Stephens says it requires "a shared willingness to develop a common language and vocabulary that will enable business, education, and community

---

8 Hinckley, Mills, and Cotner, *Adult Career Pathways*, p. 83.

partners to communicate with one another."[9] Stephens further states that there should be an "agreement on expected outcomes, to ensure alignment and integration of the stakeholder's end product need" and "clear evidence that the proposed program will increase worker productivity." His position moves the conversation closer to an ideal situation in which Programs of Study-specific advisory committees take ownership of the curriculum and of its ultimate outcomes.

One Community's Approach to Strengthening Partnerships and Improving Educational Outcomes

In 2006, Waco, Texas, Mayor Virginia DuPuy convened a committee of community leaders to consider barriers that were keeping high school students from going to college. The effort was rooted in a community visioning project led by the previous mayor, Mae Jackson. The group convened by Mayor Jackson formulated five action categories:

- Strengthen the heart of the community
- Increase economic opportunities
- Engage leaders
- Enhance life outside the workplace
- Develop our distinct advantage

Mayor DuPuy's Education Initiative Committee, which ranged from a handful of participants to as many as 50, met monthly to consider educational barriers, quickly moving from obvious topics such as high dropout rates and lack of tuition dollars to less obvious ones such as early childhood education, health, and parental involvement. In 2007, after months of gatherings, a smaller group was formed to consider action steps. This smaller steering committee began to talk about the stakeholder groups in the community that could be engaged. It noted that, while the community had higher poverty levels than the state average, it also had some strong non-profits and foundations with a history of supporting education. The committee considered the many strong organizations that operated in silos (as is often the case) and whose collective action could magnify the individual efforts of each.

---

9 Rick Stephens in Hinckley, Mills, and Cotner, *Adult Career Pathways*, p. 85.

The fuller story is best told as related in the Greater Waco Community Education Alliance Education Summit 2008 Report:

Entire careers of many Waco area citizens have been spent in the pursuit of education excellence. Individuals and organizations have, for many years, looked toward improvement of the school- and life-readiness conditions of the young people in McLennan County. Tremendous human and financial resources have been aligned and expended on behalf of future generations, and "pockets of excellence" are prolific.

Recent developments have proven the value the community places on education, such as the successful bond referendum of McLennan Community College, and Waco Independent School District. Revitalization and economic development initiatives targeting the center of Waco, funding activities of several foundation and non-profits, and school improvement initiatives underscore the commit-ment to a higher quality of life that has permeated the region.

It is with that strong background that efforts to mobilize the community toward addressing its leadership and its strategic alli-ances created the conditions that resulted in planning for the First Annual Greater Waco Community Education Summit. People, ideas, and energy had been converging, laying the groundwork, and giving voice to those who recognized a parent's need for her child's opportunity, a business owner's need for a well-trained worker, a teacher's need for a willing learner, and a child's need for help. The times were right, the urgency was building, and the community was ready.

In 2007, that readiness and the collective energy created by the Waco Community Visioning project, plans of the Greater Waco Chamber of Commerce to engage education and economic development, and the work of the Mayor's Education Initiative Committee resulted in the planning of the first of five Greater Waco Community Education summits.

The Mayor's Education Initiative was considering the barriers to students achieving high school graduation and entry to postsec-ondary education, while the Chamber was considering how a well-educated workforce strengthens area businesses and employ-ment opportunities. Statistics were being gathered to describe the issues and opportunities. Work of the Mayor's Education Initiative Committee led to the research that resulted in the eight summit assumptions, providing the framework for identifying and engaging the community stakeholder groups.

Greater Waco Community Education Alliance—Mission, Core Goals, Strategies, and Assumptions

Mission: Develop the understanding that the entire community shares the responsibility of educating every citizen.

Core Goals:

　1) Send children/youth to school ready to learn

　2) Ensure students graduate fully prepared

　3) Ensure student post-high school success

Strategies:

　1) Engage and mobilize the community to reach the goals

　2) Use research and data to inform strategies and measure success

Eight Assumptions: Our community will best equip each student ensuring children:

　1) Develop learning readiness and social skills before entering school (ages 0–4)

　2) Read at grade level by the third grade (ages 5–8)

　3) Master math concepts (ages 9–14)

　4) Are aware of and plan for postsecondary education opportunities options (ages 13–16)

　5) Expect to graduate and are optimistic about completing high school (ages 13–19)

　6) Develop a plan for accessing financial resources to reach education goals (ages 13–19)

　7) Graduate well prepared for careers and college education (ages 17–19)

　8) Succeed in reaching post-high school education goals (ages 18+) (http://www.educatewaco.com)

This story of one community has not ended. Visit *www.educatewaco. com* to learn that there have been four annual summits, with no plans to stop at five. Read about the Alliance's eight assumptions (also given below) and view its summit programs and annual reports. This is one example of how communities can utilize partnerships of groups within their own localities to address their own issues of education. The Education Alliance that was formed from the 2007 meetings now has full-time staffing and an operating budget supported by community groups.

Creating Partnerships as the Basis for a Career Pathways Transformation

Educators do not have all the tools or dollars necessary to create and maintain the education-to-careers pipeline. They must build effective partnerships throughout their communities to be effective in recruiting, teaching, and placing students into rewarding careers. While partnerships are generally initiated by the education community, it is not uncommon for other groups to reach out to education. The outreach can be the result of a businessperson being elected or appointed to a school board, for example. However, educators should be proactive in developing partnerships.

What is the first step? The education community must have its own priorities set and determine what partnering could do to enhance the success of its students, thus providing a strong return on the investment of time and energy expended in forming or strengthening the partnership. It must take a holistic view of the community's need for economic and workforce development as a means of improving the lives of each and every person in the community. It requires the creation of a sense of urgency that can motivate a broad spectrum of people in the community to grapple with problems and issues and coalesce around solutions. The process of successfully convening community leaders and sector business and industry representatives consists of the following:

1. Inventory the community, its industry, and its current workforce development and support structures.
2. Study the labor market projections and needs analysis reports from governmental, organizational, and industrial sources for the region.
3. Determine which occupational clusters are represented within the industries.
4. Identify the key persons within the community, industry, education, and workforce development.
5. Establish a plan of action.
6. Convene the top business leaders representing the identified Career Clusters™.[10]

---

10 Adapted from Hinckley et al., *Adult Career Pathways*, pp. 79–81.

Education should start with an inventory of areas in which a partnership could assist as well as an inventory of the existing groups and entities in the community with whom partnerships could be developed. The inventory and list of groups should be matched and then ranked according to potential for partnering.

For example, the process of building a Career Pathway in health care would initially involve convening a forum of CEOs from local healthcare and healthcare-related employers to determine the current and future need for nurses, respiratory therapists, physicians' assistants, phlebotomists, and related positions. The education community would consider its current Programs of Study and the mechanisms needed to develop additional programs. For programs that it is not fully equipped to develop, it should be ready to seek the assistance of business and industry.

Structures to Develop

In establishing the plan of action, the planners should consider the structures and meeting agendas needed to convene the required personnel and agree upon goals, objectives, timelines, and agendas. The plan may call for the establishment of a steering committee, a board, and advisory committees. Further, the plan should include strategies for seeking and adding regional and state-level involvement.

Overall, the intent is to create partnerships that serve as advocates for Career Pathways programs and services, to embed the programs within the community, and to leverage the resources of the partnership to enhance the curriculum. At the very least, establishing new and/or strengthening business-education advisory committees is a first step. Advisory committees, consisting of individuals with experience and expertise in the career field that the program serves, can provide these benefits:

- Promote communication among education, business, and industry;
- Identify new and emerging fields and modify existing programs;
- Strengthen programs by providing student competency lists and reviewing curriculum;

- Ensure that each Career Pathway academic ladder matches the corresponding industry career ladder;
- Review student outcomes (completion rates, placement rates, and state licensing examination outcomes);
- Ensure that programs are relevant and up-to-date;
- Assess the equipment and facilities available and make recommendations as needed;
- Provide work-based learning experiences for learners;
- Provide training opportunities for educators;
- Advocate programs to communities and legislators;
- Assist with placement of program completers;
- Promote Career Pathways and inform communities about them;
- Seek legislative support for Career Pathways; and
- Leverage community resources (equipment, facilities, materials, and broker community partnerships).[11]

While it is typical to find general CTE advisory committees that gather business and industry advisors from all the school's career programs into one committee, the model followed by community and technical colleges works best for Career Pathways support. Career Cluster™- or Career Pathway-specific advisory groups provide the best and most concentrated focus and assistance. Where possible, committees should combine representatives of both secondary and postsecondary to provide the most effective, efficient, and seamless articulation.

The establishment and nurturing of effective advisory committees will take some time. A great deal of planning should take place ahead of selecting advisory committee members, and consideration must be given to who should chair the committee, how it will be maintained and evaluated, and how it will be fashioned to best serve the region's education and business community.

---

11 Debra Mills, *Career Pathways Advisory Committee Toolkit* (CORD, 2011). For an online version, visit www.ncpn.info.

Action Plan for Employer Partnerships

As stated earlier, partnerships between education and business and industry can produce significant results for students and the local economy. An action plan for partnering with area employers should include the following:

1. Development of and agreement upon the career ladders(s) needed by industry for each Career Cluster™ area. Elements of the plan would include:

   • Formation of a career ladder task group with education (secondary and postsecondary) and business membership.

   • Agreement upon a ladder curriculum.[12]

   • Agreement upon the necessary courses, certificates, and degrees.

   • Establishment of the delivery mechanisms.

   • Training of the instructional and career guidance staff as needed.

2. Inventorying the community for existing public and private programs for services required to assist students through their programs. Devise a matrix matching existing programs and services to areas of student need. Elements of the plan should include:

   • Forming a support program task group with secondary, postsecondary, business, and community membership.

   • Identification of gaps in services.

   • Preparation of a plan to address the gaps.

3. Development of a funding/resource acquisition campaign to provide backing for the programs and services needed to ensure student success. Elements of the acquisition plan should include:

   • Development of a case for support for needed programs, services, and facilities that addresses the needs of the community, not just the desires of the educator.

---

12 A *ladder curriculum* "consists of a series of occupational levels that students are expected to attain as they move through their programs" (Hinckley et al., *Adult Career Pathways,* p. 133).

- Testing of the support levels in the community through partnership channels.
- Training of those who will lead and assist with the campaign.

4. Providing opportunities for students within the work setting. For each Program of Study, establish the business support structures. Elements of the plan should include:

- Determination of the where, when, and how according to which internships and related work-based learning will be provided.
- Establishment of an effective mentorship program.[13]

Sustaining Partnerships

To be effective and sustainable, partnerships should be formalized in writing. Formal agreements provide for a working framework for each partner, setting expectations and the desired outcomes. When approved by an education board and signed by each partner, the formal agreement elevates the partnership and its work. Each agreement should state the purpose of the partnership and describe its benefits to the partnering entities. It should include the broad strategic direction of the partnership and the outcomes expected. The agreement should form the basis of active management of the partnership and provide meaningful action plans and guidelines for meetings and communication. It must be built with an eye toward building trust and mutual respect as a foundation for future endeavors.

Beyond the formal agreement, collaborative partnerships should

- Create written memoranda of understanding that specify the roles and responsibilities of the partnership's members.
- Conduct ongoing analysis of economic and workforce trends to identify which statewide/regional Programs of Study should be created, expanded, or discontinued.
- Link into existing initiatives that promote workforce and economic development, such as sector strategies and other

---

13 Adapted from Hinckley et al., *Adult Career Pathways*, p. 101.

activities supported by the Workforce Investment Act as administered through the U.S. Department of Labor.

- Identify, validate, and keep current the technical and workforce readiness skills that should be taught within each Program of Study.

Keep in mind that every partnership should be of equal advantage to all participants. Too often education seeks a one-sided relationship and does not consider the strategic, long-term advantages to each partner, nor does education typically recognize the value of improvement of the ROI for all concerned.

Case Study: Gateway Technical College

Many strong partnerships have emerged across the country. Gateway Technical College, headquartered in Kenosha, Wisconsin, is well ahead of most comparable colleges in its strategic partnerships. Its journey can provide a roadmap for others.

Like many community and technical colleges in America, Gateway serves a population that for many years has enjoyed strong industrial employment opportunities but is now facing the challenges of a changing economic base. Located in southeast Wisconsin midway between Milwaukee and Chicago, Gateway had opportunities to build partnerships with local industry, yet for years had not established a process for leveraging those partnerships to gain an economic and educational advantage for both the community and the college. In 2006 newly appointed President Bryan Albrecht set out to change what business and education partnerships meant to the college and in turn could mean for the nation.

For over 100 years Kenosha had been grounded by the automotive manufacturing industry. Most recently the area was one of Chrysler's engine production plant locations, and prior to Chrysler it was the home of American Motors. Kenosha's deep roots in the automotive industry historically provided the technology, training, and innovation needed to support a regional economy. Gateway also has an extensive history in training related to the automotive industry, with two separate programs located on two campuses. Often, however, the college programs competed with one another for funding and students, which in turn diminished the output of qualified technicians. Faced with increasing demand upon college resources, Gateway closed both automotive programs and established a new vision for automotive training and community investment.

In an initial meeting between executives of Snap-on Tools Corporation, headquartered in Kenosha, and President Albrecht it was clear that this new vision was shaped by the shared interests of Gateway and Snap-on. Snap-on had partnered with schools for decades. As the world's most recognized brand of automotive tools and equipment, Snap-on also saw the future changing for its customers. But even though hand tools will always be essential to technicians, it was also becoming increasingly clear that diagnostic technology was the next generation of skills needed by technicians.

Snap-on had already established itself as the world leader in the sale of diagnostic equipment but had not found a systematic way to deploy the training needed by incumbent technicians whose companies were purchasing the new equipment. The transition to computer-driven solutions to service and repair was creating a gap between existing and needed skills. These issues were discussed at the meeting, at which Dr. Albrecht stated, "To solve this gap we must build a bridge connecting Gateway with Snap-on. We each have a need and the solution is not resting on either side but in the middle."

That initial meeting has led Gateway to national training activities for Snap-on and was the foundation for a national consortium of colleges called the National Coalition of Certification Centers, or NC3. The need for diagnostics training helped to identify the differentiating skill set that Gateway was looking for to increase investment in faculty development and heighten student interest in automotive training. It defined a roadmap that led to the development of Gateway's Horizon Center for Transportation Technology, a new advanced technology center devoted to the industry.

The concept was powerful because each of the leading entities, along with an additional 150 community partners, embraced the vision and found ways to leverage the partnership to benefit their particular needs. Local automotive dealers received more highly skilled technicians, local banks found young entrepreneurs to invest in, and local municipalities found a place to demonstrate new technologies such as hybrid vehicles. The change had built momentum that carries on today throughout multiple programs and partnerships at Gateway.

141

Developing the platform for solving the basic problem of diagnostics technology training is still the defining challenge in moving forward. From the beginning the curriculum and certification programs related to the technologies were jointly developed by Gateway faculty and Snap-on industry experts. This shared responsibility secured everyone's involvement and commitment to success. Teaching the latest technology and having access to the designers and creators of that technology add immeasurable value to the quality of the instruction and performance of the students. In an industry that is fast paced and changes with every new model, it is imperative that Gateway instructors work hand-in-hand with the industry professionals who are developing this technology.

The Horizon Center concept was established to solve a problem that Gateway had with competing automotive programming and to serve as a means for Snap-on to begin building capacity for the introduction of an emerging technology in the automotive industry. The Horizon Center was the first Snap-on branded diagnostic training center in the country, and now there are over 60 colleges with Snap-on diagnostic partnerships, including one in Morocco that Gateway assisted in establishing. While they are not all called Horizon Centers, they all share the common elements of the partnership through curriculum and training certifications. Gateway uses the name "Horizon" to represent three industries in which training is delivered in a single building — automotive, diesel, and aviation. Hence the idea of the horizon, where sky and land meet. As a result of the unique perspective of a shared training center, the vision for certification across industries was created. Through NC3, certifications now exist in automotive, diesel, torque, electronics, and aviation. NC3 creates common core knowledge and skills that enhance the qualifications of students and technicians while strengthening the bridge between all partnering colleges and supporting industries. Snap-on and Gateway have led the way, but many colleges are now leveraging the vision and accessing certification and training resources through partners such as Snap-on, Trane Corporation, and the Federal Aviation Administration.

Strategies for sustaining the Gateway/Snap-on partnership were designed into the model from the beginning. Benchmarks, progress reports, and a governance model established through a 501(c)3 independent organization have allowed for colleges to help shape the future direction of the partnership. For Gateway it has meant increased student enrollment, enhanced community visibility, integrated training opportunities for faculty and students, and opportunities for other programs and disciplines to replicate the model. Gateway has replicated the model by (among other means) securing anchor industry partners in

- Horticulture with Bacho Tools,
- Cosmetology with Andis Tools,
- Industrial maintenance with Insinkerator,
- Energy systems with Ingersoll Rand and Trane,
- Computer numerical control with HAAS,
- Information technology with IBM,
- Surgical technology with Bradshaw Medical,
- Career boot camps in manufacturing with SC Johnson Company, and
- Fire service with Pierce Manufacturing.

Sharing solutions and the responsibility for sustaining those solutions has transformed the way Gateway establishes and improves programs. According to Dr. Albrecht, "Our future will be built upon anchor partnerships that drive curriculum and change in our culture at Gateway." Further, according to Nick Pinchuk, CEO of Snap-on, Inc.,

> Technical education is a key differentiator in keeping the United States competitive in the world economy. Snap-on is proud to partner with Gateway and our nation's community and technical colleges to enhance the skills for America's workforce.

Success can be measured in several ways and is reported through metrics established by the partners. Enrollment, student success and completion, and student and employer satisfaction surveys are the traditional metrics by which Gateway measures progress. Added to that are the number of certifications earned, return on investment back to the colleges for products sold by industry partners, replicated models within Gateway, community outreach through engagement activities held at the center, increased training and credentials for faculty, leveraged business sponsorships, and increased grant resources through college-to-college collaboration. One element that should be highlighted but cannot be measured is local branding of the program and college through the leveraging of the world brand of Snap-on. Snap-on has co-branded the colleges in the NC3 network and features them in its international marketing strategies.

In recognizing Gateway's work with the awarding of a U.S. Department of Labor High Growth grant, the former assistant secretary of the department's Employment and Training Administration stated,

> Leadership must come from all corners for a region to be successful, and you're fortunate that Gateway Technical College has risen to the occasion. Their High Growth grant was a little less than a million dollars and they could have been satisfied with simply producing the curriculum and training program that had been outlined. But they were able to leverage an additional $2 million from the private sector to build a state-of-the-art center.[14]

Getting Started

Gateway's example is extensive and has taken exceptionally focused work to achieve. It started with good ideas and willing partners and through the diligence of those involved has become its own engine of creative change and improvement of programs at the college.

Many resources exist and more are being developed to assist the education community in developing and sustaining effective partnerships. An online professional development course in building strategic partnerships is available at *www.acp-sc.org* courtesy of the Designing Instruction for Career Pathways project as funded by the U.S. Department of Education's Office of Vocational Adult Education (OVAE) Division of Adult Education and Literacy. The document *Thriving in Challenging Times*, available at *http://www.ncpn.info/ thriving-in-challenging-times.php*, provides 17 examples of career pathways models built on business and industry partnerships. Attesting to the influence of partnerships, the following quotations are excerpted from that document:

> Partnerships are paramount in the development and implementation of successful career exploration programs. In providing career

---

14 National Career Pathways Network and the Institute for a Competitive Workforce, *Thriving in Challenging Times: Connecting Education to Economic Development through Career Pathways*, 2012 (http://www.ncpn.info/ downloads/Thriving_in_Challenging_Times.pdf), p. 38.

exploration experiences for thousands of Southern California high school students in the last 20 years, this program has proven that lesson many times over. (The Graphic Communications Academic Challenge Program, Southern California, p. 25)

Success depends on the involvement of top-level administrators and business representatives. It takes two to three years of steady effort for career pathways programs to succeed. The keys to success are consistency, persistence, and patience. (The Brunswick County Health Sciences Career Pathway, Supply, North Carolina, p. 31)

Align high school curriculum at the onset with community college competencies for dual credit; high school students will form postsecondary relationships from the beginning. Find passionate business leaders who are willing to fund the startup; other businesses and the public sector will follow. (The Advanced Manufacturing Technology and Aerospace Initiative, Snohomish County, Washington, p. 13)

This project demonstrates the value of partnerships and the importance of including the community from the onset. Strong partnerships and community involvement create a broad base of support and help ensure that the project meets the needs of the constituents it is designed to serve. (The Horizon Center for Transportation Technology, Kenosha, Wisconsin, p. 39)

Years of intense Tech Prep support structure development yielded countless examples of 2+2+2 intergovernmental agreements, dual credit arrangements, and collaborative working relationships among business/industry, education, labor, workforce entities, and community organizations that can serve as Career Pathways building blocks. Collaboration was manifested in high school area career centers, high schools on college campuses, and secondary districts utilizing college campus laboratories, to name only a few of the creative and effective partnerships that gained a foothold in the 1980s and 1990s. A strong recent example was featured in the National Career Pathways Network newsletter, *NCPN Connections,* volume 21-3. Mortenous A. Johnson's article "An Adaptable Model That Prepares Students for College and Workforce Credentials While in High School" describes the work of the partnership between the Dayton Public Schools' Ponitz Career Technology Center and Sinclair Community College (OH) in addressing the call for improvement in high school graduation rates.

Among the article's key points is that "the model fosters collaboration between postsecondary and secondary partners and community and workforce agencies."[15]

Other Resources

A growing body of literature is being assembled by organizations such as the Office of Community College Research and Leadership (OCCRL) at the University of Illinois Urbana-Champaign. Their June 2010 document titled *Promising Practice: A Community College and Employer Partnership* provided this example:

> Oakton Community College (OCC) partnered with Presbyterian Homes to develop a bridge course to prepare a cadre of their employed Certified Nurse Assistants (CNAs) to enter a college-credit level prerequisite course to a Practical Nursing program. Three strategies for supporting their initiative were described, including: 1. Commitment to Working Through Issues, 2. Shared Provision of Support Services, and 3. Frequent and Open Communication. Evidence-of-success data points were described and success was measured at the organizational level (college/employer partnership) and at the student level. Fifteen of 17 students completed the course, 14 enrolled in the next course in the prerequisite sequence and at the time of the article were on track to graduate.

In another resource, the *In Brief Newsletter,* OCCRL featured "Bridges Across the P-16 Continuum: The Role of Educational Partnerships" by Pamela L. Eddy, College of William and Mary, and Marilyn J. Amey, Michigan State University. The article accumulates and synthesizes studies of and research on educational partnerships, including the utilization of change models and the recognition of critical stages in partnership development.

Partnerships are an essential component of Perkins IV and are at the very core of developing successful Career Pathway programs and services. Effective partnerships extend the classroom into the workplace and the community, to the advantage of students, teachers, and employers. They are an essential key to establishing comprehensive Programs of Study, as will be discussed in the next section of this book.

---

15 http://www.cordonline.net/connections/21_3/.

SECTION III CHECK-UP

After reading the **PARTNER** section chapters, complete this initial formative assessment to determine where your schools, colleges, and region stand regarding the organization and structures needed to support Career Pathways implementation, evolution, and sustainability. How you rate your readiness may indicate the need for a deeper analysis, including a comprehensive self-evaluation and external evaluation.

PARTNER Checklist		Disagree			Agree	
	NA	−2	−1	0	1	2
(1) A collaborative partnership (comprising secondary and postsecondary education, business/industry/labor, appropriate economic and workforce agencies, and community- and/or faith-based organizations) has been established and supports Career Pathways.						
(2) A written agreement (MOU, charter, or by-laws) outlines the basic elements of the partnership and roles and responsibilities for each stakeholder.						
(3) The partnership has a shared vision and decision-making process.						
(4) The partnership conducts ongoing analyses of economic and workforce trends to identify regional POS to be created, expanded, or discontinued.						
(5) Duplication of effort has been reduced by merging overlapping existing advisory committees or developing a cross-representation structure.						

Section IV. Deliver

CTE is delivered through comprehensive Programs of Study aligned to the National Career Clusters™ Framework.

The chapters in the previous sections have described the nuts and bolts of moving forward in the classroom and securing community support services. While we consider how the best Programs of Study are delivered, the word comprehensive takes center stage. CTE is a system, not a program. It has well-conceived underpinnings and involves a distinctive framework.

The CTE system considers where it has been and where it must go. It considers more than instructional methodology by formalizing services for the whole student, such as guidance and counseling, instructional rigor and relevance, and real-world experiences.

This section includes five chapters in which the main initiatives moving CTE are discussed. A chapter on the National Career Clusters™ Framework relates the process that determined a structure for Career Pathways. A chapter on standards discusses the Career Cluster™ knowledge and skills statements and provides further discussion of the Common Core State Standards and the Common Career Technical Core roll-out across the states and the incorporation of specific company/industry technical skills standards. A chapter on course sequences discusses the POS design process and provides examples of CTE delivery system characteristics and implementation strategies. A chapter on teaching and learning considers contextual, innovative teaching and learning techniques as a cornerstone to sound educational practice. The final chapter in this section considers the importance of guidance and counseling in its formal and informal contexts and provides a strong list of recommendations.

POS Framework Components Supported

College and Career Readiness Standards • Course Sequences
Credit Transfer Agreements • Teaching and Learning Strategies
Guidance Counseling and Academic Advisement
Professional Development

The National Career Clusters™ Framework

Ron McCage and Dean Folkers

The National Career Clusters™ Framework provides a vital structure for organizing and delivering high-quality CTE programs through learning and comprehensive Programs of Study (POS). The Framework also serves to support career awareness and exploration by providing a common language. In total, there are 16 Career Clusters™ in the National Career Clusters™ Framework, representing 79 Career Pathways designed to help students navigate their way to greater success in college and careers.

As an organizing tool for curriculum design and instruction, the Framework provides the essential knowledge and skills for the 16 Career Clusters™ and their Career Pathways. It also functions as a useful guide in developing POS, bridging secondary and postsecondary curriculum, and for creating individual student plans of study for a complete range of career options. As such, it helps students discover their interests and their passions, and empowers them to choose the educational pathways that can lead to success in high school, college, and careers.

And because the knowledge and skills encompass both secondary and postsecondary education, the Framework informs efforts to strengthen and improve students' transition from secondary to postsecondary education and ultimately into careers of their choice.

Early History of the Career Clusters™

While credit for coining the term "career education" and the initiation of the career education movement is often given to Commissioner of Education Dr. Sidney P. Marland, Jr., it was the previous Commissioner, Dr. James E. Allen, who first used the term "career education" in a 1970 speech to the National Association of Secondary School Principals, almost a year before Marland's now famous *Career Education Now* speech to the same group in 1971. Later that year, Marland delivered an address to the National Association of State Directors of Vocational Education (now NASDCTEc) during which he stressed the necessity of constructing a sound, systematized relationship between education and work through which it would be standard practice to teach every student about occupations and the economic enterprise to better meet the manpower needs of the country.[1]

While both Allen and Marland can be credited with the establishment of the concept of career education, Marland clearly brought about its acceptance and implementation as a way of organizing education around the "world of work" using career development as the major context for guiding students within the system. Consequently, Marland directed the U.S. Office of Education (USOE; now U.S. Department of Education, ED) in developing and disseminating fifteen career clusters that identified the major business and industry sectors in existence at the time so that everyone could see where they fit into the broader context of the "world of work." The career clusters were:

- Agribusiness and natural resources occupations
- Business and office occupations
- Communications and media occupations
- Construction occupations
- Consumer and homemaking occupations
- Environmental control occupations
- Fine arts and humanities occupations
- Health occupations

---

1 L. Bailey and R. Stadt, *Career Education: New Approaches to Human Development* (Bloomington, IL: McKnight Publishing Company, 1973).

- Hospitality and recreation occupations
- Manufacturing occupations
- Marine science occupations
- Marketing and distribution occupations
- Personal services occupations
- Public service occupations
- Transportation occupations

In the early 1970s, USOE defined *career education* as "an effort aimed at focusing American education and the actions of the broader community in ways that will help individuals acquire and use the knowledge, skills and attitudes necessary for each to make work a meaningful, productive, and satisfying part of his or her way of living."[2]

In addition to creating the first set of career clusters, Marland also directed USOE's research arm, the National Institute for Education, to fund four experimental models for the purpose of determining the best ways to implement the career education concept:

- School-based Model I
- Employee-based Model II
- Home-community-based Model III
- Rural-residential-based Model IV

As the Director of Research and Development for the Illinois Department of Adult, Vocational, and Technical Education, one of the authors of this chapter (Ron McCage) was the national project director for School-based Model I. As an outcome of the project, Illinois developed one of the first state-level models (simplified version shown below) for career education, and virtually every other state followed suit shortly thereafter. As the figure illustrates, career education was presented as a lifelong pursuit that involved all aspects and levels of education. The model is also one of the first that clearly illustrated that vocational education had an important connection to elementary and middle school and led beyond high school and into the world of work via multiple exit points.

---

2 Bailey and Stadt, *Career Education.*

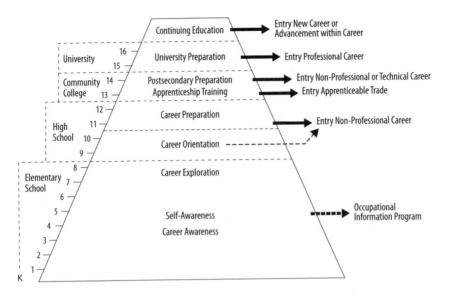

Ken Hoyt, an authority on career guidance and later the director of the Office of Career Education, provided his definition of "career education," which merges his definitions of "career" and "education":

[One's "career" is] the totality of the work one does in his or her lifetime. "Education" is the totality of experiences through which one learns. Based on these two definitions, "career education" is the totality of experiences through which one learns about work as a part of his or her way of living. "Career" is a developmental concept beginning in the very early years and continuing well into the retirement years. "Education," as defined here, obviously includes more than the formal educational system. Thus, this generic definition of career education is purposely intended to be of a very broad and encompassing nature. At the same time, it is intended to be considerably less than all of one's reasons for living.[3]

Because of the growing interest in career education, Congress amended Public Law 93-380: The Educational Amendments of 1974, as follows:

Section 406, Title 1V, Public Law 93-380 (Educational Amendments of 1974), made career education a law of the land while establishing a National Advisory Council on Career Education.

---

3 Bailey and Stadt, *Career Education.*

- Every child should, by the time they have completed secondary school, be prepared for gainful employment and for full participation in society according to his or her ability.

- It is the obligation of each LEA [local education agency] to provide that preparation for all children (including handicapped children and all other children who are educationally disadvantaged) within the school district of such agency; and

- Each state and local educational agency should carry out a program of career education options which are designed to prepare each child for maximum employment and participation in our society according to his or her ability.

In 1977 Congress passed Public Law 92-207 (The Career Education and Incentive Act). Its primary purposes were as follows:

- To assist states and local educational agencies and institutions of postsecondary education including collaborative arrangements with the appropriate agencies and organizations in making education a preparation for work, and as a means of relating work values to life roles and choices (such as family life), a major goal of all who teach and all who learn by increasing the emphasis they place on career awareness, exploration, decision making, and planning. And to do so in a manner which will promote equal opportunity in making career choices through the elimination of bias and stereotyping in such activities, including bias and stereotyping on account of race, sex, age, economic status, or handicap.

- To create an office of career education with a director and provide funding, though modest when compared to the Vocational Education Appropriation.

The main focus of career education at that time (as defined in the legislation) was on providing career guidance and helping students to see the importance of work as a lifelong pursuit. There was very little focus on developing classroom-related materials such as curriculum or assessments. More importantly, the Marland Career Clusters created a world of work umbrella under which everyone could theoretically fit given a broader context. Consequently, those teaching academics could see how what they taught was used in the real world, and students could see how their choices of occupations might lead to more meaningful careers. For a period of time everyone seemed to want to work together for the betterment of students and the larger community. However, when the Career Education Incentive Act was passed and began to be implemented, there was a breakdown in the level of cooperation because career education, which now had its own office and funding source, began to be viewed as a competing program to vocational education and other fields in education and workforce development. Consequently, the concept began to die.

During the first cycle of career clusters, John P. Gnadinger, president, founder, and CEO of Soil Testing Systems, Inc. (an internationally successful civil engineering firm), created a set of sixteen career clusters representing economic sectors. The project his foundation co-funded in partnership with CTECS produced 16 booklets representing the economic sectors as he saw them from his perspective as a highly successful CEO. What is fascinating about Gnadinger's understanding of the "world of work" is how far he was ahead of his time. Some of the clusters he identified weren't even on the radar until recently. These include Arts, Culture and Religion, Communications, Education, Energy, Finance, Government Service, Hospitality, Insurance, Natural Resources and Transportation along with the more traditional ones of Agriculture, Construction (which he called Built Environment), Health Care, Manufacturing, Personal and Business Services and Retailing and Wholesaling. Shown below are the covers for the manufacturing and education booklets.

Career Clusters™ and the Skill Standards Projects of the 1990s

The career clusters concept was given fresh momentum in 1994 with the passage of the National School-to-Work Opportunities Act, which promoted the use of Career Pathways and career majors as a framework for the delivery of work-based programs and career development strategies. This momentum was also driven in part by the 22 technical skill standards projects funded by the U. S. Department of Education (ED) (16 projects) and the U. S. Department of Labor (DOL) (6 projects) between 1992 and 1998. Each of the projects was asked to accomplish the following tasks:

1. Analyze an occupation or group of occupations to define and validate the units of work, e.g., duties/tasks and/or functions.

2. Write a set of performance standards or skill standards for the occupation or group of occupations under review.

3. Develop a means of certifying that a person possessing the knowledge and skills inherent in these standards could be certified as meeting the standards.

4. Establish a means of perpetuating the work long-term, i.e., establish an organization such as the National Institute for Automotive Service Excellence (ASE) or the National Institute for Metalworking Skills (NIMS) that could continue to update and maintain the work.

The skill standards projects were experimental, so their definitions, published outcomes, and display formats were not required to be consistent from one project to the next. In fact, using different approaches and formats was strongly encouraged by the sponsors, ED and DOL. The first major shift toward consistency occurred with the passing of the National School to Work Opportunities Act and the Goals 2000 Legislation, which contained provisions for the establishment of a National Skills Standards Board (NSSB) that featured employer-led Skill Councils made up of employers, employees, organized labor, education, and others for each industry. Consequently, uniformity of process and product became the order of the day.

How the National Career Clusters™ Initiative Came to Be and What It Has Accomplished

The Linkages Projects: Round One

Certain elements of the National Career Clusters™ Initiative can be traced to 1996, at which time the National School to Work Opportunities Office (NSWOO), NSSB, and ED's Office of Vocational and Adult Education (OVAE) formed a partnership to support an initiative originally referred to as Linkages. Each of the three agencies that were involved in sponsoring the first round of Linkages Projects had different reasons for being involved. NSSB was interested in promoting broad economic clusters, so each project was asked to address an industry or occupational sector. NSWOO was interested in promoting transportable credentials, so one of the main focuses was on creating ways to document skills so that holders could take their portfolios with them and have equal currency in the marketplace no matter where they were. OVAE was interested in the integration of academic and occupational skills, so a major focus was on relating national academic and industrial skill standards to state academic and occupational standards within the broader context of occupational sectors, the ultimate goal being to provide transportable credentials based on industry-validated standards. Another overriding requirement of the round one Linkages Projects was that each project be led by a state agency using a consortium made up of representatives from business, industry, labor, and education.

Since the initial three projects were funded as grants, a great deal of freedom was given to each grantee. However, as the effort was rolled out, the sponsors began to see that each of the projects was going down a different path in regard to processes and outcomes. For instance, Utah's Health Linkages Project was used as a vehicle to further what had been accomplished in one of the original 22 skill standards projects. Indiana's Manufacturing Linkages Project was being used as a vehicle for furthering the implementation of the Certification of Technical Achievement Initiative originally undertaken by the Indiana Department of Workforce Development working with the Career and Technical Education Consortium of States (CTECS; formerly VTECS, the Vocational and Technical Education Consortium of States). A third project was terminated during the second year because the sponsor deemed its focus as being too narrow.

The Linkages Projects: Round Two

As the first group of Linkages Projects was coming to an end in 1999, a second group was initiated by OVAE (the only remaining sponsor), which opened the process to entities other than states and vowed to monitor the projects more closely to ensure uniformity. The second RFP (request for proposal) specified that the three projects address the same fourteen predetermined tasks. The occupational sectors chosen for the second round of Linkages Projects were audio-visual technology and telecommunications (contract awarded to VTECS), which was eventually expanded to include arts and communications when the official transitions to Career Clusters™ occurred; information technology (contract awarded to Education Development Corporation (EDC); and transportation, distribution, and logistics (contract awarded to the state of Illinois).

In 1999, OVAE made a game-changing decision when it began to require the use of Career Clusters™ as a means of reporting student enrollment as a part of the Perkins accountability requirements, which meant that the Career Clusters™ had to be more clearly defined and that a framework had to be developed for each cluster to include crosswalks to ED's Classification of Instructional Programs Codes and Titles (CIP) and DOL's Standard Occupational Classification System (SOC/O*NET) to ensure that all the entities submitting enrollment information were counting people the same way.

Lack of uniformity across projects was still an issue, and it was becoming increasingly clear that uniformity could only be achieved if all the Career Clusters™ were developed under one master developer with one set of guidelines. Consequently, the chief executives of VTECS (now CTECS), CORD, and the National Association of State Directors of Career Technical Education Consortium (NASDCTEc) played a major role in convincing ED to issue an RFP that permitted the remaining eleven clusters to be addressed as a package. To that end, the board of directors of NASDCTEc submitted a proposal to address all eleven clusters. The state of Oklahoma was named the fiscal agent, and Charles Losh was appointed project director. Thus the States' Career Clusters™ Initiative was born.

Development of the Sixteen Career Clusters™ and Respective Pathways

The historical overview excerpted below appeared in the introduction to *Career Cluster Resources for Arts, A/V Technology and Communications,* one of the sixteen Career Cluster™ guides formerly published on the website of the States' Career Clusters Initiative (www.careerclusters. org):[4]

> The U.S. Department of Education Office of Vocational and Adult Education (OVAE) has identified 16 Career Clusters™ representing career opportunities for the 21st century economy. These clusters will frame student opportunities as they pursue postsecondary education and a wide range of career opportunities from front-line to professional and managerial careers.
>
> [The] Career Clusters™ initiative [was] launched June 1, 2001. Twelve lead states and the District of Columbia were partners in the development of the tools supporting eleven career clusters which, when combined with the five clusters that have already been developed, will represent all career possibilities.
>
> The National Association of State Directors for Career and Technical Education Consortium (NASDCTEc) and their Board of Directors assumed leadership for coordinating the project, [which was] designed to establish curriculum frameworks and supportive materials for each cluster, with a broad-based advisory committee for each cluster, led by a state. . . .
>
> The lead states included: Idaho and Iowa (jointly leading the Agriculture, Food and Natural Resources cluster), Pennsylvania (Architecture and Construction), Ohio (Marketing, Sales and Service), North Dakota (Finance), West Virginia (Hospitality and Tourism), South Carolina (Business, Management and Administration), Kentucky (Human Services), Arkansas (Law, Public Safety and Security), North Carolina (Science, Technology, Engineering and Mathematics), Michigan (Education and Training), and Oklahoma and the District of Columbia/Washington D.C. (jointly leading the Government and Public Administration cluster).

---

4 Today visitors to careerclusters.org are rerouted to http://www.ca-reertech.org/, the new NASDCTEc website.

The five additional Career Clusters™ included Health Science led by the State of Utah, Manufacturing led by the State of Indiana, Arts, Audio/Video Technology and Communications led by the VTECS Consortium, Information Technology led by the Educational Development Center, Inc., and Transportation, Distribution and Logistics led by the State of Illinois. . . .

Development work for the States' Career Clusters™ Initiative began June 1, 2001 [in Oklahoma City]. . . . In January of 2002, the lead state teams were brought together in Phoenix to begin the process of developing knowledge and skill statements for each of the cluster pathways and foundations. . . . The National Advisory Committee met in March of 2002, and reviewed the curriculum frameworks, credentials list, and lead state advisory committee memberships and structures. . . . The Executive Committee, made up of the Board of the NASDCTEc, also met in March, approved the materials and discussed the future actions needed to assure implementation of the cluster materials. . . .

Development of the products needed for curriculum and assessment was fast-tracked, with the knowledge and skill statements, performance elements and measurement criteria ready for validation by July 15, 2002. . . .

Given the efforts of the developmental teams, cluster advisory committee members were able to review and validate the knowledge and skills and supporting elements. Additionally, a national web-based validation was conducted from July 15 to August 15, 2002. All 50 states were invited to a dissemination meeting held in Charleston, South Carolina Sept 13, 2002, where the materials were distributed to participants for their use in updating their curriculum.

NASDCTEc provided the following definitions:

The term **Career Clusters™** represents a grouping of occupations and broad industries based on commonalities.

The Career Cluster™ Framework organized the occupations, within each Career Cluster, into Career Pathways that group the cluster occupations based on commonalities.

Within the **Career Cluster™ Framework**, each level is defined as follows:

Cluster Level
Represents the skill and knowledge, both academic and technical, that all students within the cluster should achieve regardless of their pathway.

Pathway Level
Represents the skill and knowledge, both academic and technical, necessary to pursue a full range of career opportunities within a pathway — ranging from entry level to management, including technical and professional career specialties.

Career Specialties
Represents the full range of career opportunities within each pathway.[5]

Initial Research Regarding the Grouping of the Career Clusters™

In 1994 Dr. Joan Wills, Director of Workforce Development for the Institute for Educational Leadership, asked co-author Dr. McCage to write one of the seventeen DOL-commissioned papers that were to be advisory to the yet-to-be-established NSSB. In setting the context for the paper, Dr. Wills posed the following question: "If one could group the world of work around broad occupational or industry-based clusters, how many would there be? Given a systematically determined number of clusters, how many subgroups, i.e., pathways or concentrations, would there be within each group?"

After agreeing to write the paper and after reviewing all the major systems for the classification and coding of educational programs, occupations, and/or industries, including the New North American Industrial Classification System, Dr. McCage arrived at fourteen occupational families with over sixty subgroups. In addition, a four-tier model was proposed as a way of arranging information from broad

---

5 National Association of State Directors of Career and Technical Education Consortium, *Career Clusters™: Focusing Education on the Future* (a Speakers Kit PowerPoint), February 2003.

to specific. The broadest level was originally called *occupational fami-lies,* since "families" was the most widely used term for describing the most general level in virtually all the major industrial and occupa-tional classification systems that existed at the time. The second level was called *occupational clusters,* the third *occupational specialties,* and the fourth *occupational job titles.* The original occupational family titles that emerged from this research were actually a set of combined and modi-fied CIP code titles that had been carefully cross-walked to the other coding systems for continuity across systems in terms of coverage.

CIP Codes	Original Fourteen Combined and Modified Titles Derived from the 1990 Classification of Instruction Programs
01, 02, 03	Agricultural, Forestry, Natural Resource Occupations
08	Marketing and Distributive Occupations
	Personal Service and Miscellaneous Occupations
09, 10	Arts and Communication Occupations
14, 14, 15, 41	Engineering and Science Related Occupations
08, 20, 31	Hospitality and Tourism Occupations
22, 43	Protective and Legal Services Occupations
46	Construction Trades Occupations
47	Mechanics/Technicians, Installers, Repairer Service Occupations
48	Precision and Production Occupations
49	Transportation and Material Moving Occupations
51	Health Occupations
44, 52	Business, Finance Management and Administration
13	Education and Training Occupations

To distinguish between levels, the following two-, four-, six-, and eight-digit system was proposed as a way of going from general to specific. The 1990 CIP was invaluable in arriving at this concept, since it was already structured along this line of thinking.

00.   Occupational Family/Industry
   00.00   Occupational Cluster/Programs
      00.0000   Occupational Specialties/Clusters/Skills
         00.000000   Occupational Job Titles/Programs

The second question that Dr. Wills wanted feedback on was, "How do we define industry clusters using only knowledge and skills statements, as contrasted to the traditional approach of using units of work such as duties/tasks and critical work functions?" In this context, it was concluded that both elements were needed and, in fact, were already present in most of the nationally recognized standards development approaches being used at the time. In March 1996, the VTECS Board of Directors adopted these fourteen clusters as its major framework for determining which occupations to include in an analysis based on the assumption of commonality across titles. To make it easier to understand, VTECS built its own CIP/SOC Crosswalk of the areas it was addressing or intended to address and developed a wheel for each family showing how the elements related to each other from general to specific.

In addition to being a part of the research base for creating NSSB's Industry Clusters, the research carried out by VTECS on the grouping of clusters was later shared with OVAE as it worked to decide on titles for its sixteen clusters in 1999. Once ED released its sixteen Career Clusters™, the VTECS board of directors asked that the VTECS Industry/Occupational Families be aligned with ED's sixteen Career Clusters™. This review resulted in the conversion of the original fourteen VTECS wheels into sixteen wheels using concentrations as the grouping element for occupational specialties. To the degree possible, the concentrations (now called pathways) shared a common base of essential knowledge and skills.

In arriving at its sixteen Career Clusters™, OVAE used economic sectors as their organizer rather than the commonality of knowledge and skills that is critical from a curriculum and instruction point of view. This is why some of the Career Clusters™ do not readily lend themselves to curriculum and assessment development and that certain pathways appear in more than one Career Cluster™. (This is especially critical when it comes to the occupational areas that center around hydraulics, pneumatics, electronics, and mechanical skills.) A chart comparing the Career Clusters™ identified by NSSB and ED is shown below.

ED/OVAE'S SIXTEEN CAREER CLUSTERS™	NSSB FIFTEEN INDUSTRY CLUSTERS
1. Agriculture, Food and Natural Resources	1. Agriculture, Forestry and Fishing 2. Mining
2. Architecture and Construction	3. Construction
3. Arts, Audio/Video Technology and Communications 4. Information Technology	4. Telecommunications, Computers, Arts, Entertainment and Information Technology
5. Business, Management and Administration	5. Business and Administrative Services
6. Education and Training	6. Education and Training
7. Marketing, Sales and Service	7. Retail Trade, Wholesale Trade, Real Estate and Personal Services
8. Finance	8. Finance and Insurance
9. Hospitality and Tourism	9. Restaurants, Lodging, Hospitality and Tourism, and Amusement and Recreation
10. Health Science 11. Human Services	10. Health and Human Services
12. Law, Public Safety and Security 13. Government and Public Administration	11. Public Administration, Legal and Protective Services
	12. Utilities and Environmental and Waste Management
14. Manufacturing	13. Manufacturing, Installation and Repair
15. Science, Technology, Engineering and Mathematics	14. Scientific and Technical Services
16. Transportation, Distribution & Logistics	15. Transportation

The evolution and development of the Career Clusters™ built upon the early work from the states and the efforts to identify the educational expectation within each of the industry areas. The Knowledge and Skills statements that resulted from this early work by the states provided a foundation for informing and framing the outcomes students need to achieve and served as a baseline for states to support within the context of the Framework. The work ultimately provided the foundation for the creation of the States' Career Cluster Initiative (SCCI). The collaboration and commitment among the states to support the work and continue providing leadership was critical to the evolution and sustained use of Career Clusters™ that exists today.

Career Clusters™ Today

In 2002, the States' Career Clusters™ Initiative began as a means of continuing the development and implementation of the career clusters concept. The initiative became a part of the focus of NASDCTEc.

Today the National Career Clusters™ Framework continues to serve as a critical model for organizing and delivering high-quality CTE programs through comprehensive Programs of Study (POS). The 16 Career Clusters™ in the National Career Clusters™ Framework representing 79 Career Pathways provide one of the keys to improving student achievement by creating relevant contexts for studying and learning. Career Clusters™ link school-based learning with the knowledge and skills required for success in the workplace and serve as an organizing tool for curriculum design and instruction. In addition to identifying the knowledge and skills expected by employers, the Career Clusters™ serve as a useful guide in developing POS, bridging secondary and postsecondary curriculum, and creating individual student plans of study for a complete range of career options. The role of the Framework also helps students discover their interests and even their passions to empower them to select the educational Career Pathways that can lead to success in high school, college, and careers.

The Career Clusters™ Framework supports efforts to strengthen and improve student transition from secondary to postsecondary education by helping students prepare themselves to meet industry expectations. An important aspect of the Career Clusters™ is a strong focus on the economic development and workforce priorities that ensures flexibility for states to adapt one or more of the Career Clusters™ to reflect key educational objectives, standards, or priorities.

Each Career Cluster™ represents a distinct grouping of occupations and industries based on the knowledge and skills they require.

- **Agriculture, Food and Natural Resources** — The production, processing, marketing, distribution, financing, and development of agricultural commodities and resources including food, fiber, wood products, natural resources, horticulture, and other plant and animal products/resources.

- **Architecture & Construction** — Careers in designing, planning, managing, building, and maintaining the built environment.

- **Arts, A/V Technology and Communications** — Designing, producing, exhibiting, performing, writing, and publishing multimedia content including visual and performing arts and design, journalism, and entertainment services.

- **Business Management and Administration** — Careers in planning, organizing, directing, and evaluating business functions essential to efficient and productive business operations.

- **Education & Training** — Planning, managing, and providing education and training services, and related learning support services such as administration, teaching/training, administrative support, and professional support services.

- **Finance** — Planning and related services for financial and investment planning, banking, insurance, and business financial management.

- **Government and Public Administration** — Planning and executing government functions at the local, state, and federal levels, including governance, national security, foreign service, planning, revenue and taxation, and regulations.

- **Health Science** — Planning, managing, and providing therapeutic services, diagnostic services, health informatics, support services, and biotechnology research and development.

- **Hospitality and Tourism** — Preparing individuals for employment in career pathways that relate to families and human needs such as restaurant and food/beverage services, lodging, travel and tourism, recreation, amusement, and attractions.

- **Human Services** — Preparing individuals for employment in career pathways that relate to families and human needs such as counseling and mental health services, family and community services, personal care, and consumer services.

- **Information Technology** — Building linkages in IT occupations for entry-level, technical, and professional careers related to the design, development, support, and management of hardware, software, multimedia, and systems integration services.

- **Law, Public Safety, Corrections, and Security**—Planning, managing, and providing legal, public safety, protective services, and homeland security, including professional and technical support services.

- **Manufacturing**—Planning, managing, and performing the processing of materials into intermediate or final products and related professional and technical support activities such as production planning and control, maintenance, and manufacturing/process engineering.

- **Marketing**—Planning, managing, and performing marketing activities to reach organizational objectives such as brand management, professional sales, merchandising, marketing communications and market research.

- **Science, Technology, Engineering, and Mathematics**— Planning, managing, and providing scientific research, professional and technical services (e.g., physical science, social science, engineering) including laboratory and testing services, and research and development services.

- **Transportation, Distribution, & Logistics**—The planning, management, and movement of people, materials, and goods by road, pipeline, air, rail and water and related professional and technical support services such as transportation infrastructure planning and management, logistics services, mobile equipment, and facility maintenance.

Career Clusters™: A Foundation for the Common Career Technical Core

Since 2002, the Career Cluster™ Knowledge and Skills Statements established a set of common learning expectations in CTE. In fact, technically, one could suggest that the Knowledge and Skills Statements may well be considered the first set of national, state-developed common "standards." However, as is shown in Chapter 9, which lays out the pathway to common standards, the nation wasn't quite ready for common standards in 2002. In 2002, the nation was setting national education goals but still allowing for state variation in standards and assessments. As our economy has evolved over the last decade, so too has the perception that states must collaborate if the nation is to compete in the global economy. And as a system that is responsive to changes in the workplace, CTE has risen to the challenge.

Many CTE programs transitioned from helping students prepare for entry-level jobs to helping students prepare for careers. As part of that transition, national organizations such as NASDCTEc, individual states, and even industry-based organizations created different sets of standards for student learning in CTE programs. The result was a hodgepodge of standards that vary in quality and specificity from one state to the next, putting some students at a distinct disadvantage for competing in the ever-changing global economy.

Recognizing the need for more consistency in today's global market-place, in the spring of 2010 CTE State Directors united around a vision for CTE entitled *Reflect, Transform, Lead.* That vision, as described in Chapter 1, set forth five principles and contained action steps to achieve the principles. One of the action steps was to develop a shared set of standards that meet a quality benchmark for students in CTE programs, regardless of where they live or which delivery system they use. A specific action step called for the creation of a "common technical core" (http://www.careertech.org/career-technical-education/cte-vision.html) using the National Career Clusters™ Framework.

The process was set in motion for establishing the Common Career Technical Core (CCTC) Initiative in the winter of 2011 by the NASDCTEc Board of Directors. The timing of the scheduled revision process for the Career Clusters™ Knowledge and Skills Statements created an opening for the work to begin. In the winter of 2010, the initial work of revising the Knowledge and Skills Statements began. Revision has occurred several times since 2002, including 2006 and 2008, to ensure that up-to-date, high-quality expectations for CTE are being used by the states. The revision process, along with the vision for common technical expectations, led to the development of the CCTC. The CCTC was also developed to align with other college and career ready standards efforts, such as the Common Core State Standards in English Language Arts and mathematics, while also articulating industry expectations for each of the 16 Career Clusters™. Chapter 9 shares a more detailed explanation about the rationale behind and expectations for the CCTC, as well as the process used to develop the standards and the next steps for state CCTC adoption and usage.

As the Career Clusters™ continue to evolve, the Framework continues to serve as an organizing tool for guidance and counseling, economic and workforce development prioritization, POS alignment, and supporting high-quality teaching and learning through CTE. The work of the CCTC will also contribute to a positive trajectory for Career Clusters™ and support the preparation of students in their efforts to become college and career ready.

The ongoing work of management—updating and ensuring high-quality resources for state use and implementing the Career Clusters™ in ways that support unique delivery systems and economic priorities—continues through the leadership of NASDCTEc. Additional information and resources about Career Clusters™ is available at www.careertech.org/career-clusters.

Resources

Built to Work: A Common Framework for Skill Standards. Washington, DC: National Skill Standards Board, 2000.

Career Clusters™: Focusing Education on the Future. (A Speakers Kit PowerPoint). National Association of State Directors of Career and Technical Education Consortium, February 2003.

Career Cluster Resources. National Association of State Directors of Career and Technical Education Consortium. States Career Cluster Initiative, Oklahoma CIMC, Stillwater, 2002.

McCage, R. Observations Regarding the Development of Occupational Skill Clusters. A U.S. Department of Labor Paper Commissioned by the Center on Workforce Development, Institute for Educational Leadership, Washington, DC, 1984.

VTECS Career Cluster Framework Wheels, 1999.

Reflect, Transform, Lead: A New Vision for CTE. http://www.careertech.org/career-technical-education/cte-vision.html.

www.careerclusters.org

www.careetech.org

www.ctecs.org

Standards

Kate Blosveren Kreamer and Seth Derner

The Evolution of State-Driven, Standards-Based Education Reform

The story of the standards-based reform movement is one of incremental progress punctuated by periods of rapid change. As recently as thirty years ago the concept of content standards was vague and undefined, and no state had statewide academic standards. Today every state has academic standards—and in nearly every case those standards are anchored in college and career readiness expectations.

What education and policy leaders were only beginning to understand in the early 1980s—the need for high expectations and clear learning targets—is today's reality. With the adoption of the Common Core State Standards (CCSS) by 46[1] states and Washington, DC, education and policy leaders today have turned the rhetoric of the past into reality.

The Early Days of Standards-Based Reform

Before the 1980s, the role of the state (and state departments of education) was essentially one of monitoring and compliance, not setting expectations. State departments of education monitored local education agencies (LEA) to ensure that they were upholding federal and state statutes pertaining to issues such as funding and student supports. LEAs were ultimately responsible for setting their own

---

1 Minnesota adopted the math standards but not the English Language Arts standards.

requirements and expectations. Consequently, there were literally thousands of different sets of expectations for what students had to know to advance grades and earn diplomas. Not until 1983, with the release of *A Nation at Risk*, was this highly fragmented system first called into question.

A Nation at Risk

In 1983, the National Commission on Excellence in Education issued *A Nation at Risk: The Imperative for Education Reform*, sounding the alarm that unless the United States strengthened its education system, the nation would cease to be competitive in the global economy, thereby jeopardizing national security.[2] Using alarmist language, this high-profile report drew attention to the current and future consequences of not setting high expectations: "We report to the American people that while we can take justifiable pride in what our schools and colleges have historically accomplished and contributed to the United States and the well-being of its people, the educational foundations of our society are presently being eroded by a rising tide of mediocrity. . . . If an unfriendly foreign power had attempted to impose on America the mediocre educational performance that exists today, we might well have viewed it as an act of war."

A Nation at Risk recommended that "schools, colleges, and universities adopt more rigorous and measurable standards, and higher expectations, for academic performance and student conduct. . . . This will help students do their best educationally with challenging materials in an environment that supports learning and authentic accomplishment." Given that when *A Nation at Risk* was published the United States was just coming out of the deep recession of the 1970s and that foreign countries, especially Japan, were becoming increasingly competitive in the global economy, the report struck a nerve with many people and illuminated the connection between the U.S. education system and economic competitiveness.

---

2 The report can be found in PDF at http://www.scribd.com/ doc/49151492/A-Nation-at-Risk (scanned from the original) and http:// datacenter.spps.org/sites/2259653e-ffb3-45ba-8fd6-04a024ecf7a4/uploads/ SOTW_A_Nation_at_Risk_1983.pdf (transcribed).

Time for Results and *Goals for Education: Challenge 2000*

The alarm sounded by *A Nation at Risk* woke up the entire country and jump-started the standards-based reform movement. *A Nation at Risk* changed the national conversation on education and encouraged education and state and federal policy leaders to consider their roles in setting expectations and identifying a coherent vision of what "achievement" really meant and looked like.

As a follow-up to *A Nation at Risk*, the National Governors Association (NGA) issued *Time for Results: The Governors' 1991 Report on Education*, establishing a plan for developing recommendations for the improvement of U.S. education. One of the seven areas cited was "helping at-risk children and youth meet higher education standards," which represented a relatively narrow view of standards-based reform. Governor Lamar Alexander of Tennessee, at that time the chair of the NGA, elaborated on the plan by noting that if governors established clear goals, created better report cards, and found better ways to measure what students know and can do, states could give schools and school districts more flexibility in meeting state education goals — "*if* schools and school districts will be accountable for the results."[3] The key concept was *accountability,* and accountability is impossible without *standards.*

The Southern Regional Education Board Commission for Educational Quality's 1988 report *Goals for Education: Challenge 2000* further added to the momentum. This report explicitly called for standards ("national standards" to be exact) and proposed twelve goals:

By the year 2000 …

… all children will be ready for the first grade.

… student achievement for elementary and secondary students will be at national levels or higher.

… the school dropout rate will be reduced by one-half.

… 90 percent of adults will have a high school diploma or equivalency.

… 4 out of every 5 students entering college will be ready to begin college-level work.

---

3 http://govinfo.library.unt.edu/negp/reports/negp30.pdf

... significant gains will be achieved in the mathematics, sciences, and communications competencies of vocational education students.

... the percentage of adults who have attended college or earned two-year, four-year, and graduate degrees will be at the national averages or higher.

... the quality and effectiveness of all colleges and universities will be regularly assessed, with particular emphasis on the performance of undergraduate students.

... all institutions that prepare teachers will have effective teacher education programs that place primary emphasis on the knowledge and performance of graduates.

... all states and localities will have schools with improved performance and productivity demonstrated by results.

... salaries for teachers and faculty will be competitive in the marketplace, will reach important benchmarks, and will be linked to performance measures and standards.

... states will maintain or increase the proposition of state tax dollars for schools and colleges while emphasizing funding aimed at raising quality and productivity.[4]

Despite the thoroughness of those goals, there was still little understanding of exactly what states should hold schools accountable for, and the word "standards" was barely in the day-to-day lexicon of education reformers. While there was growing interest in outcomes and goals, and increased demand for standards, those concepts had yet to come together explicitly in policy. That was about to change.

The 1989 National Education Summit and National Education Goals Panel

In 1989, then-President George H.W. Bush convened the nation's governors in Charlottesville, Virginia, to discuss the most significant education challenges the country was facing. The historic assembly marked the first time a U.S. President and each state's governor met to improve the country's locally-controlled education system in which

---

4 http://www.eric.ed.gov/PDFS/ED301966.pdf

education standards varied across states and localities.[5] The meeting of these leaders was a precursor to a national shift toward greater involvement of the federal government in education.

There were two major outcomes of what was called the "President's Education Summit with Governors": the development of six national education goals (which became the backbone of the 1994 "Goals 2000" legislation) and the launch of the National Education Goals Panel (NEGP), which would monitor progress towards those six goals.

The six goals were announced in the 1990 State of the Union address:

1. All children in America will start school ready to learn.

2. The high school graduation rate will increase to at least 90 percent.

3. All students will leave grades 4, 8, and 12 having demonstrated competency over challenging subject matter including English, mathematics, science, foreign languages, civics and government, economics, arts, history, and geography, and every school in America will ensure that all students learn to use their minds well, so they may be prepared for responsible citizenship, further learning, and productive employment in our nation's modern economy.

4. United States students will be first in the world in mathematics and science achievement.

5. Every adult American will be literate and will possess the knowledge and skills necessary to compete in a global economy and exercise the rights and responsibilities of citizenship.

6. Every school in the United States will be free of drugs, violence, and the unauthorized presence of firearms and alcohol and will offer a disciplined environment conducive to learning.[6]

---

5 Maris A. Vinovskis, "The Road to Charlottesville: The 1989 Education Summit," September 1999 (http://govinfo.library.unt.edu/negp/reports/negp30.pdf).

6 Two additional goals ("The Nation's teaching force will have access to programs for the continued improvement of their professional skills and the opportunity to acquire the knowledge and skills needed to instruct and prepare all American students for the next century" and "Every school will promote partnerships that will increase parental involvement and participation in promoting the social, emotional, and academic growth of children") were added by Congress in 1994.

One significant undertaking of the NEGP was the development of model national standards to provide benchmarks for states and LEAs. The panel also recommended that the Federal Government offer grants to support the development of academic standards. Around the same time, a number of national organizations—such as the National Council for Teachers of Mathematics (NCTM)—began developing their own model standards to support state and local efforts to raise achievement and create a degree of commonality across the nation.

1990s: The Slow Build

Following the launch of the NEGP and the release of Goals 2000, the NEGP created the National Education Standards and Assessment Council,[7] charged with ensuring that standards development activities were underway and would continue to make progress. This helped incentivize the development of national models, such as those developed by NCTM and like organizations.

As states began to develop their own standards and national models were emerging, the discussion in the reform community began to shift away from expectations and outcomes and toward fully aligned systems. One major event contributing to this shift was the 1993 launch of the New Standards Project, a joint effort of research institutions and over 20 states designed to support the development of aligned systems of performance standards and assessments.[8]

1994: Goals 2000 and the Reauthorization of the *Elementary and Secondary Education Act* (ESEA) as the *Improving America's Schools Act*

Early in President Clinton's first term, he introduced the Goals 2000: Educate America Act,[9] which codified the six original NEGP goals and added two goals addressing professional development and parental involvement. Goals 2000 aimed to improve the nation's progress by

---

7 http://www2.ed.gov/pubs/Prog95/pt3fed.html

8 Commission on Behavioral and Social Sciences and Education, *International Comparative Studies in Education: Descriptions of Selected Large-Scale Assessments and Case Studies*, 1995 (http://www.nap.edu/openbook.php?record_id=9174&page=74).

9 http://www2.ed.gov/legislation/GOALS2000/TheAct/index.html

laying out a framework that would establish academic standards and require participating states to show measurable improvement of student outcomes to achieve the eight National Education Goals. States opting to participate submitted improvement plans to the Federal Government as part of their grant applications. Also, the law was a change of pace for K-12 education in the United States because it shifted the main focus onto the outcomes of student learning rather than the resources put into education. This legislation also created competitive grant programs to support the development of state standards; over 40 states applied for and were awarded money.

Soon after the passage of Goals 2000, ESEA was reauthorized in 1994, reinforcing Goals 2000 and the NEGP recommendations. Title I of the Elementary and Secondary Education Act (ESEA), "Helping Disadvantaged Children Meet High Standards," stated that the purpose of the reauthorization was to "enable schools to provide opportunities for children served to acquire the knowledge and skills contained in the challenging state content standards and to meet the challenging state performance standards developed for all children." The legislation required that all states demonstrate how they had developed, or will develop, challenging content and student performance standards and aligned assessments for all students.[10]

States that didn't already have standards were given a year to develop them and four years to develop aligned assessments or risk losing Title I funds. The bill also required that states administer assessments at least once in elementary, middle, and high school and report "adequate yearly progress." The bill accelerated state efforts to adopt academic standards and ensure that their assessments reflected those standards, but it still marked little change in states that wanted to maintain local control of standards — largely from lack of federal enforcement and political pushback against any effort toward the creation of national standards.

Although *Goals* 2000 gave states the option to apply for grant funding, it ultimately failed because, though the governors were heavily involved in the conceptualization, the initiative became a federally driven program. The failure of *Goals 2000* made clear that state leaders, in collaboration with local entities, would most successfully drive this type of reform.

---

10 http://www2.ed.gov/legislation/ESEA/toc.html

1996 National Education Summit

By the mid-1990s nearly every state had adopted academic standards. However, concerns about the success of the reforms were beginning to emerge for two major reasons—the perceived intrusiveness of the federal government in the reform movement, and the realization that states had adopted standards of differing (and often unverified) quality. In addition, the nation had not met any of the eight education goals set forth in 1990. Between 1995 and 1998, the American Federation of Teachers, the Thomas B. Fordham Foundation, and the Council for Basic Education all issued reports that ranked the rigor and quality of state standards. While there were differences in both the scoring and findings, all three reports found the standards to be average (with a few exemplary sets) and disparate.

Around this same time, business leaders and governors began to draw more attention to the perceived gap between what students were likely to know at the time of their graduation and what was demanded of them in the workplace. Most state standards focused on mastery requirements for each grade but did not utilize real-world anchors to ensure that the standards had value outside and beyond the classroom.

It was these concerns that led governors and business leaders to host the 1996 National Education Summit to address the issues of standards, assessments, and technology. Describing the need for such a summit, then Nevada Governor Bob Miller said, "The nation's governors and CEOs are fed up with passive acceptance of mediocrity."[11] A major outcome of the summit was the launch of Achieve, a non-profit organization charged with addressing this "expectations gap" and providing states with support for and evaluation of their standards and assessments.[12]

2001–2004: Laying a New Foundation for Standards-Based Reform

The next major impetus in the standards-based reform movement was the 2001 reauthorization of ESEA as *No Child Left Behind* (NCLB).

---

11 Charles Bierbauer, "Now That Johnny Can Read, Can He Get a Job at IBM?" March 26, 1996, CNN News (http://www.cnn.com/US/9603/education_summit/index.html).

12 For more on Achieve, see www.achieve.org.

NCLB had the strongest focus on accountability of any ESEA reauthorization and required that all states have standards and aligned assessments by tying student, school, district, and state outcomes to federal accountability targets.

Clearly, NCLB has had both positive and negative consequences. On the positive side, there was a focus on building data systems and for states, districts, and schools to utilize disaggregated reporting, thereby shining a light on student achievement across all demographics. On the negative side, NCLB created perverse incentives, making the floor the ceiling in many states. Even in states where standards were already strong, the law unintentionally created incentives to keep proficiency levels on assessments low to ensure higher pass rates and fewer federal sanctions.

The American Diploma Project[13]

From 2002 to 2004, Achieve, in partnership with the Education Trust, the Thomas B. Fordham Foundation, and the National Alliance of Business, worked closely with representatives from K-12, postsecondary, and business in Indiana, Kentucky, Massachusetts, Nevada, and Texas to identify the English and mathematics knowledge and skills high school graduates need for success in college and careers. As the first step of the project, economists analyzed labor market projections to identify the most promising jobs—those that pay enough to support a family and provide real potential for career advancement—and reviewed high school transcripts and other longitudinal education data to determine what preparation workers in those occupations had received in high school.

The American Diploma Project (ADP) then partnered with postsecondary faculty members from two- and four-year broad-access institutions in the five partner states to determine the prerequisite English and mathematics knowledge and skills required for success in entry-level credit-bearing courses in English, mathematics, the physical sciences, the social sciences, and the humanities. The ADP benchmarks, an ambitious set of academic content standards reflecting

---

13 The American Diploma Project benchmarks can be found online at http://www.achieve.org/american-diploma-project. The final ADP report, *Ready or Not: Creating a High School Diploma That Counts,* can be found online at http://www.achieve.org/ReadyorNot.

the convergence of both employer and postsecondary expectations, emerged from this research.

The ADP benchmarks defined the knowledge and skills in English and mathematics that all students must acquire in high school if they are to be prepared to meet the challenges that await them on college campuses and in the workplace. ADP eventually "back-mapped" the end-of-high school standards into the earlier grades, offering a full K-12 set of benchmarks in math and ELA.

- In **English**, the ADP benchmarks focus not only on literature and writing but also explicitly on reasoning, logic, and communication skills. The English benchmarks demand strong oral and written communication skills because these skills are staples in college classrooms and 21st-century jobs. They also contain analytical and reasoning skills that formerly were associated with selective honors high school courses.

- In **mathematics**, the ADP benchmarks include number sense and numerical operations; algebra; geometry; data interpretation, statistics, and probability; and mathematical reasoning. The mathematics benchmarks equate roughly to the knowledge and skills students should acquire in four-year high school mathematics programs — as typically taught in algebra I, geometry, and algebra II, as well as data analysis, statistics, and probability — and the content and skills needed in the earlier grades to prepare students to meet the high school benchmarks. A fourth year of meaningful mathematics is considered critical by college faculty and employers alike to ensure that students continue to develop and hone their facility in mathematics.

2005–2009: States Embrace College and Career Readiness

Beginning in 2005, Achieve began working directly with states to help them align their standards to *college and career ready* (CCR) expectations, using the ADP benchmarks as a roadmap. Achieve conducted alignment institutes with 22 states, offering an opportunity for K-12, higher education, and business representatives from each state to come together to ensure that the state's standards were aligned with CCR expectations.

Similarly, a number of other states began to undertake CCR alignment on their own, either using the ADP benchmarks as an anchor or some other state-developed process. These states engaged higher education faculty (not just colleges of education) and business/workforce representatives to provide a broad, real-world context for the K-12 expectations. The process of developing and verifying academic standards was clearly experiencing a shift, and CCR was at the center of that shift. For the first time, states were putting in place expectations that were anchored in what students needed to be able to know and do to succeed after they left K-12, not just what they needed to succeed at each grade level.

According to an Achieve report, by 2008 over a dozen states had adopted a common core of mathematics and/or ELA standards because of their independent work in aligning their standards to the expectations of employers and higher education.[14] The report went on to say that "the ADP Core has become the 'common core' as a byproduct of the alignment work in each of the states." This finding demonstrated that commonality in state standards was not only possible but was already taking shape, opening the door to a national, but state-led, movement.

2009–Today: The Common Core State Standards

In 2009 the Common Core State Standards (CCSS) Initiative was launched by the Council of Chief State School Officers (CCSSO) and the National Governors Association (NGA) Center for Best Practices. Through this initiative, governors and state commissioners of education from 48 states, two territories, and the District of Columbia agreed to develop a common core of state K-12 English Language Arts (ELA) and mathematics standards.

The goal of the initiative was to develop common standards that were focused, coherent, clear, and rigorous; internationally benchmarked; anchored in CCR; and evidence- and research-based. The evidence used included standards from high-performing countries, leading states, and nationally regarded frameworks, as well as

---

14 Achieve, *Out of Many, One: Toward Rigorous Common Core Standards from the Ground Up,* 2008 (http://www.achieve.org/OutofManyOne).

research on adolescent literacy, text complexity, mathematics instruction, and quantitative literacy.

Over the course of about 14 months, writing teams in English Language Arts and mathematics drafted end-of-high-school CCR standards and comprehensive K-12 academic standards. External and state feedback teams provided ongoing feedback to the writing teams throughout the process. In March 2010 the draft of the K-12 standards was released for public comment and over 9,600 comments were received (the vast majority from classroom teachers). Following a final review of the draft standards by an expert-led validation committee, which took into account the feedback from the state and public reviews, the final standards were released June 2, 2010.[15]

During the same period, the U.S. Department of Education created the Race to the Top (RTTT)[16] competition, leveraging $4.35 billion of the American Recovery and Reinvestment Act stimulus funds earmarked for education. The majority of this funding was allocated to a state competition in which states needed to demonstrate how they would make substantive improvements in four areas: standards and assessments, teacher and leader effectiveness, longitudinal data systems, and lowest-performing schools.

Specifically, the standards and assessments assurance area called upon states to demonstrate (1) past progress in developing and adopting common standards and common, high-quality assessments and (2) future plans for supporting the transition to enhanced standards and assessments. The promise of the RTTT funding incentivized and accelerated states' adoption of the CCSS, even with no funding guarantees or federal mandates in place.

As of August 2012, 46 states and Washington, DC, have adopted the Common Core and plan to implement them fully by the 2014–2015 school year. Additionally, all four of the states that have not adopted the Common Core (Texas, Virginia, Nebraska, and Alaska) have adopted state-developed CCR standards.

The CCSS represent a major step forward in the standards-based reform movement. For the first time the United States has a common set

---

15 See www.corestandards.org for the Common Core State Standards and more information on their development.

16 For more, see http://www2.ed.gov/programs/racetothetop/index.html and http://www2.ed.gov/programs/racetothetop-assessment/index.html.

of expectations, allowing for more sharing of materials and resources among states, and for economies of scale to be realized. States have already begun joining together to develop instructional resources and common rubrics for evaluating the quality of instructional materials. In addition, the CCSS are more rigorous than most existing state standards. According to research by the Thomas B. Fordham Foundation, the K-12 Common Core in English Language Arts/literacy and math are clearer and more rigorous than today's ELA standards in 37 states and today's math standards in 39 states. In 33 of those states, the CCSS score higher than both the ELA and mathematics standards.[17]

The CCSS include the end-of-high-school knowledge and skills necessary for success in credit-bearing, college-level coursework and in the 21st-century workplace. In fact, certain skills — such as perseverance in problem solving, research, and communication — are embedded throughout the standards. Finally, the CCSS include a number of key advances in organization and delivery of content that address inadequacies in current state standards and meet stated demands of the higher education and business communities.

Key Advances in the CCSS in Mathematics

- The CCSS *focus* on key topics at each grade level to allow educators and students to go deeper into the content.

- The CCSS emphasize *coherence* at each grade level — making connections across content and between content and mathematical practices.

- The CCSS emphasize *progressions* across grades. The goal of each progression is *fluency* — the ability to perform calculations or solve problems quickly and accurately.

- **The *Standards for Mathematical Practice*** describe mathematical "habits of mind" or mathematical *applications* and foster reasoning, problem solving, modeling, decision making, and engagement.

- Finally, the CCSS require students to demonstrate *deep conceptual understanding* by applying them to new situations.

---

17 Sheila Byrd et al., *The State of State Standards — and the Common Core — in 2010*, July 2010 (http://www.edexcellence.net/publications-issues/publications/the-state-of-state.html).

Key Advances in the CCSS in English Language Arts/Literacy

- In reading, the major advances are the shift away from litera-ture-focused standards to a *balance of literature and informa-tional texts* to reflect CCR expectations. There is also a greater focus on *text complexity* and at what levels students should be reading.

- In writing, there is a strong emphasis on *argument and infor-mative/explanatory writing*, along with an emphasis on writing about sources or *using evidence* to inform an argument.

- The CCSS include *speaking and listening* expectations, which can be met through presentations and group work, both formal and informal.

- The language standards emphasize *both general academic* and *domain-specific vocabulary*.

- The CCSS address *reading, writing, and literacy across the cur-riculum*, and include literacy standards for science, social stud-ies, and technical subjects. These standards complement rather than replace content standards in those subjects and are the shared responsibility of teachers in those disciplines.

Assessments Aligned to the Common Core State Standards

As state and local education leaders learned long ago, standards, on their own, will not bring about change or improve student achieve-ment. Rather, it is how the standards are implemented—and their impact on the education system as a whole—that determines the impact of those academic expectations. In recognition of this, the U.S. Department of Education put aside $350 million of the Race to the Top (RTTT) funding to incentivize the (state-led) development of common assessments aligned to the CCSS. Two consortia of states applied and were awarded RTTT Common Assessment funds—the Partnership for Assessment of Readiness for College and Careers (PARCC) and Smarter Balanced Assessment Consortiums (SBAC).

Both consortia will develop K-12 assessment systems in math-ematics and ELA/literacy that measure the full range of the CCSS, and the full range of student performance. Both systems will be tech-nology-based and will include components administered throughout the year so that the assessments can become an integral component of instruction, rather than a disconnected mandate. The assessments from both assessment consortia will be ready for use in the 2014–2015 school year. Below is a comparison outlining the differences in approaches between the two assessment consortia.

Comparison of CCSS Assessment Consortia

PARCC	SBAC
Summative assessment will include a performance assessment plus an end-of-year assessment.	Summative assessment will include performance tasks and computer adaptive assessments.
Assessments will primarily be given on computers or other digital devices.	Assessments will primarily be given on computers or other digital devices.
Performance assessments will primarily focus on hard-to-measure standards.	Performance task assessments will measure the ability to integrate knowledge and skills and will be administered in a two-hour sitting, computer delivered during the final twelve weeks of school.
Performance assessment results are estimated to be returned within two weeks.	Performance assessment results are estimated to be returned within two weeks.
The end-of-year assessment will be given once.	Students can take the summative assessment twice.
End-of-year assessments will be scored by computer for fast results.	Summative assessment results will be available at the end of the assessment.
Scores from the performance assessment, plus the end-of-year assessment, will be combined for annual accountability.	Scores from the performance assessment, plus the end-of-year assessment, will be combined for annual accountability.
For English/Language Arts, a speaking and learning assessment is required but will not be used for accountability.	N/A
Supports formative early assessment, as well as formative mid-year performance tasks.	An optional system of computer adaptive interim assessments will be available.

Next Generation Science Standards

Finally, as states are working to implement the CCSS and related resources and tools, another state-led process is developing the Next Generation Science Standards (NGSS). Utilizing lessons learned from the development of the CCSS, this initiative aims to produce common science standards that are internationally benchmarked, lead to student readiness for college and careers, and are evidence-based.

The Next Generation Science Standards (NGSS): K-12 Science Standards for Today's Students and Tomorrow's Workforce[18]

The NGSS will be K-12 science standards created through a collaborative, state-led process. To date, 26 lead partner states are providing leadership to the writing teams and to other states and have agreed to strongly consider adopting the NGSS upon their release in 2013.

The new science standards are being drafted based on the *Framework for K-12 Science Education*, developed by the National Research Council, the staffing arm of the National Academy of Sciences. The vision laid out in the framework identifies what students need to know and be able to do to be functional citizens, which includes being scientifically literate and effective members of the U.S. workforce.

Briefly, the framework established three dimensions of scientific proficiency:

- Science and engineering practices (*major practices that scientists and engineers employ as they investigate and build models and theories about the world*);
- Crosscutting concepts (*concepts have application across all domains of science*); and
- Disciplinary core ideas (*those ideas with broad importance across multiple sciences or engineering disciplines or key organizing principles of a single discipline*). (http://www.nextgenscience.org)

---

18 For more information, see www.nextgenscience.org.

Looking Forward

Widespread adoption and implementation of the CCSS and aligned assessments will not mean that the standards-based reform movement has accomplished its purpose and that the education and reform community can move on to the next big thing. Over time, states will recognize and respond to the need to reevaluate the effectiveness of the CCSS and adapt them to best practices. This time, however, states will be able to share lessons learned and best practices more easily, given that all 50 states and DC share a common college and career ready context within their mathematics and ELA expectations.

Parallel Developments in Career Technical Education

The introduction of federal funding to support vocational agriculture programs in public schools in 1917 through the Smith-Hughes Act initiated a series of activities that could be seen as early precedents for the development of common CTE standards. Within ten years of the enactment of the Smith-Hughes Act a number of vocational agriculture programs had founded corresponding youth organizations designed to give students the opportunity to compete in fairs and contests and to gain leadership experience by running their own clubs. As the popularity of these clubs grew, teachers looked for opportunities for their students to compete against students at other schools. In 1926, teachers from several states brought students to participate in the American Royal, a livestock expo in Kansas City, Missouri. This led in 1928 to the formation of the Future Farmers of America (FFA), which grew into a nationwide system of state associations and local chapters. It also led to the creation of national student competitions and national criteria for local leadership development. While none of these activities were officially recognized as efforts to establish common standards, their practical impact was just that. In all likelihood, a vo-ag student/FFA member in Delaware would follow the same criteria for evaluation of dairy cattle or public speaking as a student in California.

As decades passed and other vocational fields were included in federal legislation—each with a corresponding student organization—the model of national competitions and national guidelines for local leadership development was replicated and is still intact. In a manner of speaking, student organizations—FFA; Future Business Leaders of America; SkillsUSA; Family, Career and Community Leaders of America; Health Occupations Students of America; Technology Student Association; and others—have been responsible for the acceptance of some level of de facto common expectations for CTE for many years.

Many educators, however, would be quick to point out that competition guidelines were only a small component of the curriculum in any given CTE program, and that programs were expected to use *local* advisory councils to identify the skills and competencies required to inform curricula that would in turn produce the workers and entrepreneurs needed in their *local* communities. Efforts to establish national standards for CTE were resisted almost universally until the 1990s. However, many leaders in CTE recognized that efforts to develop national standards in math, science, and English language arts in the 1990s would eventually lead to the expectation that other disciplines—CTE included—would follow suit. Sensing the growing interest, national organizations in each of the CTE disciplines began to discuss the feasibility of establishing common curriculum standards. Many state CTE agencies began efforts to identify and define common, statewide curriculum "frameworks." As the term "standards" was highly politicized in the 1990s, its use was avoided. Nonetheless, discussion of the value of and need for common CTE standards had begun.

As discussed in previous chapters, during this era, federal agencies piloted initiatives designed to develop a clearer, more unified understanding of career preparation across educational institutions and agencies. In 1996 the aforementioned Building Linkages Initiative was launched as a collaborative effort of the U.S. Department of Education, the Office of Vocational and Adult Education, the National School-to-Work Office, and the National Skill Standards Board.[19] The purpose of the initiative was to establish linkages among state educational agencies, secondary and postsecondary educational institutions, employers, industry groups, other stakeholders, and federal agencies. The goal of those linkages was to create national curriculum frameworks, each designed to help students transition from high school to postsecondary education and employment in a given

---

19 For more on the Building Linkages Initiative, see chapter 8.

career area. The project began with working groups in four clusters—manufacturing, transportation, retail, and construction. By 1999, the initiative had settled on a model comprising 16 *clusters* subdivided into 81 *career pathways* (now 79 Career Pathways). The model became known as *Career Clusters* (a trademarked name). Federal funding was used to support the National Association of State Directors of Career Technical Education Consortium (NASDCTEc) to convene national advisory committees representing industry, labor, secondary and postsecondary education, and CTE administrators to complete frameworks for all the clusters and pathways.

NASDCTEc used the Building Linkages pilot to design the process for identifying and vetting the elements to be included in the frameworks. To prevent the misperception that national curriculum standards were being created, the term "Knowledge and Skill Statements" was used to describe what students should know and be able to do. The term became the common name for the frameworks themselves.

The Knowledge and Skill Statements differ in key ways from most state and local frameworks.

- The Knowledge and Skill Statements are organized according to the 16 Career Clusters™, while most state and local frameworks are organized by CTE programs—family consumer science, construction, and so on.

- The Knowledge and Skill Statements are not curriculum objectives but performance expectations. They have the tone and terminology of job descriptions rather than lesson plans.

- Unlike state and local curriculum frameworks, the Knowledge and Skill Statements address foundational competencies for entire Career Clusters™ rather than narrow roles within Career Clusters™. For example, a Knowledge and Skill Statement in the Architecture and Construction Career Cluster™ applies to any role in that cluster, from bricklayer to architect. One of the goals of the Career Clusters™ initiative was to prepare students to be flexible and employable within entire industries so that changes in technology or the economy would not leave them without marketable skills.

- Unlike state and local curriculum frameworks, the Knowledge and Skill Statements are not designated for any particular level (middle school, secondary, postsecondary). This gives educators the flexibility to apply the statements at the levels they deem appropriate.

The national advisory committees commissioned by NASDCTEc completed their work on the first complete set of Knowledge and Skill Statements in 2002. The entire collection underwent a national validation process and was ready for the field in late 2002. Many states began making plans to use the new Knowledge and Skill Statements to create or re-evaluate their own curriculum frameworks. Many of the national advisory committees remained intact, shifting their focus to dissemination of the Knowledge and Skill Statements and identifying pilot projects and samples of work to share with other schools and colleges.

In 2006 and 2008 the national advisory committees were called into action again. The 2006 revision effort examined the extent to which (if any) recent changes in technology and the economy might necessitate adjustment of the Knowledge and Skill Statements. The 2008 effort focused on ensuring consistency in the presentation and format of the statements and developed the "Essential Knowledge and Skills" – a consolidation of the numerous similar expectations found throughout the Career Clusters™.

The 2011 revision efforts were initiated to ensure that the statements aligned with current expectations. Many of the elements of the process used in the development of the CCSS were employed. The most significant changes occurred in the Essential Knowledge and Skills and the 16 collections of Career Cluster™-level statements. The Essential Knowledge and Skills were reconfigured as "Career Ready Practices," so-called because they apply across entire programs of study. The second most significant change was the reduction of the number of statements in each Career Cluster™-level collection to no more than 12, to ensure that the statements were limited to the most critical.

In the decade that has followed since the initial release of the Knowledge and Skill Statements a number of important trends and ideas have laid the groundwork for the development of common standards for CTE.

The release of the initial Knowledge and Skill Statements was met by a variety of responses. The Career Clusters™ model and the corresponding Knowledge and Skill Statements were made available to all but were never mandatory. Generally, each state responded to the Knowledge and Skill Statements in one of four ways:

- Some states used the Knowledge and Skill Statements to inform their own state curriculum standards for CTE. Some required that all the Knowledge and Skill Statements be cross-walked to at least one state CTE standard. Others used the statements verbatim or required that the Knowledge and Skill Statements be addressed in the state's curriculum.

- Some states used the Knowledge and Skill Statements as a resource when developing state curriculum standards for CTE. The Knowledge and Skill Statements were considered in the development and adoption of the state standards.

- Some states promoted the Knowledge and Skill Statements as a resource for the local education agencies responsible for establishing local curriculum standards for CTE.

- Some states did not use Knowledge and Skill Statements at all.

At the time of the Career Clusters™ initial release (2002), state and local agencies varied widely in their expectations of the rigor and content of CTE programs. Consequently, the need for a resource such as the Knowledge and Skill Statements varied widely from place to place. Moreover, at the time there was little dialogue about the need for common expectations across state lines. A number of factors, however, have begun to change the environment for CTE and, thus, perception of the need for common standards. Following are the most important three of those factors.

(1) The most significant change is the recent emphasis on POS. Every recipient of Perkins IV funds must offer at least one POS. Naturally, this has shifted the focus of planning and curriculum development from CTE programs to POS. As POS continue to emerge as the preferred vehicle for delivery of CTE instruction, recognition of the need for national standards in the design of POS will grow.

(2) Perkins IV places new emphasis on academic skill attainment by CTE students. In many states, NCLB assessment data were used as a performance measure for CTE programs. With the emergence of the CCSS, many states and local entities—particularly at the secondary level—are seeking a more thorough integration of CTE and academic instruction. The presence of CCSS for mathematics and

English Language Arts (and science in 2013) has raised interest in having common standards for CTE, especially at the secondary level. Common standards for CTE would facilitate the development of sharable models and tools, best practices would be easier to identify and leverage, and data on integration efforts would be more useful in determining which methods are most effective in improving student performance.

(3) Today's increasing interest in common standards has led to increased interest in methods for assessing the attainment of technical skills. Several methods of assessment have been proposed, but a number of logistical challenges remain — the cost to the student and school or college, the value of the certification, and the appropriateness of certifications for given POS, to name a few. The development of common standards for CTE will not automatically lead to the development of common assessments of technical skill attainment, but the standards are a step in that direction.

Toward a Common Career Technical Core

In response to changes in the economy, many CTE programs have transitioned from helping students prepare for entry-level jobs to helping students prepare for careers. As part of that transition, national organizations such as NASDCTEc, individual states, and even industry-based organizations created different sets of standards for student learning in CTE programs. The result was a hodgepodge of standards that varied in quality and specificity from one state to the next, putting some students at a distinct disadvantage for competing in the ever-changing global economy.

Recognizing the need for more consistency in today's global marketplace, in the spring of 2010 CTE State Directors united around a common, shared vision for CTE. The *Reflect, Transform, Lead* vision[20] (as described in Chapters 1 and 8) set forth a series of action steps that includes the development of a shared set of standards that meet a quality benchmark for students in CTE programs, regardless of where they live or which delivery system they use. The concept led to the development of the Common Career Technical Core (CCTC).

---

20 http://www.careertech.org/career-technical-education/cte-vision.html

The concurrence to develop common CTE standards happened just as the Career Cluster™ Knowledge and Skills were poised for revision and validation in 2011. The revision and validation process has occurred several times since 2002 (as described earlier in the chapter, including 2006 and 2008) to ensure up-to-date and high-quality expectations are being used by the states for CTE. The revision process, along with the vision for common standards led to the development of the CCTC, to be coordinated by NASDCTEc but driven by the states.

The CCTC, a state-led initiative designed to establish rigorous, high-quality program-level CTE standards that states can adopt voluntarily, started in the winter of 2010 with the approval of the NASDCTEc Board of Directors. The development of the CCTC was a multi-step process that incorporated input from approximately 3,500 individuals representing K-12 education, business and industry, and higher education from across the nation and built from the decade of work in the states with the Knowledge and Skills. The CCTC was developed to align with other college and career ready standards efforts, such as the Common Core State Standards in English language arts and mathematics, while also articulating industry expectations for each of the 16 Career Clusters™.

The 17-month process began with the revision and revalidation of the 2008 Knowledge and Skills. The use of an online review and ratings system removed barriers from subject matter expert (SME) participation in the process and worked to ensure an engagement from as many states as possible and people as possible. The revisions to the Knowledge and Skills, informed by preliminary feedback from SMEs and a set of benchmark standards from industry, curriculum, state, and postsecondary education resources, were finalized through an online validation process.

The resulting statements were then provided to a set of CCTC working groups that represented the 42 supporting states, District of Columbia, and Palau that signed a Declaration of Support for the development of the CCTC. The 16 different working groups—with over 320 representatives—convened virtually three times over the course of three months. The virtual meetings ensured the engagement of participants and were facilitated through the consensus review and refinement process by Marzano Research Laboratories. A version of the standards was also provided online for public comment. The input was used to refine the final standards that were released at the Career Clusters™ Institute in June 2012, in Washington, DC, after NASDCTEc Board adoption.

The final standards represent the most rigorous, high-quality program-level standards for CTE available to date. The CCTC includes a set of standards for each of the 16 Career Clusters™ and their corresponding Career Pathways that define what students should know and be able to do after completing instruction in a POS. The CCTC also includes an overarching set of Career Ready Practices[21] that apply to all POS. The Career Ready Practices include 12 statements that address the knowledge, skills, and dispositions that are important to becoming career ready.

The Career Ready Practices component of the CCTC provides a framework for the developmental experiences necessary to become career ready—experiences that can be "practiced" using many different approaches in a variety of settings. Students refine these practices throughout their full continuum of learning—through their journey in school, college, and the workforce and when they return to advance their education. Each Career Ready Practice includes an overarching statement along with a more detailed description. Below are the 12 overarching statements:

- Act as a responsible and contributing citizen and employee.
- Apply appropriate academic and technical skills.
- Attend to personal health and financial well-being.
- Communicate clearly and effectively and with reason.
- Consider the environmental, social, and economic impacts of decisions.
- Demonstrate creativity and innovation.
- Employ valid and reliable research strategies.
- Utilize critical thinking to make sense of problems and persevere in solving them.
- Model integrity, ethical leadership, and effective management.
- Plan education and career paths aligned to personal goals.
- Use technology to enhance productivity.

---

21 See *Career Ready Practices* (http://www.careertech.org/career-technical-education/cctc/info.html).

- Work productively in teams while using cultural/global competence.

The Career Ready Practices are intended to establish goals for CTE programs, yet the practices are relevant for all students. At the high school level, for example, the Career Ready Practices enhance the CCSS by more clearly illustrating what it means to be career ready. If a student's course experience embeds both Career Ready Practices and lessons aligned to CCSS, they gain a learning experience with the academic rigor and career-context that will prepare them to be college and career ready.

The CCTC standards reflect a broader program-level set of targets to be achieved across an entire Program of Study. The broader nature of the expectations supported the fewer, higher, clearer objectives, while supporting an opportunity for states to align the state, curriculum, and other frameworks reflecting the diversity of delivery of CTE within each state along with the economic and workforce priorities of the state. The CCTC serves as the common target among states using the National Career Clusters™ Framework.

Provided below is a sample from the Agriculture, Food & Natural Resources Career Cluster™ and a subsequent Career Pathway in Animal Systems. The CCTC are also aligned with performance elements and sample indicators from the revision of the 2008 National Career Clusters™ Knowledge and Skills statements. For more information about these resources, go to http://www.careertech.org/career-technical-education/cctc/.

Common Career Technical Core Standard Samples

Agriculture, Food & Natural Resources Career Cluster™

AG2—Evaluate the nature and scope of the Agriculture, Food & Natural Resources Career Cluster™ and the role agriculture, food, and natural resources (AFNR) play in society and the economy

Animal Systems Career Pathway

AG-ANI3—Design and provide proper animal nutrition given desired outcomes for performance, development, reproduction, and/or economic production

From http://www.careertech.org/career-technical-education/cctc/

How Will States Adopt the CCTC?

Over the course of 2012–2013, NASDCTEc will launch an initiative to coordinate a comprehensive gap analysis to compare each state's current course-level standards against the CCTC program-level standards to determine alignment. The gap analysis will be conducted by a team of third-party experts to ensure quality and consistency across the states. Based on the gap analysis, each state will decide whether or not to adopt the CCTC and identify a plan for aligning current state expectations to the CCTC.

States have the option to adopt some or all of the Career Clusters™ that comprise the CCTC, but any area that is adopted must be adopted in its entirety. States that choose to adopt any of the Career Clusters™ must also adopt the Career Ready Practices. To learn more about the CCTC, visit www.careertech.org/career-technical-education/cctc/.

The use of the program-level standards as a common alignment tool supports the diversity of implementation, the economic and workforce priorities, and the rich and diverse delivery methods of high-quality CTE within the states. Below is a model demonstrating the opportunities for alignment to the CCTC among the states and connecting the state course standards, industry standards, and other content standards used to ensure high-quality teaching and learning in the classroom.

The CCTC

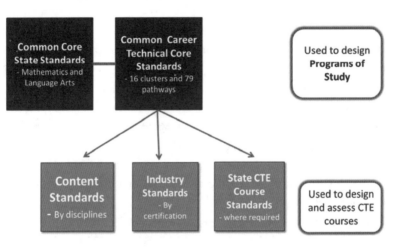

Course Sequence and Delivery Systems

Lyle Courtnage, Reba Poulson, and Annette Severson

Introduction

Course sequencing is the foundation of Programs of Study (POS). Through appropriate course sequencing, students progressively gather valuable knowledge and skills, building higher-level skills as they proceed through increasingly advanced work. A planned sequence of courses within a POS prevents duplication of coursework.[1] At the secondary level, the academic content should enable students to meet state graduation requirements and support the POS's technical content. At the postsecondary level, POS should indicate the coursework students would pursue to satisfy requirements for certifications, degrees, and other credentials. The nonduplicative sequence of secondary and postsecondary courses in a POS is intended to ensure that students transition to postsecondary without having to repeat courses or enroll in remedial courses.

Creating high-quality POS for selected pathways requires the use of the POS design framework components as building blocks.[2] The 10 components support the four statutory requirements of the Carl

---

1 MPR Associates, Inc., *Programs of Study: Local Implementation Readiness and Capacity Self-Assessment,* 2010 (prepared for the Office of Vocational and Adult Education, U. S. Department of Education) (http://cte.ed.gov/docs/POSLocalImplementationTool-9-14-10.pdf).
2 MPR Associates, Inc., *Programs of Study.*

D. Perkins Career and Technical Education Act of 2006 (Perkins IV).[3] This chapter focuses on how course sequences and delivery systems support implementation of the POS design framework.

The POS Design Process

The design process follows a continuum that begins with very broad concepts and progresses toward increasingly narrow concepts. It provides a structure for the development of a seamless delivery system for Career Technical Education (CTE). Understanding the steps on the continuum will help practitioners design the course sequences necessary to build POS.

Table 1 illustrates the relationships between the four required elements of a POS as defined in Perkins IV and the 10 components of the POS design framework.

Table 1. A Comparison of the Perkins POS Requirements and POS Framework Components

Perkins POS Requirements	POS Framework Components
A. Incorporate and align secondary and postsecondary education elements	• *Legislation and Policies* • *Partnerships*
B. Include academic and CTE content in a coordinated, non-duplicative progression of courses	• *College and Career Readiness Standards* • *Course Sequences* • *Guidance Counseling and Academic Advisement* • *Teaching and Learning Strategies*
C. Offer the opportunity, where appropriate, for secondary students to acquire postsecondary credits	• *Professional Development* • *Credit Transfer Agreements*
D. Lead to industry-recognized credential or certificate at the postsecondary level, or an associate or baccalaureate degree	• *Accountability and Evaluation Systems* • *Technical Skills Assessments*

The components are not in every case exclusive to the Perkins requirement with which they are aligned in the table. For example, both professional development and teaching and learning strategies may be needed to support several of the requirements. Policies at

---

3 Public Law 109–270 — AUG. 12, 2006, 120 STAT. 689.

the state and local levels may be necessary to ensure that secondary students receive postsecondary credit and to align secondary and postsecondary levels.[4]

Equip Your Toolbox

In the ensuing paragraphs we use the term "toolbox" to refer to an inventory of items needed to begin the design process. Designing and building effective POS goes well beyond filling in charts with the names of existing courses. The toolbox for each state, region, or community will vary, depending on state and local policies, but the types of tools available and the outcomes achieved will be generally the same.

Each toolbox should include the items described below. Together those items will provide the assistance necessary for states and school districts to design and support effective POS.

- *The National Career Clusters™ Framework* (http://www.careertech. org/career-clusters/glance/clusters.html) provides a structure for organizing and delivering high-quality POS. The framework consists of 16 Career Clusters™ representing 79 Career Pathways. Some states have developed frameworks specific to their needs. For example, Illinois developed a "fan" graphic for the 16 Career Clusters™ and Nebraska created a wheel.[5]

- *The POS design framework* contains 10 supporting and interdependent components.[6] These components are instrumental in the creation and implementation of high-quality, comprehensive POS. If all the elements of the POS design framework are implemented, the POS is considered a *Rigorous Program of Study* (RPOS). Understanding this framework is critical as you embark upon the design of your POS. The framework illustrates that designing and

---

4 MPR Associates, Inc., *Programs of Study*.

5 See N. A. Jankowski et al., *Illinois' Career Cluster Model*, 2009, Urbana-Champaign, IL: OCCRL, Univ. of Ill. at Urbana-Champaign (http://occrl.illinois. edu/files/Projects/perkins/Report/POSmailerFINAL.pdf), p. 12; and *Preparation for College & Career: Nebraska Standards for Career Ready Practice*, 2011, Nebraska Dept. of Ed. (http://www.education.ne.gov/nce/documents/ NCECareerReadinessStandards.pdf), p. 3.

6 MPR Associates, Inc., *Programs of Study*.

building a POS in a specific career pathway goes well beyond filling in a chart with the names of courses. Chapter 5 addresses the framework in more detail. Table 2[7] provides a synopsis for reference.

Table 2. The POS Design Framework Components

1. *Legislation and Policies*—Federal, state, and local legislation or administrative policies promote POS development and implementation.

2. *Partnerships*—Ongoing relationships among education, business, and other community stakeholders are central to POS design, implementation, and maintenance.

3. *Professional Development*—Sustained, intensive, and focused professional development opportunities for administrators, teachers, and faculty foster POS design, implementation, and maintenance.

4. *Accountability and Evaluation Systems*—Systems and strategies to gather quantitative and qualitative data on both POS components and student outcomes are crucial for ongoing efforts to develop and implement POS.

5. *College and Career Readiness Standards*—Content standards that define what students are expected to know and be able to do to enter and advance in college and/or their careers comprise the foundation of a POS.

6. *Course Sequences*—Non-duplicative sequences of secondary and postsecondary courses within a POS ensure that students transition to postsecondary education without duplicating classes or requiring remedial coursework.

7. *Credit Transfer Agreements*—Provide opportunities for secondary students to be awarded transcripted postsecondary credit at the time the credit is earned and are supported by formal agreements between secondary and postsecondary education systems.

8. *Guidance Counseling and Academic Advisement*—Guidance counseling and academic advisement help students to make informed decisions about which POS to pursue.

---

7 MPR Associates, Inc., *Programs of Study.*

Table 2 (cont.)

9. *Teaching and Learning Strategies*—Innovative and creative instructional approaches enable teachers to integrate academic and technical instruction and students to apply academic and technical learning in their POS coursework.

10. *Technical Skills Assessments*—National, state, and/or local assessments provide ongoing information on the extent to which students are attaining the necessary knowledge and skills for entry into and advancement in postsecondary education and careers in their chosen POS.

- *Examples of CTE Delivery System Characteristics.* Table 3 contains an array of CTE delivery system models, but is not an exhaustive list of the ways CTE is delivered across the country. Some models vary only slightly, and some terms are used interchangeably. The delivery model adopted by a given state or institutions within that state will most likely be a hybrid, modification, or continuum of one or more of the basic delivery models, and will be reflective of the structures, culture, and resources in the state.

Table 3. Examples of CTE Delivery System Characteristics

Elective courses as part of a high school curriculum

Definition/key attributes: Historical model associated with "vocational" education.

Considerations: May be seen as only appropriate for students at risk, or for students who are academically challenged.

Does not reflect a coherent set of courses that prepares students in a specific way or for a specific career.

Delivery can occur at a comprehensive high school, a regional/area technical center, or a technical high school.

Dual Enrollment/Dual Credit (Transcripted Credit, Advanced Standing, Youth Options)

Definition/key attributes: High school students enrolled in postsecondary courses, taught either at the postsecondary institutions or at the high schools by either postsecondary faculty members or HS teachers (credentialed as postsecondary adjunct faculty). Students earn postsecondary and secondary credit concurrently.

Considerations: High school teachers deliver the college course curriculum and use the same assessment methodology as college faculty.

Table 3 (cont.)

Generally there are financial arrangements between the secondary and postsecondary institutions that keep the courses at "no cost" to the student.

Transportation and scheduling issues are generally a barrier to multiple course enrollments in a given semester or year.

Programs of Study

Definition/key attributes: A coherent sequence of rigorous, seamless, non-duplicative courses that prepare students for college and career readiness.

Considerations: Aligned to the POS design framework.

Require strong partnerships between high schools, postsecondary institutions, and business and industry.

Career Academies

Definition/key attributes: Characterized by small learning communities:

- Cohorts of secondary students take classes together for at least two years and remain with core groups of discipline-specific teachers
- Students take discipline-specific courses
- Courses meet high school graduation requirements, provide technical skill development, and earn college credit (as appropriate)
- Develop partnerships with employers, the community, and colleges, thereby increasing opportunities for students to engage in internships and workplace learning

Considerations: Centralization of discipline-specific focuses within the academy model helps to realize operational efficiencies (one curriculum, one set of technology tools to support the discipline, etc.).

The difficulty of maintaining minimum class size (in enrollment and retention) and transportation issues within large school districts can be barriers.

Employer involvement is essential.

Table 3 (cont.)

Delivery Partnerships with Industry

Definition/key attributes: Similar to Career Academies but more narrowly focused on specific industries within targeted Career Clusters™ and Career Pathways.

Considerations: Employer engagement (which may involve both financial and programmatic support) provides the benefit of *real world* projects for student learning.

Can be perceived as too limiting if the industry is very narrow — and not portable to other industries or industry sectors.

Promotes the mindset that all education is a form of career preparation.

Employer engagement is critical to success and provides benefits to both the employer and student; however, time demands are a barrier to full employer engagement.

Work-based learning opportunities allow students to experience the application of knowledge and skills to workplace relevance.

Registered Apprenticeship Programs

Definition/key attributes: Apprenticeship programs provide on-the-job training and related classroom instruction and are employer sponsored. Some programs collaborate with postsecondary institutions to allow students to earn certificates or degrees.

Considerations: Certifications earned through registered apprenticeship programs are recognized nationally.

Apprenticeship programs are not always aligned with a college program so that credit is awarded and credentials earned.

Middle College

Definition/key attributes: Are typically housed on postsecondary campuses and offer at-risk students the opportunity to earn postsecondary credit, but not necessarily with the goal of completing associate degrees or technical certifications.

Courses meet both high school graduation and college degree requirements.

Considerations: At-risk students often thrive in environments that provide real-world learning, relevance, and relationships in small settings. Students on college campuses, through *controlled* exposure to college life, may be better equipped to manage the transition to postsecondary education in their post-high school years.

Table 3 (cont.)

Some high school students may lack the maturity to be integrated into the *culture* of postsecondary learning communities. Transportation and course schedules are less of a concern than in other dual enrollment models.

Early College

Definition/key attributes:	"Early college high schools blend high school and college in a rigorous yet supportive program, compressing the time it takes to complete a high school diploma and the first two years of college." (Early College High School Initiative; http://www.earlycolleges.org/)
	Students earn both high school diplomas and associate degrees.
Considerations:	Some would argue that earning two years of college credit in high school is beyond the intellectual and developmental capacity of adolescents, and could suggest a *weakening* of the college level content. But others contend that students who might not fit in at comprehensive high schools tend to gain a sense of belonging and self-confidence in more focused programs. (http://mb2.ecs.org.reports/Report.aspx?id=1317)
	The coursework may be either academic or CTE.
	If students are required to pay for the courses, they are generally at substantially reduced rates, with significant cost savings for the students.

- *State/Local Regulations and Policies.* Effective policies support and promote the development and implementation of POS. Policy efforts are key to establishing formal procedures for the design, implementation, and continuous improvement of POS. Examples of such efforts are found in Chapter 5.

- *Communication tools and guidelines.* The development process will require a system for communication among participating parties. Communication will probably involve both formal and informal settings. Program designers should agree to a process that makes optimum use of technology without going beyond participants' comfort level. Guidelines should be in place for variables such as frequency, length, leadership, and agendas of meetings; how materials are to be distributed prior to and following meetings; collective decision-making; record keeping and reporting; ways to keep participants apprised of trends in relevant career fields (e.g., via electronic newsletters). If the development process is likely to extend over a period of months or more, a dedicated website provides an excellent means of housing relevant documents.

* *Up-to-Date Labor Market and Demographic Information.* In order for any POS to succeed it must be relevant to "facts on the ground" — the real needs of employers, the availability of suitable candidates for enrollment, and the feasibility of creating cooperative agreements between participating institutions, to name a few. That information can be obtained only through partnerships between educational institutions, the business community, and other stakeholders. Partnerships ensure community ownership and build local support, commitment, and resources. Making the necessary effort to grow and sustain stakeholder partnerships is fundamental for successful POS. Certain states (e.g., Minnesota) have placed more emphasis on the role of partnership advisory committees, groups of local employers and community representatives who advise educators on the design, development, operation, evaluation, and revision of POS. The knowledge and support provided by committee members helps to ensure that the POS reflect employer needs and current economic conditions.[8]

The Implementation Plan

Designing and carrying out the implementation plan involves ensuring that the criteria specified in the POS design framework are met. Successful implementation will ensure that educational offerings within the POS align with industry and thus provide the surest pathway to success in the workplace.

To promote adoption of the POS design framework and the creation of more consistent, high-quality POS, the U.S. Department of Education's Office of Vocational and Adult Education (OVAE) awarded six state grants under its *Promoting Rigorous Career and Technical Education Programs of Study* project. The project was designed

---

8 J. Simser, D. Smith, and D. Mills, "Minnesota Program Advisory Committees: Invigorated with Perkins IV!" 2010, *NCPN Connections,* Vol. 20, no. 3, p. 4.

to test the implementation of POS using the POS design framework and to include an in-depth evaluation of implementation consistency and outcomes. Grant recipients were Arizona, Kansas, Maryland, Montana, Utah, and Wisconsin. Each state formed partnerships of local school districts and postsecondary institutions in urban, rural, and suburban settings to implement their POS. On the following pages, we share information on the experiences of **Montana** and **Wisconsin** in designing and implementing POS using the POS design framework.

Plan Design and Implementation—Strategies from the Field

Montana began its participation in the RPOS project by selecting the Architecture and Construction Career Cluster™ and the Construction Pathway as its focus and forming a partnership consisting of the following entities:

- Two state agencies: the Office of Public Instruction (OPI; secondary) and the Office of the Commissioner of Higher Education (OCHE; postsecondary)
- Four high school districts of varying sizes
- A two-year college

Before students started down their pathway, the participating schools and state agencies needed a tool that would enable them to assure the students, their parents, counselors, and teachers that their POS was indeed rigorous. That tool—the POS design framework, described earlier in this chapter—enables practitioners to self-assess the extent to which their POS satisfy the requirements for rigor.[9]

After Montana completed the self-analysis and analyzed the state's strengths and weaknesses, the project team decided to build an RPOS around the concept of course sequences, one of the 10 components of the POS design framework. The self-assessment tool describes the course sequences component as one that "illustrates the secondary to postsecondary sequence of courses that reflect an aligned POS." Montana then followed the alignment process for its Construction Pathway to conform to the POS framework.

---

9 MPR Associates, Inc., *Programs of Study.*

The RPOS team assembled each school's construction teachers, counselors, academic teachers, and administrators to complete the alignment analysis. The process began by comparing knowledge and skills identified by industry as critical for career readiness to the knowledge and skills taught at the high school and college levels. By following this plan the team was able to learn the breadth of the Construction Pathway and identify how, when, and to what depth the knowledge and skills statements are taught.

The tool Montana employed for the alignment process was the National Career Clusters™ Knowledge and Skills Statements,[10] a component of the National Career Clusters™ Framework. In the 2008 version of the Knowledge and Skills, each Career Cluster™ was organized into four levels of knowledge and skills statements:

A. *Foundational Academic Expectations* — Form the basis for all subsequent levels and meet state academic requirements

B. *Essential Knowledge and Skills* — Pertain to all careers in all clusters

C. *Cluster (Foundation) Knowledge and Skills* — Apply to all careers in the targeted Career Cluster™

D. *Pathway Knowledge and Skills* — Apply to a given pathway within the targeted cluster[11]

Each secondary school worked independently from the others but, by comparing its offerings to the Career Cluster™ standards, was able to determine whether it was teaching the knowledge and skills necessary for college readiness. Through the close collaboration of postsecondary construction instructors, a six-year course sequence model — four years of high school and two years of college — was created that covered all of the knowledge and skills required for career readiness.

The product of the process described above is a *gap analysis*. The gap analysis reveals which knowledge and skills are poorly addressed, or not at all, in the six-year plan. Once the gaps were understood, each school developed and implemented a strategy for closing them.

---

10 http://www.careertech.org/resources/clusters/knowledge-skills.html
11 In 2012 a transition to the Common Career Technical Core (CCTC) occurred and different levels of knowledge and skills have been developed. For a review of the latest information, go to http://www.careertech.org/career-technical-education/cctc/.

In Montana, team members discovered two significant gaps that were causing many students to enter college with inadequate math and literacy skills. Studies of students entering Montana two-year colleges revealed that nearly 60 percent of recent high school graduates required remedial math or English or both. Of greater concern was that nearly half of the remedial students did not finish the classes and consequently went no further in their college education.

The course sequence model not only helped to identify gaps but also showed how to close them. The foundation of any Career Pathway is a planned sequence of courses. Every POS sequence starts with broad foundational courses in the early secondary years. As students continue along their pathways, they take CTE courses and related academic courses that focus more narrowly but also go into greater depth. Once students graduate and enter college, their courses narrow to the occupationally specific technical skills required to embark on careers.

Each participating Montana school reviewed its construction course sequences to make sure they conformed to the progression described above—from broad and general to narrower and more in-depth. After aligning the knowledge and skills taught at the secondary level with those taught at the postsecondary level, both urban and rural schools could assure their students that they would enter college prepared to learn the material needed to qualify for construction careers.

The real challenge did not involve CTE per se but mathematics and literacy skills—or the lack thereof—and the high need for remediation in mathematics and English Language Arts at the entering college level. Moreover, anecdotal evidence from Montana's construction teachers indicated a larger problem than the need for remediation in mathematics (math) and English Language Arts was that some students were avoiding the remedial classes altogether and consequently were not acquiring the math and reading skills necessary to keep up with the technical concepts presented in their college programs.

The question was how to help students acquire the necessary math and reading skills *before leaving high school*. The schools already had math and English Language Arts classes. The challenge was to find a new way to help students master certain skills without significantly changing the curriculum. Montana's answer came in the form of a two-pronged attack on low academic skills, especially in math. The high schools adopted two methods for integrating math into existing construction classes.

The larger urban school district had the benefit of a dedicated career center, where the district's three high schools enrolled students in CTE classes (including construction). The center blocked two class periods, one for geometry and one for an introductory construction class. The geometry class period could be allocated to any combination of two sophomore courses, Geometry in Construction and Technical Geometry. The class followed a process that involved learning math, then learning technical skills, and then applying the skills and repeating the process. The purpose of teaching both academic and CTE skills in the sophomore year is to enable students to move easily into more advanced construction classes later in their high school pathways and continue to apply the math learned.

The smaller high schools took a different approach that required a smaller investment of financial resources but a larger investment of teacher time. These schools brought in the National Research Center for Career and Technical Education (NRCCTE) "Math-in-CTE" professional development program, which is designed to pair math and CTE teachers for the purpose of finding math concepts embedded in CTE lessons. The math teacher helped the construction teacher learn new ways to teach the math concepts as part of the existing construction class. The math teacher was also able to learn new practical uses for math skills, lessons that could be used to show students the role of math in careers.

Mastery of each math element was assessed in three ways. First, could students apply the math concepts to the construction skills they were learning? Second, were students able to adopt math lessons to non-construction applications? And finally, could students use the math they had learned for construction to solve questions from standardized exams such as the ACT, exam questions they would later see when they were applying for college?

To further assist students in mastering the math they needed for construction (as well as all technical careers), the Montana high schools added a dual-credit technical math class for seniors. The two-year college math instructors worked with the high school math teachers to offer the college-level technical math used as a prerequisite for the college's technical skill programs. There were four benefits to the students. First, they learned the math in a just-in-time fashion for the senior-level construction classes they were taking. Second, they knew the math required for the college classes they would be taking the next year. Third, they were less likely to require remedial math at the college. And fourth, they received postsecondary credit for the class and did not have to repeat it at the college.

In the area of literacy, high schools followed a similar process; each adopting NRCCTE's Literacy-in-CTE program. The participating English and construction teachers worked together in devising reading skills strategies they could apply in the classroom.

Strategies for Communication

Once the components of the POS have been designed and are ready for implementation, communicating them becomes the priority. Clear, concise, and user-friendly formats for communicating the POS to stakeholders facilitate widespread adoption and use of the POS components. In Wisconsin, the communication of information about POS and their associated sequences of courses to teachers, faculty, counselors, students, parents, and other stakeholders is accomplished through the Wisconsin Career Pathways website (http://www.wicareerpathways.org). The website's tools enable high school career prep coordinators to link their POS to technical college or university curricula in such a way that high school students can easily see the sequences of courses they should take and how those courses earn college credit and/or prepare students for college-level work. Students can see the college curriculum and look at labor market and earnings forecasts, along with admission criteria, tuition and fees, and other general information. The established POS are searchable by cluster, pathway, school district, and high school.

Students can explore the POS offered at their high schools and take one or more occupational interest inventories. When the inventories have been completed, Career Clusters™ that match the students' interests are listed. Students can then build their own educational plans, entering the high school courses they have taken or plan to take, and track their progress in completing their POS. Discussion forums are available; planned upgrades include the ability to access the site via iPad or smart phone. Individual student information is kept in students' secure "MiLocker" areas and can be accessed by the students and their parents and, with the students' permission, the students' guidance counselors.

The website is in its third year of development and implementation. As of spring 2012, a total of 328 high schools (or about 66 percent of Wisconsin's public high schools) have created 4,575 POS. The student section was added in fall 2011, and after only a few months 8,634 students have created "lockers" and have begun the process of creating their educational plans.

Optimize Instruction Through Dual Credit Models

Research indicates that students who earn college credit in high school are more likely to earn high school diplomas and persist to college completion.[12] Among the benefits of awarding college credit to high school students is that it provides "academic momentum" and a clearer vision of the continuum of work- and college-readiness.[13] Many phrases have been used to capture the experience of earning college credit in high school — "credit bearing transition programs," "dual credit," "dual enrollment," and "concurrent enrollment," among others. The terminology is complicated still further by the fact that, within the broad umbrella of dual enrollment, there are several subcategories.

---

12 M. M. Karp et al., *The Postsecondary Achievement of Participants in Dual Enrollment: An Analysis of Student Outcomes in Two States*, 2007 (National Research Center for Career and Technical Education: St. Paul, Minn.); T. North and J. Jacobs, *Dual Credit in Oregon 2010 Follow-Up: An Analysis of Students Taking Dual Credit in High School in 2007–08 with Subsequent Performance in College*, 2010 (Oregon University System: Eugene, Oregon); J. Swanson, "An Analysis of the Impact of High School Dual Enrollment Course Participation on Postsecondary Academic Success, Persistence and Degree Completion," 2008 (paper presented at the meeting for the National Association for Gifted Children, Tampa, Florida, and the National Alliance of Concurrent Enrollment Partnerships, Kansas City, MO). The National Alliance of Concurrent Enrollment Partnerships (NACEP) offers an excellent online teacher resource that includes links to research regarding the enhanced outcomes for high school graduates who participate in dual enrollment programs along with resources for the development and implementation of concurrent (dual) credit opportunities (http://nacep.org/).

13 Swanson, "An Analysis of the Impact of High School Dual Enrollment."

When the concept of dual enrollment is discussed, many people assume that the conversation is about College Level Examination Program (CLEP) or Advanced Placement (AP) credit. That assumption is reinforced by reports such as the *8th Annual AP Report to the Nation* conducted by the College Board (2012).[14] The report states that in 2011, 616,412 students from 12,926 public high schools submitted one or more AP exam results intended to demonstrate their acquisition of the competencies required to earn postsecondary credit to 3,293 postsecondary institutions. However impressive those numbers might be, they reflect only a portion of dual enrollment participation. National data on the prevalence of high school students earning college credit in CTE courses is less readily available.

The creation of dual credit opportunities requires several tools. The federal toolbox includes Perkins IV, in which one statutory requirement states that a POS should offer the opportunity, *where appropriate,* for secondary students to acquire postsecondary credits. Elsewhere the law states that POS "*may* include the opportunity for secondary education students to participate in dual or concurrent enrollment programs or other ways to acquire postsecondary education credits."[15] The phrases "where appropriate" and "may include" are critical in setting the tone of negotiations with postsecondary partners. Words such as "must" and "will" can trigger a negative response from college faculty if they perceive a threat to their academic freedom. This is particularly true in Wisconsin, a "local control" state, where state statute does not require alignment of secondary or postsecondary curricula. A more positive outcome can be expected by framing the conversation between secondary and postsecondary faculty around "possibilities" for earning dual credit. Discussions about dual enrollment opportunities can be fruitfully initiated with the right questions: Is some of the college course content appropriate for high school students? Is it likely that a high school student can achieve the course competencies? If so, is it appropriate to award them college credit for their work?

---

14 College Board, *8th Annual AP Report to the Nation*, February 8, 2012 (http://media.collegeboard.com/digitalServices/public/pdf/ap/rtn/AP-Report-to-the-Nation.pdf).
15 Perkins §122(c)(1)(A)(iii).

As the economy continues to improve, the demand for "globally competitive" skills will continue to rise, as will recognition of, and public and private investment in, CTE as a way to meet that demand. Dual enrollment in CTE courses will be a key strategy in preparing students to fill skill gaps, especially in "middle-skilled jobs."[16]

In the state toolbox, dual enrollment can take different forms based on statute and protocols that have been developed by high school and postsecondary partners. AP is an example of a traditional, well-established dual credit program. Effective dual credit programs, locally grown by partnerships between high schools and four-year institutions, generally result in *credit transfer agreements* that detail dual credit options, criteria that must be met (e.g., end-of-course assessment, faculty credentials), and the mechanism for dually reflecting credit on high school and college transcripts.[17] Generally speaking, dual enrollment courses should be taught at high schools by faculty who are appropriately credentialed (usually to the same level as the college faculty), and students should be assessed in the same way as students who take the courses on college campuses.

Montana's CTE STatewide ARTiculation (START) program is an example of a highly systematized state-level approach to dual enrollment. Using Montana's common course numbering system, the START program integrates postsecondary course objectives into one or more high school courses in technical math, technical writing, and computer applications.

Because of Wisconsin's reliance on local control, several types of dual credit are available throughout the state—international baccalaureate programs, early and middle college high schools, and traditional CLEP and AP courses. Wisconsin is near the national average in AP exam participation (27.8 percent versus 30.2 percent) and above the national average in AP exam performance (19.4 percent versus 18.1 percent).[18] In the Wisconsin Technical College System, dual enrollment programs that focus on CTE courses include youth options, youth apprenticeship programs, advanced standing, and transcripted

---

16 H. J. Holzer and R. I. Lerman, *The Future of Middle-Skill Jobs*, 2009, Center on Children and Families, Briefing #41 (Brookings Institution: Washington, D.C.).

17 MPR Associates, Inc., *Programs of Study*.

18 College Board, *8th Annual AP Report*, p. 13.

credit programs. In 2010–2011, 18,252 high school students earned college credit through transcripted credit courses.[19] Transcripted credit courses are articulated courses within RPOS that allow for college courses to be taught by "credentialed" high school teachers using college curricula and assessments. High school teachers, in addition to their state secondary teacher's license, must meet the college system's certification standards for the course(s) they teach. High school teachers and college instructors jointly review curricula, assessments, and processes for generation of college transcripts, and culminate their work in articulation agreements. The college faculty members meet with the high school classes on the first day of the school year to discuss the importance of the transcripted courses in preparing to enter postsecondary education. The transcripted credit courses are clearly noted to help counselors, students, and parents make decisions on the students' educational plans.

Valuing Technical Skill Attainment

The ability to determine, with accuracy, whether students, through their participation in POS, have achieved sets of skills that are valued by business and industry is a powerful accountability tool that should be in the toolbox of every high school and postsecondary institution.

For the past several years secondary schools have focused on demonstrating student progress in response to "No Child Left Behind," which emphasizes academic performance. Perkins IV includes measurement of technical skills, thereby helping to broaden the focus of both secondary and postsecondary education to include CTE. The Knowledge and Skills statements that are part of the National Career Clusters™ Framework standardized the expected outcomes for CTE programs across the nation and national groups, like NOCTI, have developed assessment tools aligned to these Knowledge and Skills statements.

The final piece of the course sequence strategy is *technical skills assessment* (TSA). Montana looked beyond the Knowledge and Skills statements that are part of the National Career Clusters™ Framework to the standards published by the National Center for Construction

---

19 WTCS 38.04(21) Report (2011, January 24), Wisconsin Technical College System: Madison, Wisconsin.

Education and Research (NCCER). Using the NCCER standards as a point of reference, the college instructors compiled a list of competencies associated with their fundamental construction class. The list represented a cross-section of knowledge and skills that qualify an individual to start a postsecondary construction program.

The team worked with NOCTI to create assessments. Knowledge competencies were measured using multiple-choice exams. For testing technical skills, the group developed a performance assessment administered by the college instructors. Each participating college set aside days on which secondary construction students would demonstrate skill mastery at the college. Students who passed both the knowledge assessment and the technical skill assessment were awarded college credit at the institution giving the exam. Because of the credibility added by NOCTI and the NCCER standards, the state of Montana approved the assessment process for any student completing a construction program. The credit, transcripted at the college, was also transferable to any Montana college offering the course.

In Wisconsin, instructors and educational leaders felt it was important to be intentional in the language they used to refer to the federal requirements for TSA. As their development work progressed, the initial federal term "technical skill assessment" morphed into "technical skill *attainment*." The distinction is important. In a state that favors local control, there is little support for the idea that there is only one way to do any given thing. Assessment of the *attainment* of skill(s) was seen as the right thing to do but was not perceived as an attempt to enforce a one-size-fits-all approach, since it does not mandate the method of assessment. Philosophically, assessing the *attainment* of a skill is more palatable because once you know what skill you want the student to attain, there are many ways to assess whether attainment has taken place, and that translates into local control and academic freedom.

To make the transition from assessment to attainment work, instructors must commit to standardizing the skill(s) of interest and the performance standards by which they will be assessed. The skills, and the indicators of their performance, are standardized across similar programs in the technical college system. The skills to be demonstrated and/or measured are supported by business and industry, but the way in which the skills are assessed is a local decision. College faculty can assess the skills through portfolios, demonstrations, essays, exams, or multiple-choice tests. As long as the assessments are valid, reliable, and fair, the *types* of assessments used are not as important as the ability of those assessments to determine whether the students have actually attained the skills.[20]

Whether created by third parties or developed locally, effective technical skills assessments include the following attributes:

- Measure student attainment of technical skill proficiencies at multiple points during a POS.

- Employ industry-approved technical skill assessments based on industry standards, where available and appropriate.

- Employ state-developed and/or -approved assessments, particularly where industry-approved assessments do not exist.

- Result in the awarding of secondary credit, postsecondary credit, or a special designation on a student's high school diploma.

- Incorporate performance-based assessment items, to the greatest extent possible, where students must demonstrate the application of their knowledge and skills.[21]

The success of any POS and the associated TSA is, at its core, based on the degree to which local employers find the knowledge and skills that students attain at the end of the process a value to their organizations. Even though Perkins IV requires that a state-approved assessment be used to measure technical skill attainment, if that assessment is not supported by industry, it serves little purpose.

Through its RPOS grant, the three participating Wisconsin LEAs (Local Education Agencies) and their local technical colleges, in partnership with the Department of Public Instruction and the Wisconsin Technical College System, created a technical skill assessment for high school CTE students who are concentrators in the Manufacturing Career Cluster™ Production Career Pathway. The assessment is based on the Career Cluster™ Knowledge and Skills and the Critical

---

20 For a more complete summary of the TSA development work in Wisconsin, see *A Unique Approach: Going Beyond Carl D. Perkins Compliance* (http://www.wids.org/Portals/0/PDF_Docs/A_Unique_Approach.pdf).

21 MPR Associates, Inc., *Programs of Study.*

Core Manufacturing Skills (CCMS), an industry certification created by Wisconsin-based manufacturers. Key Wisconsin manufacturers (John Deere, Sub-Zero, Harley-Davidson, among others) partnered with the technical college system to identify core manufacturing skills that are essential to the effectiveness of manufacturing operations. Four certification areas were identified: productivity skills, problem-solving skills, team skills, and adaptability skills. While the work was initially carried out and vetted by manufacturers, the certification has come to be seen as applicable and useful in several industry sectors.

The four industry-recognized CCMS certifications were cross-walked to the Manufacturing Career Cluster™ Knowledge and Skills, and to each of the courses within the Manufacturing Production RPOS. The resulting matrix enables teachers and students to know what knowledge and skills will be taught in which courses, how those skills relate to the CCMS certifications, and at what point in their pathways the students' attainment of the knowledge and skills will be assessed.

The RPOS project team, uncomfortable with the idea of high-stakes tests for high school students, decided that students would be assessed several times throughout their high school careers, using both formative and summative assessments. To facilitate the multiple-assessments-multiple-times methodology, the RPOS team has been engaged in the development of an application (App) for the iPad. The App will allow high school teachers to access a secure database of student information to identify the CCMS skills that students have already demonstrated and those that remain to be demonstrated. Over the course of the semester, the high school teacher uses the App to guide learning activities and assessments. When a student success-fully demonstrates a skill, the relevant information is entered into the App and uploaded to the database, where it is then available for the next teacher to see and use. It is hoped that, by creating a track record of student success, the App will provide positive reinforcement for students and teachers alike.

Evaluation

This chapter highlighted the building blocks necessary to construct an effective sequence of courses, essential to implementation of the POS Framework, in addition to credit transfer agreements and technical skill attainment. Each block has unique criteria for measuring effectiveness. The evaluation process should inquire as to whether the sequence of courses within the POS operates within a culture of continuous process improvement. A strong commitment by administrators to support continuous process improvement is critical to the success of CTE courses and POS, both in terms of the integration of core academic content and in response to rapidly changing business and industry needs.

Non-duplicative sequences of secondary and postsecondary courses within a POS ensure students transition to postsecondary education without duplicating classes or requiring remedial coursework. *Programs of Study: Local Implementation Readiness and Capacity Self-Assessment*[22] describes the criteria for a well-developed sequence of courses that could be used as one evaluation component:

- Map out the recommended academic, and career and technical courses.

- Begin with introductory courses at the secondary level (broad foundational knowledge and skills) and progress to occupationally-specific courses at the postsecondary level.

- Offer opportunities for students to earn postsecondary credit for coursework taken during high school.

The following is based on that document's evaluation tool for course sequences. This assessment can be used as an effective tool for continuous improvement.

---

22 MPR Associates, Inc., *Programs of Study*, p. 20.

Course Sequences—Implementation Capacity Analysis

Self-Assessment Reflection and Action Planning

In the section below, identify your current capacity assets in the area of Course Sequences by responding to the question prompts. Give equal analysis to local capacity barriers, items of critical importance, and steps needed to remedy these capacity concerns.

State or Local Self-Assessment	Items of Critical Importance/ Action Steps
• What's working well that is worth keeping? • What goals do you have to sustain and enhance the level of collaboration among the partners? • What strategies will you use to sustain the engagement of partnership members? • How will you know if your partnership is being successful?	• What will be new or needs to be revised? • What strategies will you use to address items identified as being of critical importance? • What are the indicators you will use to measure your improvement? • How will you know if you are successful? And when?
Notes	Notes

In addition to inventory-style evaluation tools and other objective measures of success, qualitative data can help fill in the gaps about POS and their usefulness to students and teachers. For example, a high school CTE teacher in Wisconsin, as part of his experience in teaching within an RPOS, summarized his experience by saying:

The RPOS experience is something that every teacher should have the opportunity to go through as it allows the teacher to reflect cognitively on what is being taught and why they are teaching the current curriculum to the students in class. Too many times teachers fall into what is easy and what the teacher has the most background in in their personal life. This results in students learning curriculum or skills in the way the teacher was taught sometimes many years prior. Through the RPOS the teacher investigates the true knowledge gained by the learner at every step in an effort to gain as much efficiency as possible. This efficiency is needed because the teacher has now worked with other teachers and representatives from industry and possesses a greater knowledge of the subject than previously held. Once more people are involved in the curriculum decisions there is inherently an opportunity for further learning and a reigniting of the desire to learn inside the teacher who then passes this new knowledge on to the students.

Conclusion/Summary

A POS is a *plan* — for finishing school and entering a career. All students should have a plan that involves postsecondary education to some extent. Montana and Wisconsin described their processes/methodology for the development of course sequencing and delivery systems using the POS design framework. Well-defined course sequencing can ensure students have a clear path to follow from education to careers. POS can reduce duplication and the need for remediation, a major stumbling block to millions of American college students and a huge drain on educational resources that could be more productively used elsewhere. This basic fact should be of great interest to all educational stakeholders — teachers, administrators, counselors, businesspeople, policymakers, and community leaders, not to mention students and their families. Today we are witnessing demographic and economic trends (high and rising high school dropout rates, high unemployment, the technological transformation of the workplace, globalization of commerce) that make postsecondary education more important than ever. Any increase in the percentage of American youth and adults who enter and complete some type of postsecondary program is beneficial to the American economy and the individuals and their families. POS are designed to make that increase a reality.

Teaching and Learning

David Bond and Agustin Navarra

This chapter is dedicated to Dr. Dale Parnell, who in 1985 wrote The Neglected Majority, *which launched a tidal wave of interest in students in the middle 50 to 65 percent as represented on traditional measures of academic success. At the time of its first printing, Dale was President of the American Association of Community and Junior Colleges (now AACC). Since that time he has taught education at universities and written several books (including* Why Do I Have to Learn This? *and* Contextual Teaching Works) *to promote contextual teaching and learning.*

Why Do I Have to Learn This?

Educators all over the world are often asked, "Why do I have to learn this?" Too often the response is, "Because you might need it someday." Or worse, "Because it will be on the test." Neither answer is satisfying to students, and neither inspires interest in learning.

What is the purpose of education? Should schools, especially public schools, be primarily in the business of instilling facts and developing so-called intellectual skills? Shouldn't they have a more practical focus as well, preparing students for their "real world" of careers, grocery shopping, marriage, and the like? American education has always favored the priority of a "classical subject-matter education" in the tradition of the Greek philosopher Plato over the more practical, problem-oriented approach favored by Aristotle, and the inquiry method favored by Socrates. We hold to a broad definition of education that includes an understanding of how knowledge may be applied to real-life situations. The realities of living in today's economy require students to experience a deeper and more meaningful education than has ever existed in our history. If we believe the primary purpose of education is to help each student become a fully competent, contributing, self-motivating, self-fulfilling member of our society, it is time to redirect our goals discussions toward a broader, more inclusive view.

No longer can the debate about academic education and Career Technical Education (CTE) be allowed to degenerate into an either/or argument. They are both important, but, unfortunately, we have allowed a wide gap to exist between the two.

Why Are U.S. Students Falling Behind Other Countries?

The findings of the National Commission on Mathematics and Science Teaching for the 21st Century reflect what parents and employers have been saying for many years. Mathematics and science education are crucial. Unfortunately, it is not up to the standards needed. In reaction to our children's poor performance on the Third International Mathematics and Science Study (TIMMS) and the National Assessment of Educational Progress (NAEP), the commission stated, "…It is abundantly clear…that we are not doing the job that we should do — or can do — in teaching our children to understand and use ideas from these fields. Our children are falling behind; they are simply not "world-class learners when it comes to mathematics and science."[1]

In Chapter 3, and in the Harvard Graduate School of Education project report *Pathways to Prosperity*, William Symonds et al. use data from 2009 to confirm what was already true in 2000.[2] The 2009 assessment report by the Organisation for Economic Co-operation and Development (OECD) and the Programme for International Student

---

1 National Commission on Mathematics and Science Teaching for the 21st Century, *Before It's Too Late: A Report to the Nation from The National Commission on Mathematics and Science Teaching for the 21st Century* (Jessup, MD: Education Publication Center, 2000), p. 4 (www.ed.gov/americacounts/glenn).

2 William C. Symonds, Robert B. Schwartz, and Ronald Ferguson, *Pathways to Prosperity: Meeting the Challenge of Preparing Young Americans for the 21st Century*, Pathways to Prosperity Project, February 2011, Harvard Graduate School of Education (http://www.gse.harvard.edu/news_events/features/2011/Pathways_to_Prosperity_Feb2011.pdf).

Assessment (PISA) reveals that the performance of U.S. students in science and math has not compared well with other countries (ranked 17th in science and 25th in math achievement).

Population, Environmental, and Other Changes

At the beginning of the last century, only 6 percent of appropriate-aged youth were graduating from high school. Seventy years later that had grown to about 75 percent. Because of compulsory education requirements, with almost all youth being educated, we are driven to attempt to deal with a vast array of individual differences: in intelligence levels, in family and economic background, in cultural background, and in the ways individual students learn. The following diagram may show the challenge teachers are facing every day.

Is this your classroom?

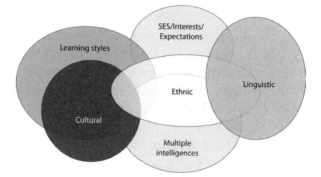

Yet, despite huge population changes in schools over the past 100+ years, the teaching process has changed little. Many teachers continue to use traditional teaching methodologies. However, the world has changed, the technology has accelerated its pace, global markets are more complex, and global competition is tougher. Are teachers in sync with new requirements?

What Are the Challenges?

The "flat" world is asking for less content, deeper understanding, and a problem-solving attitude. A number of faulty ideas and unsound practices stand in the way of cultivating excellence throughout our schools.

- Faulty images of excellence — There is little agreement among educational leaders about the definition of excellence in education.

- A diverse population — Anyone who has spent much time in a public school classroom can attest to the awesome array of individual differences among the students. The varieties of student aspiration and the multiplicity of socioeconomic and cultural backgrounds and experiences require multiple pedagogical approaches.

- "High standards" — Many ignore the fact that having "high standards" is only half the solution. The more important half is designing programs that help students **meet** those high standards.

- Fragmentation — Students are expected to go from class to class, subject to subject, even from grade to grade and school to school, with little sense of connection or continuity.

- Will it be on the test? — The testing movement, by and large, defies rational observation about how individuals learn and how effective education works. In fact, the word *test* has become a four-letter word for many teachers. Many tests provide few ways of evaluating whether students can solve problems, apply knowledge, or see things in the mind's eye — all vital skills both for ongoing education and for success beyond the classroom.

- Too much to cover! — Exposing students to more material does not mean they will learn more. More likely, attempting to "cover the material" in a packed curriculum usually means that the students receive only a superficial exposure to a massive amount of information and learn nothing in depth. As W. James Popham[3] says, "excessive curricular aspirations have an unforeseeable but devastating impact on educational quality." Contextual learning advocates moving away from the "more is better" theory in curriculum building, teaching, and learning, toward a theory of "go deeper rather that wider."

---

3 W. James Popham, *Unlearned Lessons: Six Stumbling Blocks to Our Schools' Success* (Cambridge, MA: Harvard University Press, 2009).

- What to leave out? — A natural consequence of the "too much to cover!" compared to the "never enough time to teach" is that a portion of the content is usually left out (or in the best of the cases, it is "covered" in the last week or so). A more contextual and sense-making approach calls for re-sequencing the content, in order to teach first what is important for the life of the students, then teach what is going to be on the test (and is maybe useful for life), and finally teach what is left. If this last portion is "not covered," the damage to the students has been minimized.

- Conventional pedagogy prepares a relatively small number of students — those considered "smart" — to use "head skills," while relegating everyone else to the acquisition of "hand skills." Unfortunately, the two groups are not considered merely *different*. Those who can easily learn "head skills" are considered superior. This is clearly a case of *pedagogical inequity*.

  Pedagogical inequity is unfair and irrational. It is a very real problem that demands a solution. One cause of the problem is that conventional pedagogy mistakenly views "head skills" and "hand skills" as incompatible. They are not. It is possible to teach in such a way that both types of skills are developed — and fairness demands that we try to do so.

False Assumptions About Learning

Many educators tend to interpret the learning environment according to their own experience as students. In other words, they teach the way they have been taught — usually through traditional abstract lecture methods. As part of these abstract lecture methods, we found that teachers strongly believe and trust that only when they talk about a topic, students miraculously learn it. Those faculty members may base their methods on one or more false assumptions:

- *People automatically transfer learning from one situation to another.* Contextual teaching methods would allow students to have experiences where they can see how knowledge from academic classes is used in a potential career field.

- *Learners are passive receivers of wisdom — empty vessels into which knowledge is poured.* Students in a passive classroom may miss the most important means of learning — exploration, discovery, and invention.

- *Learning is the strengthening of bonds between stimuli and correct responses.* This misconception is based on a behaviorist approach to education, which tends to reward response instead of understanding. This way may be good for a minority of students — not more than 15 percent.

- *What matters is getting the right answer.* Students who focus primarily on getting the right answer tend to rely on memorized shortcuts instead of acquiring the problem-solving skills they will need in a real-life setting. Maybe if problems were defined as in the real world, there would be no need for a unique right answer. This would help students to think about the practical significance of the answer.

- *Skills and knowledge, to be transferable to new situations, should be acquired independent of their contexts of uses.* The process of abstracting knowledge, or taking it away from this specific context, has long been thought to make that knowledge more useful to a number of situations. However, such decontextualization can easily rob students of a sense of motivation and purpose.

Measuring Success Involves More Than Rote Memory

How do you know that they know? Most educators understand that the most important part of learning is what students can do with what they know. Yet, paper-and-pencil tests are identified as the primary method for determining a student's grade. Renate and Geoffrey Caine suggested that, by overextending the rote memory capacity of students through memorization with no connection to application, educators impoverish the learning and interfere with the development of understanding.[4] Assessment may be considered authentic if

---

4 Renate Nummela Caine and Geoffrey Caine, *Making Connections: Teaching and the Human Brain* (Alexandria, VA: Association for Supervision and Curriculum Development, 1991).

226

the assessment is an activity that is known to occur in areas of life other than school.

Schools must define their expectation for student learning so that they may decide what will be taught. Business and industry can help schools decide "what" to teach, or at least what to teach **first**. Once a determination is made as to which student expectation should be taught, the critical question arises: what level of proficiency indicates success? To assess how well students are doing, educators must look at a variety of sources that provide evidence of student performance. Classroom-based measures include profiles, portfolios, exhibitions, projects, diagnostic assessments, and assessments that cover subject skills, concepts, and knowledge. Teachers need to identify which data to collect and decide how to analyze that data to support the ultimate goal of focusing school improvement efforts. [5]

The most valuable form of assessment reflects the students' current understanding of key concepts and simulates authentic life-related tasks. Assessment is authentic when it is focused and based on what people do in real situations. It is only in using knowledge in challenging situations that replicate or are based in day-to-day life that students truly demonstrate what they know. Authentic assessment is a key ingredient in contextual teaching and learning. Assessment should not be based simply on rote memory.[6]

Common Vision and Goals Needed

According to Dr. Willard Daggett, Founder and Chairman of the International Center for Leadership in Education, the rate of change in society is four to five times faster than the rate of change in our schools. As we decide how to respond to our changing world, we must understand that the rest of the world will not stand still while we think about how to address our challenges.

It's been almost thirty years since the release of *A Nation At Risk* which accentuated the need to provide *all* students with academically rigorous and relevant education. Most people would agree that this

---

5 Willard Daggett, *Rigor and Relevance from Concept to Reality* (International Center for Leadership in Education, 2008).

6 Sandra H. Harwell, and William E. Blank, *Promising Practices for Contextual Learning* (Waco, TX: CCI Publishing, Inc., 2001).

is the direction in which American education needs to go; however, we are finding it easier to conceptualize change than to implement it.[7]

What Does the Research Say?

It is important that educators fully understand the breathtaking power of the human brain to make meaningful connections between knowledge and the application of that knowledge, between knowing and doing, and between content and context. Since the brain tends to discard information for which it finds no connection or meaning, many students find their education meaningless.

A computer, like an instructor, can supply knowledge and information, but it cannot help students make connections between their lives and that knowledge and information. It is the major task of the instructor to help students make connections so that the purpose of learning is immediately understandable.

The process of what is now called "brain-based learning" calls for making connections. Psychologists, philosophers, and educators from William James to John Dewey to Jerome Bruner—all the way to Howard Gardner and Robert Sternberg—have made the case for making connections in education. In the past few decades, neuroscientists have shown the need for making connections in the teaching and learning process.

In 1989, the Secretary of Labor's Commission on Achieving Necessary Skills (SCANS) was formed under the leadership of Secretary of Labor Elizabeth Dole and Assistant Secretary Robert Jones. Representatives from business, industry, labor, government, and education labored mightily to shed light on the question, "What does work require of schools?" The Commission staff studied the cognitive science research literature related to the importance of **contextual teaching**. They also interviewed a number of cognitive scientists and more that 500 private and public employers to discover what they expected of educational institutions and what kind of education and training they thought would be required to meet future needs. As a result the Commission formed the following mission statement:

---

7 Daggett, *Rigor and Relevance.*

We believe that these skills (SCANS-recommended skills and competencies) are best learned in context and especially in the context of realistic workplace problems. Thus the teaching of functional skills will require the most radical change in educational practices since the beginning of this century. (SCANS 1991)

The contextual approach to teaching and learning is not a new pedagogical method. There have always been highly effective teachers who motivate their students to achieve academically by connecting content to context. One of the first educational tools for teaching mathematics contextually was called *Applied Mathematics,* developed in 1986–1988 by a consortium of over 40 state education agencies led by CORD.

The first large-scale test of *Applied Mathematics* was administered during the 1992–1993 school year, when 326 students completing *Applied Mathematics* at 20 schools in 13 states were tested in algebra I concepts and compared with 843 traditional algebra I completers. Results showed no significant difference in the scores of the two groups, despite the fact that the Applied Mathematics students had significantly lower entry-level skills.[8] This means that the applied group improved at a higher rate.

During the same school year, four researchers from the University of Georgia studied the *Applied Mathematics* curriculum as it relates to college preparatory credit. One of their findings dealt with the motivational impact of teaching contextually. Teachers attributed the very high rate of success of students who had not previously been successful in mathematics, to the positive attitudes students had toward the activity-oriented approach to teaching.[9]

Multiple Intelligences

As stated earlier, there is nothing new about contextual learning. There have always been teachers who intuitively understood how to teach concepts so that all learners could grasp them—through

---

8 Candace Todd, *A Report on the Attainment of Algebra I Skills by Completers of* Applied Mathematics *1 and 2* (Waco, TX: CORD, July 1993).

9 William D. McKillip, Edward J. David, Thomas R. Koballa Jr., and J. Steve Oliver, *A Study of* Applied Mathematics *and* Principles of Technology *Relative to the College Preparatory Curriculum Final Report* (University of Georgia, July 1993).

example, illustration, and hands-on application. But even these naturally effective teachers can benefit from understanding the findings of cognitive research and from learning how to put these findings to use. The results of research explain the success of contextual teaching and learning approaches in the classroom.

Howard Gardner, professor of education and psychology at Harvard University, challenged traditional thinking by questioning whether intelligence is a single, measurable capacity. Gardner posited instead that the human capacity for learning is much broader than traditional measurements of intelligence would indicate. Gardner argued for as many as seven forms of intelligence: linguistic, logical/mathematical, musical, spatial, kinesthetic, interpersonal, and intrapersonal. He based his theory on his observation of the wide range of capabilities of adolescents.[10] Further investigation led Gardner to add two additional forms of intelligence—naturalistic and existential. In 2008, on the 25th anniversary of the publication of his original report on multiple intelligences, Gardner reflected on its impact on education. In 1983 he did not expect that his ideas about multiple intelligences in the field of psychology would be picked up by educators all over the globe. He now believes that any serious application of multiple intelligences ideas should entail at least two components:

1. An attempt to individuate education as much as possible. The advent of personal computers should make this goal much easier to attain.

2. A commitment to convey important ideas and concepts in a number of different formats [11]

In his discussion of the variety of learning styles, learning theorist David Kolb observes that learners tend to perceive information either abstractly (by conceptualizing/thinking) or concretely (by experiencing/feeling) and then process that information either actively (by experimenting/doing) or reflectively (by observing/watching). Kolb's construction, like Gardner's, clearly indicated that most

---

10 Howard Gardner, *Frames of Mind: The Theory of Multiple Intelligences* (New York: Basic Books, 1983).

11 Howard Gardner, "The 25th anniversary of the publication of Howard Gardner's *Frames of Mind: The Theory of Multiple Intelligences,*" 2008 (http://pzweb.harvard.edu/pis/MIat25.pdf).

students do not fit neatly into one category or the other. All students can learn by and benefit from all four experiences (thinking, feeling, doing, and watching). Most students will show a preference for one or two particular kinds of learning, and this preference will indicate the individual's primary learning style(s).[12]

The emphasis for contextual learning is to use this process for effective learning to reach the strengths of all students. However, as Kolb's studies indicate, most students have a tendency to learn in a concrete manner (with an emphasis on feeling and doing), while the school system tends to teach in an abstract manner (with an emphasis on thinking and watching). This may not be the best allocation of public money.

Striving for Connectedness

Despite the individual differences in learning styles and intelligences, all learners strive for connectedness. Learning is cumulative. Isolated bits of information normally are not processed and retained by the mind for meaningful use unless connections are made and points of reference or relationships are established between what is known and what is not known.

Learning theorists Caine and Caine explain this "connectedness" theory by pointing out that all knowledge is "embedded" in other knowledge.[13] Academic "subjects" such as English, math, and chemistry are at best artificial distinctions within a single body of knowledge. Allowing these subjects to overlap and integrating them into a single curriculum can therefore provide a better, more connected understanding.

In addition to making connections between different school subjects, educators can enhance the learning process by engaging students in hands-on activities and concrete experiences as other ways of reinforcing the usefulness of the knowledge. Lab activities, experiments, and projects that require students to be actively involved in the community usually stimulate interest and motivation to learn.

---

12 David A. Kolb, *Experiential Learning: Experience As the Source of Learning and Development* (New Jersey: Prentice-Hall, 1984).
13 Caine and Caine, *Making Connections.*

Integrating work-based learning with school subjects is another effective way to ground learning in actual experience.

Constructivism

John Dewey and Jean Piaget, among others who studied how students learn, contributed to the modern view of learning called *constructivism*. Education researchers, psychologists, and cognitive scientists have published hundreds, perhaps thousands, of research articles about various aspects of constructivism. It is a view of learning that people construct new knowledge and understandings based on what they already know and believe. Teaching strategies based on constructivism include exploration and active learning. These strategies include using hands-on activities, encouraging students to think and explain their reasoning instead of merely memorizing and reciting facts, and helping students to see the connections among themes and concepts rather than presenting them in isolation.[14]

Additional Research

If educators really want all students to master rigorous academic standards, they must use instructional strategies that have been empirically documented to be effective. Dolores Perin conducted a literature review on the "evidence of contextualization."[15] The purpose of the review was to consider whether low-skilled students can learn more effectively and advance to college-level programs more readily through contextualization of basic skills instruction. The presence of large numbers of low-skilled students in colleges, especially community colleges, along with low rates of retention and progress in course work and recent findings that traditionally low graduation rates are not increasing suggests that the method of instruction of academically underprepared college students needs to be reformed. An analysis of the 27 studies found in the review suggests that contextualization

---

14 Michael L. Crawford, *Teaching Contextually: Research, Rationale, and Techniques for Improving Student Motivation and Achievement in Mathematics and Science* (Waco, TX: CORD, 2001).

15 Dolores Perin, *Facilitating Student Learning Through Contextualization* (New York: Community College Research Center, Teachers College, Columbia University, 2011).

has the potential to promote short-term academic achievement and longer-term college advancement of low-skilled students. These strategies are familiar to effective teachers.

What Are Some Teaching Strategies That Work?

REACT—A Better Way

CORD developed an acronym, REACT, for describing the five elements of contextual teaching. Through years of teaching, supervising and developing curricula, CORD has observed many outstanding teachers creating exceptional learning environments. These teachers used five teaching methodologies at least some of the time. CORD called them *contextual teaching strategies:* relating, experiencing, applying, cooperating, and transferring. These elements focus on teaching and learning in context. REACT is an easily remembered acronym that represents methods used by the best teachers and also methods supported by research on how people learn best.

- Relating (Learning in the context of life experiences)
- Experiencing (Learning in the context of exploration, discovery, and invention)
- Applying (Learning in the context of how the knowledge and information can be used)
- Cooperating (Learning in the context of sharing, responding, and communicating with other learners)
- Transferring (Using knowledge in a new context or novel situation—one that has not been addressed in class)

Relating

Relating is *learning in the context of one's life experiences or preexisting knowledge.* Given that learning is the challenging process of going from what is known to what is not known by presenting problems within a situation or context known by the students, teachers help students when linking a new concept (to be learned) to something completely familiar to them (previous knowledge), thus connecting what students already know to the new information. When the link is successful, students gain almost instant insight. Caine and Caine call this reaction "felt meaning" because of the "aha!" sensation that often accompanies the insight.[16] Felt meaning can be momentous, as when a student first sees the solution to a problem that he or she has spent significant time and effort in solving. Felt meaning can also be subtle, as when insight leads to a milder reaction, such as, "Oh, that makes sense."

Excellent contextual teachers plan carefully for learning situations in which students can experience felt meaning. Careful planning is needed because often students do not automatically connect new information to the familiar. Research shows that, although students may bring memories or prior knowledge that is relevant to a new learning situation, they can fail to recognize its relevance. When teachers both provide environments in which students activate memories or prior knowledge *and* recognize the relevance of the memories or knowledge, they are using relating.

Experiencing

Relating connects new information to life experiences or prior knowledge that students bring with them to the classroom. But this approach is not possible if students do not have relevant experience or prior knowledge. Teachers can overcome this obstacle and help students construct new knowledge with orchestrated, hands-on experiences that take place inside the classroom. This strategy is called *experiencing*. It is *learning by doing – through exploration, discovery, and invention*. In-class hands-on experiences can include the use of manipulatives, problem-solving activities, and laboratories. The process of collecting data and getting information needed to solve a certain problem gives students a sense of ownership and direction that help motivation, which is the key to learning.

Applying

We define the *applying* strategy as *learning by putting the concepts to use*. Obviously, students apply concepts when they are engaged in hands-on problem-solving activities and projects like those described above. Teachers also can motivate a need for understanding the concepts by assigning *realistic* and *relevant* exercises. These exercises are "word problems" like those found in all textbooks. But they have two major

---

16 Caine and Caine, *Making Connections.*

differences: They pose very realistic situations, and they demonstrate the utility of academic concepts in some area of a person's life. Both are important for application problems to be motivational.

Cooperating

Many problem-solving exercises, especially when they involve realistic situations, are complex. Students working individually sometimes cannot make significant progress in a class period on these problems. They can become frustrated unless the teacher provides step-by-step guidance. On the other hand, students working in small groups can often handle these complex problems with little outside help. Teachers using student-led groups to complete exercises or hands-on activities are using the strategy of *cooperating—learning in the context of sharing, responding, and communicating with other learners.*

Working with their peers in small groups, most students feel less self-conscious and can ask questions without feeling embarrassed. They also will more readily explain their understanding of concepts to others or recommend problem-solving approaches for the group. By listening to others in the group, students reevaluate and reformulate their own sense of understanding. They learn to value the opinions of others because sometimes a different strategy proves to be a better approach to the problem. When a group succeeds in reaching a common goal, student members of the group experience higher self-confidence and motivation than when students work alone.

Transferring

In a traditional classroom, the teacher's primary role is to convey facts and procedures. The students' roles are to memorize the facts and practice the procedures by working skill drill exercises and, sometimes, word problems. Students who can recall and repeat the appropriate facts and procedures score well on the end-of-unit or end-of-semester test. By contrast, in a contextual classroom, the teacher's role is expanded to include creating a variety of learning experiences with a focus on understanding rather than memorization. Contextual teachers use the strategies discussed above (relating, experiencing, applying, and cooperating) and they assign a wide variety of tasks to facilitate learning for understanding. In addition to skill drill and word problems, they assign experiential, hands-on activities and realistic problems through which students gain intuitive initial understanding and then deepen their understanding of concepts.

Students who learn and understand can also learn to transfer knowledge. *Transferring* is a teaching strategy that we define as *using knowledge in a new context or novel situation — one that has not been addressed in class.*

Research shows that, when teachers design tasks for novelty and variety, student interest, motivation, engagement, and mastery of academic goals can increase. Excellent teachers seem to have a natural ability to introduce novel ideas that motivate students intrinsically by invoking curiosity or emotions.

Promising Practices in Contextual Learning

There are several classroom teaching strategies that can be identified as including some or all of the REACT elements. Here are a few:[17]

Problem-Based Learning

With problem-based learning, the educational experience is organized around problems and themes rather than subject-matter disciplines. Problem-based learning is a strategy many teachers use to create a student-centered learning environment in the classroom. Teachers create or encourage students to identify an ill-defined problem or issue that is grounded in the students' experiences. The class-room teacher then serves as a guide as the students work through solving the problem through a discovery-based, research-rich learning process. When students solve problems rather than learning passively, they take ownership of the knowledge and skills they are gaining. They develop an intrinsic motivation based on the satisfaction of accomplishment.

Project-Based Learning

Project-based learning has become a time-proven approach for providing rigorous, relevant, contextual, learning in a manner consistent with how learning takes place beyond the walls of the school and is also compatible with how the brain learns more efficiently. In project-based learning, individual students, small groups, or the entire

---

17 Harwell and Blank, *Promising Practices.*

class focus on creating a useful product or service or similar tangible outcome that is of authentic value to someone outside the classroom. It is similar to problem-based learning in terms of the constructivist process in which students engage, however, project-based learning goes an important step beyond problem-based learning: creation of a tangible outcome. Ideally, projects should closely resemble the kinds of accomplishments performed by adults in the "real world."

Service Learning

Many educators believe that young people should be connected with their community and their own humanity through service. The added notion of linking service with learning has made the concept of service even more attractive as a vehicle for better connecting what happens in school with what happens in the real world. Service learning is a form of experiential education and is a powerful vehicle for achieving the goals of character education. Learning is facilitated when it is personally relevant and contextual and when the learners can see application in their own lives of what they are being asked to learn. Service learning usually takes the form of project-based learning with the project being something that serves the good of some element of the community (e.g. working with a non-profit or local government agency).

Cooperative Learning

Cooperative learning involves deliberately structuring working groups to replicate the population in the classroom. The heterogeneous nature of a truly cooperative group may be one of the most significant factors. Students learn from each other, building understanding and tolerance of differences and at the same time learning to value the diversity. The group functions as an interdependent unit to solve a problem, reach a goal, or create a project. The cooperative learning teacher structures activities in such a way as to create a need for students to depend on each other. At the same time, the students are reminded that they have an individual responsibility to contribute to the group outcome. These cooperative methods have been used successfully in industry settings all over the world.

Work-Based Learning

Work-based learning is a critical component of a system capable of preparing students for life. Work-based learning is knowledge, skills, and attitudes taught in the context of work or life settings. This type of student-centered learning goes beyond the classroom by engaging students through direct contact with the workforce. Work-based learning experiences such as internships and apprenticeships place students in realistic work environments, engaging them with real-world problems and empowering them to find real-world solutions. Mentorship, both workplace-based and off-site, provides adult role models and benefits for students and supervisors. Research shows that mentees improve their job skills, employability skills, academic performance and attendance rates in addition to gaining self-esteem and finding more relevance in their education. Mentors benefit from training future workers and improving their supervisory skills, in addition to the high-quality work they get from mentees.[18] Work-based learning connects the skill or knowledge with the real application.

School-Based Enterprise

A school-based enterprise is any activity through which students produce goods or services for sale to or use by people other than themselves. It is important to realize that participating in the establishment and operation of a school-related business is preparation for both careers and postsecondary education. Some examples of school-based enterprises are sales of refreshments, school supplies, or other merchandise like furniture or recycled materials. Also, a student-run bank is another example. Students learn creation of a business plan, marketing, accounting, manufacturing, distribution, etc.

Integrating Academic and Career Technical Education

An often overlooked resource for academic teachers who might be searching for ways to better connect what they teach in the classrooms with the real world is the Career Technical Education (CTE) instructors located in their own schools. In the absence of integration, academic courses are likely to be more focused on covering vast numbers of

---

18 Jean Rhodes, *Research Corner: Work-Based Mentoring* (Boston: National Mentoring Partnership, July 2003) (http://www.mentoring.org/downloads/mentoring-1310.pdf).

facts and concepts without much regard to context or application. On the other hand, CTE may be more focused on equipping graduates with the specific skills needed for employment. Integration is an attempt to address the major criticisms of both areas of study. Forming teams with other instructors, workplace representatives, and experts on specific subjects can create a well-rounded instructional base from which students can apply what they are learning to concrete experience.[19]

Smaller Learning Communities

The term "smaller learning communities" has been used with schools which have a small population and with small groupings of students and teachers within a larger school. These small groupings have been referred to as an academy, a pod, a building, a team, or a cohort. Students normally stay with an interdisciplinary team of teachers. Several personalized strategies used in the smaller settings have resulted in improved behavior and attendance while students perform as well or better than large school students. The U.S. Department of Education awarded Smaller Learning Communities grants from fiscal year 2000 through 2009 to encourage the development of, and research on, the practice.

Career Academies

A career academy is a type of smaller learning community. The use of career academies is a very promising practice used by a growing number of high schools. However, career academies are more than just a classroom teaching strategy. Career academies are a way to restructure schools. They typically operate as schools within schools with each academy focused on a career theme in which there are good employment opportunities and sufficient businesses in the area that can provide advice to the academy as well as job shadowing and internships to the students. An example of the kind of learning experience typically found in a career academy is project-based learning. One of the reasons academy students find their learning experiences

---

19 Stephanie Kalchik and Kathleen Marie Oertle, *The Theory and Application of Contextualized Teaching and Learning in Relation to Programs of Study and Career Pathways* (Urbana-Champaign, IL: Office of Community College Research and Leadership in "Transition Highlights," September 2010).

so rewarding and relevant is that extensive use is made of real-world connected experiences. Two organizations which provide direction and services to career academies are the National Career Academy Coalition (www.ncacinc.com) and the National Academy Foundation (NAF; www.naf.org). NAF reports that more than 97 percent of NAF students graduated from high school—compared to 50 percent of non-academy students in the urban areas where the NAF academies are located.

In a report on career academies funded by several independent foundations, MDRC (a nonprofit, nonpartisan research organization) studied nine urban high schools over a 15-year period. The study followed randomly assigned students from entering high school until eight years after their scheduled graduation. One of the most significant findings is that career academy graduates had 11 percent more sustained earnings than individuals in the control group, and these impacts on earnings are concentrated among young men and students at risk of academic failure. [20]

Self-Directed Learning

Learning how to become independent, self-directed learners is perhaps the most important skill students can acquire. Such skills will prepare them well for the demands of lifelong learning they will face as adults. In the world beyond the classroom, adults often engage in self-initiated, self-directed, context-rich learning aimed at locating information or mastering skills they want to learn. People engaged in self-directed or independent learning are typically learning something they want to learn, in a manner they choose. Independent study typically involves self-directed learning, as do distance learning, online courses, and competitive projects.

Delivery methods for education and worker training must also continue to expand, particularly in ways that more efficiently help to retrain displaced or underskilled adult workers. Online learning, a rapidly growing methodology, is one way this is likely to occur. Online learning enables students to connect with course materials they might not otherwise be able to access, at times and in ways that are more convenient to them, which is of particular importance to

---

20 James J. Kemple. *Career Academies: Long-Term Impacts on Labor Market Outcomes, Educational Attainment, and Transitions to Adulthood* (MDRC, 2008).

working adults and students in rural areas. The number of elementary and secondary students taking online courses increased tenfold between 2000 and 2007, as documented by the Sloan Consortium[21], and a study from the National Research Center for CTE finds that almost half of community colleges offer credit-granting online occupational programs in which at least 50 percent of course content is delivered online.[22]

Online learning isn't just convenient and flexible. It works. Research from the Center for American Progress concludes that online learning provides high-quality instruction,[23] while the Department of Education has found that students who take courses online perform slightly better than those who receive face-to-face instruction.

Within CTE, some course content such as web design can be delivered entirely online. Other CTE programs require a hybrid approach that includes work-based learning activities such as internships and, in some cases, on-campus skill acquisition through laboratory courses. Whether content is delivered entirely online or in a hybrid format, online learning has proven itself an effective strategy for CTE and workforce training in schools such as Auburn Career Center (OH).

In addition, mastering the use of digital technology is an important part of career readiness for almost any workplace. When technology is embedded into classrooms, students are not just engaged. They also learn how to effectively use digital tools on a daily basis, as they often will in the workforce, and how to participate in our world as digital citizens.

---

21 Anthony Picciano and Jeff Seaman, *K-12 Online Learning: A Survey of U.S. School District Administrators* (Needham, MA: Sloan Consortium, 2007), p. 17.

22 Rod Githens, Fashaad Crawford, and Timothy Sauer, *Online Occupational Education in Community Colleges: Prevalence and Contextual Factors* (Louisville, KY: National Research Center for Career and Technical Education, 2010), p. 14.

23 Cathy Cavanaugh, *Getting Students More Learning Time Online: Distance Education in Support of Expanded Learning Time in K-12 Schools* (Washington, DC: Center for American Progress, 2009), p. 3.

How Can Teacher Effectiveness Be Improved?

A Fundamental Paradigm Shift

Most educators are not equipped to use contextual teaching methodologies effectively. Doing so calls for a fundamental paradigm shift that most are unable to make without a well-crafted professional development program — not just an isolated activity now and then but a strategically sustained professional development process designed to help teachers master contextual teaching. The paradigm shift is so deep that it cannot be carried out without this long term process. Experience shows that it is very hard to depart from the deep-rooted culture of teaching which follows traditional methods of lecture and memorization.

Some Characteristics of Contextual Learning Goals

Before teachers can begin to make a paradigm shift of this magnitude they must understand the goals/purposes of contextual learning. Here are some essential characteristics of contextual learning goals:

Contextual learning goals are application oriented.

Embedded deeply within the philosophy of contextual learning is the idea that every student must have the opportunity not only to acquire knowledge, but also to develop the competencies required to function effectively in his or her real-life roles. Thus, there is a profound shift in emphasis from what is to be taught to what is to be learned. This is probably the most basic and powerful characteristic of contextual learning goals: They are application oriented.

Contextual learning goals are learner centered.

Are our educational institutions addressing the highest-priority needs of the students to become problem solvers, critical thinkers, and life-long learners? Contextual learning offers the ability to make connections that give the student a touchstone of reality upon which to build solid and meaningful learning.

Contextual learning goals are time-flexible.

In contextual learning, how long it takes a student to master a given competency is not as important as the mastery itself. As a result, contextual learning goals provide for considerable flexibility when it comes to scheduling. Less emphasis is placed upon completing a specified unit of study in a specified time period. Students are allowed to move and recycle through the instructional process easily, and time is used flexibly. Not all learners are nine-week or eighteen-week learners; in fact, rate of learning is one key difference among learners.

Contextual learning goals are purpose centered and "up front."

A fourth characteristic of contextual learning goals is that clear statements of purpose must precede expected result statements and must be placed "up front" as guides for both instructors and learners. There should be no surprises in the instructional or evaluation process. This aspect of contextual learning goals helps to correct a common problem encountered with stimulus and response behavioral objectives — their narrow focus. Behavioral objectives tend to keep teachers and learners so focused on the minuscule that the connection is never made to the larger purposes of a lesson or the even larger purposes of the educational organization. Today's students' needs are not met by only behavioral objectives. Contextual learning insists that no matter what is being taught, students should always know how that subject matter fits into larger purposes.

Improving Support Systems

Whatever specific policies they influence, contextual learning goals are the beginning point in making *meaning* the focal point of education at all levels. As education leaders begin to bring a greater degree of congruence between purposeful goals, anticipated results, and the teaching-learning process, the work of creating a continuous and coherent learning experience for students becomes easier. At the same time, students are empowered to develop their competencies to higher levels and become more capable of coping with complexity and change. But for all this to happen, leaders, teachers, and policy makers alike must keep a clear and constant vision of what education is supposed to accomplish in the long run—to serve the society of which it is a part.

Successful schools can be built, but they cannot be sustained simply through the leadership of just one individual, or even a few individuals. To sustain successful schools' reform, create leadership teams that include individuals from multiple levels of the organization, including central administration, building-level administrators, classroom teachers, parents, students, and community leaders. They must work as a team together to encourage each other as they encounter people or groups that fight change or as unforeseen bumps in the road add new challenges.[24]

Implementing contextual learning in the classroom does not require just new equipment. It requires not only new teaching techniques but a new definition of school and teaching. For contextual learning to have its maximum effect on students, teachers must be empowered to effectively implement contextual teaching methodologies. This empowerment can come only through professional development.

Teacher Professional Development: It's Not an Event, It's a Process

Too little attention has been paid to what actually goes on in the classroom. As long as teachers continue to teach the way teachers have taught for years, we cannot expect students to change what they do. The problem has not been a lack of professional development opportunities, but is that the quality of programs has been inconsistent, not strategically thought out, and there has been no consensus on what constitutes quality. What then are the characteristics of high-quality effective teacher professional development and the factors that contribute to its success?[25]

Context (or Setting)

- Supports professional development and the changes it is intended to bring about

- Is characterized by a shared sense of need for change

- Encourages agreement among teaching professionals on answers to basic questions regarding the nature of learning and the teacher's role in the classroom

- Creates an environment in which teaching professionals consider learning a communal activity

24 Daggett, *Rigor and Relevance.*
25 Sandra H. Harwell, *Teacher Professional Development: It's Not an Event, It's a Process* (Waco, TX: CORD, 2003).

Content

- Deepens teachers' subject matter knowledge
- Sharpens classroom skills
- Is up-to-date with respect to both subject matter and education in general
- Contributes new knowledge to the profession
- Increases the ability to monitor student work
- Addresses identified gaps in student achievement
- Centers on subject matter, pedagogical weaknesses within the organization, measurement of student outcomes, and inquiry regarding locally relevant professional questions
- Focuses on (and is delivered using) proven instructional strategies

Process

- Is research based
- Is based on sound educational practice such as contextual teaching
- Supports interaction among master teachers
- Takes place over extended periods of time
- Provides opportunities for teachers to try new behaviors in safe environments and receive feedback from peers

While it is important for the teacher to be in the classroom, it is just as important for the teacher to be given the tools necessary to unlearn ineffective teaching methods and replace them with effective teaching methods. One way to accomplish this without huge commitments of time and money is online professional development programs that combine face-to-face and online interaction. Following an initial face-to-face session, participants interface with one another and with the course facilitator asynchronously via the Internet, which means that they can work almost entirely at home and at their convenience. Online courses can span several weeks, giving participants ample time to practice what they are learning and reflect on its effectiveness.

Also, orientation for students and parents about this new style of teaching and learning is essential to gaining acceptance and leads to better adjustment of the student-teacher relationship in the classroom. Teaching is both an art and a science that should be practiced with a certain amount of empathy so that students do not become frustrated with new expectations for learning.

The Role of Business and Industry

Chapter 7 reviewed the benefits and requirements of education and business/industry partnerships. The role of business and industry in teaching and learning is paramount. Business and industry partnerships with education provide most of the context for learning—and this is done in several ways.

It's obvious that a benefit to students is that there may be the opportunity for employment after graduation or program completion, but **during** the education process there are several ways in which employers provide context and motivation to teachers and learners:

- Employers work collaboratively with faculty to improve or develop curriculum when needed as industry trends change. This includes the review of materials, equipment, and textbooks before purchases are made.

- Employers provide work-based learning opportunities such as field trips, job shadowing, cooperative education, internships, as well as in-school exhibits and presentations.

- Employers provide professional development including allowing faculty to have work-site experiences.

- Employers sometimes provide financial support such as scholarships and equipment donations which provide opportunities for continued learning that would not otherwise exist.

When you read or hear about outstanding career pathways programs or hear about schools that have excellent graduation rates, you can bet that there are well-developed business/industry relationships that support contextual teaching and learning. This is true not only in the United States, but in other countries as well. Chapter 3 mentioned some of the work-based learning that takes place in other countries, and CORD has experienced outstanding results in Latin American countries such as the Dominican Republic and Brazil. In these countries, employers have taken the lead in improving education by becoming more involved with teachers and students. After intensive teacher professional development, students in those countries are showing increased graduation rates and finding better employment due to the investment of employers.

Working Toward Contextualization

Most teachers have natural tendencies to teach the way they were taught, the way their teachers were taught, and so on. Despite the dramatic transformation throughout our society over the last half-century, teaching methods in mathematics and science classes have remained unchanged for many. A growing number of teachers have begun to capitalize on the many dimensions of the learning process. Those teachers are motivated to devote the additional time and effort to see their students enjoy learning.

Where Is It Working?

There are many good examples of how contextual teaching and learning are being practiced. Below are just a few.

Elementary and Middle School

- An excellent example of a **contextual teaching** program is the *If I Had a Hammer* program founded by master carpenter, Perry Wilson. He created a curriculum which teaches math (e.g. fractions and geometry) to third through eighth grade students using the context of construction of a scale model house. The *Hammer* program has reached over 500,000 young students. Today, college students are being trained to deliver the lessons.

- At B. Michael Caudill Middle School, in Richmond, Kentucky, a new cohort of 7th graders enters a STEM-enriched Career Pathway each year — the *Applied Engineering Technology Education Career Pathway*. Science, math, and engineering technology education teachers work together to create and teach an **integrated curriculum**. One 7th grade student asked math teacher, Ashlie Griggs, "When will I ever use this?" Because of the professional development she was provided and the integrated lesson planning, Ms. Griggs was able to reply, "Next week in

Mr. Marionneaux's engineering technology class," and then proceeded to tell the class several other ways that the study of X, Y, and Z coordinates would come in handy in the world of engineering and manufacturing. Teacher, Steve Marionneaux was able to reinforce the potential contexts for the same math concepts. Plans are for this pathway to be coordinated and continued through high school and college.

High School

- As mentioned earlier, the **career academy structure** is being used by more and more high schools as a means to deliver contextual teaching. An excellent example of a high school with a career academy structure is the A. J. Moore Academies at University High School in the Waco (TX) Independent School District. A. J. Moore is a magnet school which offers students a choice of seven academies (engineering; environmental technology; finance; health professions; hospitality and tourism; information technology; and public service administration). Several of the academies have been recognized as top programs in the country by the National Academy Foundation and the entire school has been recognized as a model school by the International Center for Leadership in Education. A. J. Moore reports a 99.3 percent graduation rate — more than 18 percentage points above the other non-academy schools in the district.

- Combining **project-based learning** with **service learning** is a winning combination for students in Scot McAtee's Interactive Media class at Twin Lakes High School in Monticello, Indiana. His students thought that video creation was for making funny stuff for YouTube and for ways to embarrass others. That is, until he got them involved in doing projects that had a positive impact on their community. Since then, Mr. McAtee's students have won awards for their media projects and have learned they can make their community a better place using the same "toys" they had been playing with all along.

- The North Carolina Department of Public Instruction (DPI) studied the success of a pilot program at a single school and then expanded it to 12 more schools across the state. The pilot used a two-teacher approach with combined lesson plans, discipline, parent contact, and decision making—the ultimate **integration pilot**. English I was combined with a computer technology course which included Microsoft Word™, PowerPoint™, and Publisher™ software. Curt Miller, DPI's Business, Finance and Information Technology Education Consultant, reported that after a three-year study, the combined class structure dramatically increased the success of the students in English and computer technology. Of particular note was that the students had "limited reading proficiency" when beginning the course, but had English end-of-course scores that exceeded the scores of non-honors students in other non-integrated classes by 21 percentage points the first year and by 16 percentage points the second year. Innovative ideas gained from the pilot are shared with other teachers throughout the state in an online Moodle Professional Learning Community.

- The Bridgeport (CT) Regional Aquaculture Science and Technology Education Center (BRASTEC) accepts student applications from seven area school districts. Students attend for 2¼ hours per day and receive science and technology education credits toward high school graduation requirements. BRASTEC's **integrated curriculum** is centered around existing and emerging careers in global aquaculture. Students work on contextual projects such as boat construction, designing a prototype aquatic farm system, or operating a **school-based enterprise** such as a public seafood market that features fish grown in the school's hatchery. The school has a reputation for its highly prepared and motivated students entering either college or industry. Over 90 percent of the graduating students are accepted by colleges and universities, including the maritime academies in the Northeast.

- The Western Wisconsin STEM Consortia received a Math-Science Partnership Grant from the Wisconsin Department of Public Instruction in 2009 to implement its project, SySTEMically Improving Student Academic Achievement in Mathematics and Science. The overall project goal was to improve student academic achievement in mathematics and science by providing three years' of intensive professional development (100 hours/

year) in mathematics and science content and pedagogy for sixty (60) teachers from nine K-12 school districts. Teachers developed STEM **integrated curriculum projects** (http://www.uwstout.edu/wwsc/index.cfm) that were modeled after CORD's STEM Transitions Project (www.stemtransitions.org). The projects addressed math and science topics in the following three clusters: Agriculture, Food, and Natural Resources; Manufacturing; and Transportation, Distribution, and Logistics. Teacher evaluation data revealed statistically significant gains (.05 level) in both science and mathematics content knowledge and pedagogy in years one and two of the grant. Additionally, an analysis of student evaluation data indicates positive effects on student achievement based upon the professional development opportunity of the teachers.

Postsecondary

- Mitchell Community College, in Statesville, North Carolina, is a strong proponent of **contextual teaching** methods, which is evidenced by the creation of a unique staff position — Director of Contextual Teaching and Learning. Although some instructors had been using contextual teaching and learning for many years, more intentional efforts began in the 2008–2009 academic year. As part of Mitchell's Quality Enhancement Plan (QEP), a developmental math course was contextualized by use of the "recipe project." Students learned ratios and fractions through the real-world use of food portions. Almost 90 percent demonstrated proficiency in this project. Since that time the entire curricula has been contextualized, as in the following course examples: *humanities* (projects focused on "Race in America"); *business law* (learning history and judicial procedures); *advanced solid modeling* (using software for reverse engineering to create duplicates); and *statistics* (crime scene investigation project to learn correlation and regression). Students and faculty at Mitchell report more student motivation and learning when contextual teaching and learning is practiced.

- Houston Community College's Quality Enhancement Plan is entitled INSPIRE: INnovative Science Program Initiatives to Reform Education. At the heart of HCC INSPIRE lies the desire to facilitate changes in pedagogy from the traditional "sage on the stage" format to include a more active and collaborative, student-centered format. The goal will be to improve student learning and engagement, beginning with the sciences. For each of three targeted science courses, faculty teams will compile one comprehensive module that will address all of the core concepts of an entire textbook chapter. Modules will be framed in the **context of solving a central real-world problem**, a challenge or research question, some of which will require active and collaborative teamwork. A welcome ripple effect of the project will be the fostering of new levels of communication and collaboration among full-time and part-time faculty within and across disciplines.

Adult Education

- Blackhawk Technical College (BTC) in Janesville, Wisconsin, created a *College Readiness Bridge Program* in response to the closure of a General Motors production facility. The closure resulted in the loss of 5,000 local jobs between the plant and its suppliers, with 1,500 workers coming to BTC. The *Bridge* program was specifically designed to meet the unique needs of individuals who have been away from formal education for an extended period and tested below college level. The program provides **integrated courses** combining technical coursework with adult basic skills education, pairing a technical program instructor and basic skills instructor to team-teach the courses. Several hundred were placed into certificate programs in health care, welding, or business over two semesters, with completion rates of 60 percent. Certificate program graduates may choose to enter employment or pursue a technical or associate degree.

- Indian River State College in Fort Pierce, Florida, offers a wide variety of **contextual programs in Adult Education**. The Burlington English Career Extensions program combines content and context for various career fields by offering the linguistic bridge necessary for ESOL students to move seamlessly from general ESOL courses into their chosen career path. Learners can acquire linguistic knowledge online; applying it to contextualized texts and activities, and then extend their learning in

251

face-to-face activities which help them to further assimilate the language learned. The Career Extensions program enables students to work on two processes in a parallel manner. At one level they learn the academic English needed for their studies, while at the same time, preparing for intensive English studies in their chosen careers. By empowering these adult learners with the language needed for technical and soft skills, they can become productive members of the workforce much sooner, thus filling the available jobs in the communities in which they live.

International Experiences

A successful business education partnership initiative in the Dominican Republic supported by hard data and good results.

The Loyola Polytechnic Institute (Spanish: Instituto Politécnico Loyola, IPL) is a highly recognized public school in the Dominican Republic. Just at the high school level, IPL has almost 1400 students. With support from the Business Initiative for Technical Education (Spanish: Iniciativa Empresarial para la Educación Técnica, IEET) the school embarked on a career pathways program in 2007. During the first four-year phase, in addition to the **re-sequencing of the curriculum** to modernize and contextualize it, **intensive teacher professional development** was conducted (more than 10,000 man-hours) to ensure that the teaching paradigm shift would become a habit in the teachers and that inertia would not draw the teachers back to traditional and more familiar ways of teaching.

The experience of IPL (through IEET) shows several things:

1. IPL graduates had an 85 percent passing rate on national tests compared to a 60 percent rate for the rest of the country;

2. The learning atmosphere in the school improved dramatically (more proactive and engaged students);

3. The learning curve for students in industry settings has been dramatically reduced (from 18 months to 3 months in one company);

4. More than 50 percent of students leave high school with job offers; and

5. Other social and educational organizations are looking to apply and implement this business-directed educational model.

In 2011, INICIA Foundation (http://www.fundacioninicia.org/index.html) joined the effort and enabled the project to expand from one school (IPL) to thirteen all over the country. In addition to this quantitative indicator of growth, two other facts are worthy of mention.

First, Mr. Pedro Esteva, president and CEO of IMCA (the Caterpillar dealer in the Dominican Republic and Jamaica), was recognized by the American Chamber of Commerce in the Dominican Republic for having created IEET, a model for education-business partnerships that has made a significant impact on education since its inception in 2007.

Second, Barna Business School (http://www.barna.edu.do), a widely known tertiary education institution in the Dominican Republic, has included in its MBA programs the "IMCA case study" as an exemplary case of a successful business-education partnership.

A case in Brazil: Contextual Teaching + Business/Industry Support + Strong Leadership = Success

About 10 years ago, Embraer[26], through its Embraer Education and Research Institute (Portuguese: IEEP) launched an ambitious plan to build and maintain a high school, the Colégio Eng° Juarez Wanderley (http://www.institutoembraer.com.br/Colegio.aspx) in which, according to *Business Week*[27], "poor students have the opportunity to see their dreams take flight."

With the help of CORD, a Career Pathway project in pre-engineering was planned and implemented. To attend the school, students had to have attended public schools during the previous four years of their education. CORD proposed a comprehensive pre-engineering program based on an innovative approach to curriculum and teaching.

A challenging **curriculum enrichment** strand of 800 hours (in four semesters) was established on top of the regular high school

---

26 Embraer is a Brazilian aircraft manufacturer. For more information, visit www.embraer.com.br.

27 Geri Smith, "Embraer Helps to Educate Brazil," *Business Week,* July 31, 2006.

timetable. This enrichment strand, which was **integrated** with regular school subjects, included courses with titles such as Career Readiness, Principles of the World of Engineering, and Computer and Internet Tools for Engineers. Students were tasked with applying the scientific method in business/industry-oriented projects.

This new type of enriched and context-adapted curriculum (college-prep plus work-readiness skills and attitudes) requires that teachers be **adequately trained on contextual teaching**. The Embraer project included an intensive teacher training process, based on the REACT methodology, that produced excellent results.

The enriched curriculum and excellent team of contextual teachers were key components of the project, but two conditions were additionally required: *strong leadership* at the school level and *strong, long-term business-industry support*. Support from the Embraer Institute provided curriculum input, laboratory supplies, and assistance in annual career fairs.

It is very rewarding to see the outcomes for students who went through the program. According to a news release from Embraer, all of the December 2008 graduates, including CORD "pre-engineering students," were admitted to at least one undergraduate institution.[28]

Although these students had to stay in school two additional hours per day for four semesters, without getting a grade, they were very grateful to the school for providing them with the opportunity to enrich their abilities with knowledge, skills, and attitudes that are valued in the workplace.

Are We Up to the Challenge?

Over the last two decades, the Federal Government and states have put more emphasis on contextual teaching and learning through programs such as Tech Prep, Career Clusters™, Career Pathways, and Programs of Study. The Carl D. Perkins Career and Technical Education Improvement Act of 2006 includes a requirement that funds be used for professional development that, among other

---

28 For the Embraer press release, see http://www.embraer.com/en-US/ImprensaEventos/Press-releases/noticias/Pages/ALUNOS-DO-COLEGIO-ENG-JUAREZ-WANDERLEY-OBTEM-100-DE-APROVACAO-NO-VESTIBULAR.aspx.

things, provides opportunities for academic and CTE teachers to jointly develop and implement curriculum and pedagogical strategies including applied (contextual) learning. In spite of this emphasis, confusion regarding how to do it and what it will look like restricts development of curriculum and strategies. Helping academic and CTE teachers and instructors to work together to make connections between rigorous academics and realistic applications of academic content is a goal we can and should strive to reach if our students are to compete in a global economy.

The need to help students make connections between content and context has been the focus throughout this chapter. Isolated content taught without context is not the way people learn. All educators need to reflect on how effective current teaching strategies are in raising achievement levels of all students. While spots of excellence in contextual teaching and learning exist throughout the country, the enthusiasm and excitement for teaching in a meaningful way must be shared.

We know that the best contextual textbook, along with excellent equipment and a state-of-the-art facility, will not produce the expected results if teachers are not well prepared. That is why teacher professional development is the best investment for schools and society. An effective professional development process gives meaning and leverage to all other investments in education.

There may be many answers to the question "Why do I have to learn this?" However, the best answers are the ones that provide meaning and motivation to each learner.

Recommendations

Changing how one teaches is not easy, especially if there is no support from the leadership of institutions and partnerships. Below are a few ideas that may lead to changes that will help students—traditional and adult—persist and succeed in their pursuit of a better life.

1. Provide professional development opportunities for faculty, counselors, and administrators to learn about the theory and practice of contextual teaching and learning. This includes integrated sessions combining academic and CTE teachers.

2. Arrange for secondary and postsecondary joint meetings to discuss course-to-course transitions. This will eliminate duplication and enable students to complete programs in less time.

3. Enlist employers to provide work-based learning opportunities such as classroom presentations, mentoring, job shadowing, internships, and teacher externships.

4. Secure financial and in-kind contributions from employers to provide equipment and facilities for contextual learning activities.

5. Network with people from other educational institutions and partnerships who have successfully implemented teaching and learning practices with proven results.

6. Contact the National Academy Foundation or the National Academy Coalition for information about starting career academies.

7. Hire faculty who are not only experts in their content areas, but who understand and have used contextual teaching practices.

8. Encourage college and university schools of education to teach future teachers how to use contextual teaching methodologies.

9. Collect data to show which activities and programs result in more graduations, more transitions to college, increased job placements, and other positive outcomes that meet educational and workforce goals.

10. Help institutional leaders, parents, and other community members understand the value of contextual teaching and learning. Having everyone's support will make implementing changes much easier.

Career Guidance and Counseling

JoAnn Harris-Bowlsbey and Randy McPherson

The specialty of career guidance and counseling marked its 100th anniversary in 2009 by commemorating the publication by its founder, Frank Parsons, of his landmark book *Choosing a Vocation* (Houghton Mifflin, 1909). Since that time, the field has grown significantly in theory, in the tools necessary to implement that theory, and in the training of the professionals who assist young people and adults in choosing how to make a living, thus also making a life. The term *career counseling* will be used to refer to the services offered by certified counselors on a one-on-one or small group basis. The term *career guidance* (the primary focus of the chapter) will refer to the career development programs within a career pathways system that are administered by schools, workforce development centers, or other entities. These programs may be staffed by certified counselors, but also by career development facilitators, advisors, and teachers.

Career Guidance Theory

Parsons provided the first theoretical foundation for career guidance in *Choosing a Vocation*, in which he stated that the goal of career guidance is to enable the individual to:

1. Develop a clear understanding of [self], aptitudes, abilities, interests, resources, limitations, and other qualities.

2. Develop knowledge of the requirements and conditions for success and the advantages and disadvantages, compensation,

opportunities, and prospects associated with different lines of work.

3. Use "true reasoning" on the relations between these two groups of facts. (p. 5)

These three steps became the basis of the leading approach to career guidance throughout the twentieth century, namely, the *trait-and-factor approach*. In this approach, following the three-step model put forth by Parsons, the traits of individuals are measured, the characteristics of occupations or jobs are measured, and a "best match" is made between the two. To use this approach effectively, it was necessary to develop high-quality assessment and high-quality occupational information, both of which are addressed later in this chapter.

Though many career guidance theories were formulated between 1909 and 1956, the one that moved the field forward most significantly was published by Anne Roe in her book *The Psychology of Occupations* (Wiley and Sons, 1956). That book addressed two significant themes: (a) the organization of the world of work and (b) the influences that determine which occupations people prefer. The second part of Roe's theory — that career choices are determined by early parent-child relationships — did not stand the test of research. The first part — that occupations can be organized into eight fields of interest that collectively form a circle — has survived the test of research and time. Thus, Roe's primary contribution was the concept of an orderly organization of occupations, one highly refined later by John Holland.

The greatest milestone in the development of career guidance theory was Donald Super's book *The Psychology of Careers: An Introduction to Vocational Development* (Harper, 1957). Super proposed that career development is a lifelong process that unfolds in definable stages, each characterized by definable developmental tasks. Each of these tasks requires a certain level of what Super called "career maturity." Since everyone needs "career maturity," the need for developmental guidance is universal. Thus Super provided the conceptual basis for the creation of programs that provide developmental guidance. Later in his career Super created a graphic he called the "archway of career determinants," in which he proposed that both biographical and geographical variables determine career choice. Biographical variables include interests, aptitudes, intelligence, personality characteristics, values, and needs. Geographical variables include family, school, community, society, economy, employment practices, and the labor market.[1] Another influential construct was Super's "life-career rainbow," a semicircular graphic in which he proposed that a person's life space is filled up with life roles (son/daughter, student, leisurite, worker, spouse, parent, citizen) that interact with each other and over which one's interests, skills, and values are distributed.[2] Super's theory has been accepted and studied worldwide as a foundation for developmental career guidance programs.

The next landmark theory was that of John Holland, stated in his book *Making Vocational Choices: A Theory of Careers* (Prentice-Hall, 1973). While Super focused on the lifelong progression of career development and its characteristics, Holland focused on the dynamics of individual career choices. In his clearly stated and much researched theory, Holland stated that both personalities and work environments can be described as combinations of six types (a synthesis of Roe's eight) — *realistic, investigative, artistic, social, enterprising,* and *conventional.* He hypothesized that individuals acquire the characteristics of one or more of these types through the power of positive reinforcement. Individuals are offered a variety of activities by their parents and environments. Activities that are positively reinforced become interests. Individuals seek skills, said Holland, in areas in which they have interests. Implementation of one's interests and skills leads to the formation of sets of values. People who share these interests, skills, and values create unique environments. Further, Holland proposed that individuals of given personality types (as determined by interests, skills, and values) seek environments of the same or similar types and in so doing, to the extent possible, find job satisfaction.

Like Roe, Holland proposed (and validated by research) that occupations, jobs, postsecondary majors, and leisure activities can be organized according to his six types and that these types bear statistically defined relationships to each other that can be collectively represented by the famous "Holland hexagon." The Holland system of classification has been adopted by the U.S. Department of Labor as the basis for development of its interest inventory, *O*NET Interest Profiler,* and by the U.S. Department of Defense as the basis for its ASVAB

---

1 Duane Brown and Linda Brooks, *Career Choice and Development* (San Francisco: Jossey Bass, 1996).

2 Brown and Brooks, *Career Choice and Development.*

interest inventory. Further, the occupations defined in *O*NET* have been assigned Holland codes in that database. Holland's theory is well known by counselors internationally and serves as the basis for service delivery in private practice, postsecondary institutions, and workforce centers.

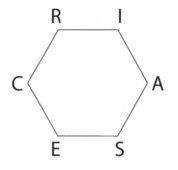

A more recent development is *constructivist* theory, which is based on the proposition that individuals make meaning out of their experiences and seek to make meaning in work by completing unfinished business in their lives or seeking to satisfy deep-seated needs or desires. (See more on constructivist theory in education in Chapter 11.) This position is championed by Savickas and many others.[3] Counselors who take this approach ask clients to describe their earliest memories and identify favorite TV and film characters and movies and/or early role models. Using that information, the counselors then identify one or more themes that run through the clients' life stories. Identification of those themes helps clients develop insights as to the meaning they want their lives to have and identify occupations that would enable them to implement or express that meaning.

In 2006 Russell Quaglia, executive director of the Center for Student Aspirations, put forth a student developmental process designed to establish a sense of purpose and belonging. The higher the level of development the more likely students are to be successful in school, college, and career and happy in all phases. His *8 Conditions That Make a Difference*™ are

- Belonging,

---

3 Mark L. Savickas, "Constructivist Counseling for Career Indecision," *Career Development Quarterly*, 43 (1995), 363–373.

- Heroes,
- Sense of accomplishment,
- Fun and excitement,
- Curiosity and creativity,
- Spirit of adventure,
- Leadership and responsibility, and
- Confidence to take action. (www.qisa.org/8conditions)

According to Quaglia, career development programs that create those conditions are conducive to mature career exploration and help students develop a sense of their purpose and place in the world.

Career Guidance Tools

Many tools have been developed to complement the theories we have briefly reviewed. Because of space restrictions, we will limit our discussion to three: assessment, career information databases, and technology-based delivery systems.

Assessment

The first psychological tests (e.g., those developed by Cattell, Binet, and Wechsler) measured intelligence. The first inventories of interest, aptitude, values, and personality traits were developed in the first half of the 20th century, partly in response to the need to classify individuals for service in the two world wars. The Kuder General Interest Survey was introduced in 1934; its scores helped survey takers identify suitable occupations. Super first developed aptitude tests for the war effort and later developed instruments designed to measure aptitudes, interests, work values, career maturity, and work salience for career guidance purposes. Holland developed his *self-directed search* in the 1950s, and many others (e.g., Campbell, Harrington, and O'Shea; ACT) developed interest and skills assessments based on the Holland typology. Dawis and Lofquist developed assessments to measure needs and the more global construct of work adjustment. Strong developed an interest inventory, also using Holland typology; Myers and Briggs developed the Myers Briggs Type Indicator. Crites developed an assessment to measure career maturity. The U.S. Department of Defense developed the Armed Forces Vocational Aptitude Battery (ASVAB) and later added an interest inventory. The U.S. Employment Service developed the General Aptitude Test Battery (GATB) to measure aptitudes and relate them to occupations. Much later the same agency developed the O*NET Interest Profiler (based on Holland typology), the O*NET Ability Profiler, and the O*NET Work Importance Profiler. Still others developed assessments to measure irrational career beliefs and thoughts.[4] These assessments and more are described and evaluated in the National Career Development Association's guide to career assessment instruments.[5]

Career Information Databases

All career guidance approaches depend on the dissemination of accurate, meaningful information about occupations and the education and training required to enter them. The United States has played a leading role in developing methodologies for identifying and classifying occupations, collecting relevant data from employers, and making career information available to the public. The expansive *Dictionary of Occupational Titles* was first published by the U.S. Employment Service in 1939 and went through four editions before being replaced in the 1990s by O*NET OnLine database (http://www.onetonline.org).

The public should also have ready access to information about postsecondary majors and training programs and the schools that offer them. The responsibility for collecting and disseminating statistics and other data related to education in the United States was officially assigned to the National Center for Educational Statistics (NCES) in 1974. NCES became part of the Office of Educational Research and Improvement when the U.S. Department of Education was established in 1979. NCES collects data from all accredited postsecondary

---

4 See, for example, J.D. Krumboltz, *Career Beliefs Inventory* (Palo Alto, CA: Consulting Psychologists Press, 1991); and G.W. Peterson, J.P. Sampson, Jr., R.C. Reardon, and J.G. Lenz, "Becoming Career Problem Solvers and Decision Makers: A Cognitive Information Processing Approach," in Brown and Brooks, *Career Choice and Development*, pp. 423-475.

5 E.A. Whitfield, R.W. Feller, and C. Wood (Eds.), *A Counselor's Guide to Career Assessment Instruments* (5th ed.) (Broken Arrow, OK: National Career Development Association, 2009).

institutions and publishes them online as the Integrated Postsecondary Education Data System (IPEDS). The IPEDS and NCES Classification of Instructional Programs databases are rich sources of information about postsecondary education in the United States. Several private publishers also collect extensive data about postsecondary institutions and make them available in print and online.

Technology-Based Delivery Systems

Career guidance information cannot be delivered to large numbers of people on a one-on-one or small group basis; technology is required. The first technology-based delivery systems emerged in the late 1960s. Some of the earliest, such as Autocoun at Pennsylvania State University and the Computerized Vocational Information System (CVIS) at Willowbrook High School in Villa Park, Illinois, were funded by the Vocational Education Act of 1963. Others, such as the Education and Career Exploration System (ECES) and the System for Interactive Guidance Information (SIGI), were funded by corporations and foundations. The Information System for Vocational Decisions (ISVD), developed at Harvard University, was funded by the United States Office of Education. Based on the theories of Roe, Holland, Super, Katz, and Tiedeman, these early systems were designed to help users learn and internalize theory, carry out formal and informal assessments, and retrieve information from databases.

In response to the information demands of a vastly expanded audience, a government agency called the National Occupational Information Coordinating Committee (NOICC) was formed in 1976 to support the proliferation of technology-based delivery systems. Following the lead of the Oregon Career Information System (CIS), those systems focused on the development of state and regional labor market information that could be delivered on a state-by-state basis. In its heyday, NOICC supported state career information delivery systems (CIDS) that served 7 million users at approximately 18,000 sites.[6] With funding cuts in the mid-1990s, the NOICC was discontinued, and many of the original State Occupational Information Coordinating Committee (SOICC) systems were replaced by custom-

---

6 V. Hopkins, J. Kinnison, E. Morgenthau, and H. Ollis, *Career Information Delivery Systems: A Summary Status Report,* 1992, National Occupational Information Coordinating Committee (NOICC) Occasional Paper No. 4.

ized versions of privately funded systems such as ACT's DISCOVER, Canada's CHOICES, and the Kuder Career Planning System.

Growth in the capability of the Internet in the early 1990s led to the transfer of these systems to the web, making them available around the clock from any web-connected computer. Some of the systems provide online research-based assessment while others offer only informal assessment or none. All, however, provide access to occupational and educational databases.

In some countries and locations, such as the United Kingdom and New Zealand, telephone call centers have been effectively used for high-volume delivery. This approach usually addresses only the specific concerns of callers and does not offer developmental career guidance, but it offers the advantage of direct human communication.

The smart phone and devices such as electronic tablets offer next-generation delivery. In some countries, such as South Africa and India, more people access the Internet by smart phone than by personal computer. The challenge of this new delivery mode is the space in which content is delivered. To be effective, content must be modularized and interfaces must be visually pleasing and intuitive.

Career Guidance Support

Legislation and Standards

The theories and tools described in the previous section are necessary components of the career guidance process, but that process also requires funding and authority through legislation and standards for content and delivery. Career guidance services are provided by professional counselors and certified *career development facilitators* (CDF; see also following paragraph) but also, unfortunately, by an array of others who lack sufficient training. Steps to meet the need for standardization are being taken by the Council for Accreditation of Counselors and Related Educational Programs (CACREP), which accredits counselor education programs that meet their stringent standards[7]. Universities thus far play a limited role. Though every American university that offers a master's degree in counseling and

---

7 See http://www.cacrep.org/template/index.cfm.

guidance offers at least one course in career development theory and practice, only nine offer specialties in career counseling.

NOICC introduced the concept of the CDF (a paraprofessional position) and funded the development of a 120-clock-hour curriculum built around 12 competencies. Taken on by the National Career Development Association after NOICC's demise, this training program and its credential have become widely accepted both in the United States and abroad. Career development facilitators can assist in a variety of settings with career exploration, retrieval of occupational and educational information, and job seeking. Their training does not equip them to interpret assessment (other than Level A) or engage in career counseling.

Legislation is often the catalyst for the development of career guidance services. The school counseling profession was birthed by the National Defense Education Act of 1958, which defined the role of school counselors and funded their training. Elementary counselors were initially funded through the Elementary and Secondary School Act of 1965. Vocational counselors were funded through the Vocational Education Act of 1973. Legislation such as the No Child Left Behind Act and the Carl Perkins Act may also provide funding for supportive tools such as assessment, web-based career planning systems, and instructional programs.

Increased emphasis on evidence-based practice in the 1990s led to the birth of *competency-based standards*. Super's development model, which depicted the career developmental tasks that people should achieve at different life stages, was in effect the first set of competency-based standards. To measure achievement of those tasks, Super developed the *Career Development Inventory* (CDI), a measure of career maturity.

In 1987 NOICC sponsored a project designed to set career guidance standards. The organization developed guidelines, published materials to help school districts implement programs, and funded four demonstration models. Since that time many states have developed their own standards for career guidance, many based on the American School Counselor Association (ASCA) National Standards, which define in measurable terms the accomplishments and behaviors that students should have at different grade levels. (See the following section for more on the ASCA standards.)

Once standards are in place, modes of delivery and methods of evaluation can be determined. Modes of delivery include one-on-one and group counseling, curriculum, computer, web- and smart-phone-based systems, and distance guidance (via telephone and email). More research is needed to determine the most cost-effective mix of these services for different populations. Whatever the modes of delivery, content must be built around standards, and, in turn, evaluation must be based on the measurable objectives included in the standards.

The American School Counselor Association National Standards

School counseling programs are collaborative efforts that benefit students, parents, teachers, administrators, and communities. School counseling programs should be an integral part of students' daily educational environments, and school counselors should be partners in student achievement. Unfortunately, that has not been the case. School counseling has lacked a consistent identity from state to state, district-to-district, and even school-to-school. This has led to a misunderstanding of what school counseling is and what it can do for a school. Consequently, school counseling programs are often viewed as ancillary rather than integral, and school counselors have not been used to their fullest potential. The question has often been asked, "What do school counselors do?" The question that should be asked is, "How are students different because of what school counselors do?"

To help answer this question, in 1997 the American School Counselor Association (ASCA) created *The ASCA National Model: A Framework for School Counseling Programs*. The ASCA model ushered in a new era of professionalization that has given school counseling a stronger identity. ASCA published its third edition of the popular framework in 2012.[8] The framework of a comprehensive school counseling program consists of four components:

1. *Foundation*—Student counselors create comprehensive school counseling programs that focus on student outcomes, teach

---

8 American School Counselor Association, *ASCA National Model: A Framework for School Counseling Programs, Third Edition, Executive Summary* (Alexandria, VA, 2012).

student competencies and are delivered with identified professional competencies.

  a. Program Focus

  b. Student Competencies

  c. Professional Competencies

2. *Management*—School counselors incorporate organization assessments and tools that are concrete, clearly delineated and reflective of the school's needs. Assessment and tools include:

  a. School counselor competency and school counseling program assessments

  b. Use-of-time assessments

  c. Annual agreements

  d. Advisory councils

  e. Use of data

  f. Curriculum small group and closing-the-gap action plans

  g. Annual and weekly calendars

3. *Delivery* (80 percent of counselors' time should be spent here)

  a. Direct Student Services

    i. School counseling core curriculum

    ii. Individual student planning

    iii. Responsive services

  b. Indirect Student Services

4. *Accountability*—To demonstrate the effectiveness of the school counseling program in measurable terms, school counselors analyze school and school counseling program data to determine how students are different as a result of the school counseling program.

When a school or district implements a counseling program based on the ASCA model, it can:

- Establish counseling as an integral component of the academic mission of the school.

- Ensure that every student has equitable access to counseling.

- Identify and deliver teaching of the knowledge and skills that all students should acquire.

- Ensure that the counseling program is comprehensive in design and is delivered systematically to all students.

National Career Development Guidelines

The National Career Development Association (NCDA) inspires and empowers the achievement of career and life goals by providing professional development, resources, standards, scientific research, and advocacy. NCDA is a founding division of the American Counseling Association (ACA). NCDA provides programs and services for career development professionals and for the public involved with or interested in career development, including professional development activities, publications, research, general information, professional standards, advocacy, and recognition for achievement and service.

The National Career Development Guidelines (NCDG) are a framework for thinking about the knowledge and skills young people and adults need to manage their careers effectively, from making decisions about school to taking that first job and beyond. Domains, goals, and indicators organize the NCDG framework. The three domains — Personal Social Development (PS), Educational Achievement and Lifelong Learning (ED), and Career Management (CM) — describe content. Under each domain are **goals** (eleven in total) that define broad areas of career development competency.

Personal Social Development Domain

- GOAL PS1 Develop understanding of self to build and maintain a positive self-concept.

- GOAL PS2 Develop positive interpersonal skills including respect for diversity.

- GOAL PS3 Integrate growth and change into your career development.

- GOAL PS4 Balance personal, leisure, community, learner, family, and work roles.

Educational Achievement and Lifelong Learning Domain

- GOAL ED1 Attain educational achievement and performance levels needed to reach your personal and career goals.

- GOAL ED2 Participate in ongoing, lifelong learning experiences to enhance your ability to function effectively in a diverse and changing economy.

Career Management Domain

- GOAL CM1 Create and manage a career plan that meets your career goals.

- GOAL CM2 Use a process of decision-making as one component of career development.

- GOAL CM3 Use accurate, current, and unbiased career information during career planning and management.

- GOAL CM4 Master academic, occupational and general employability skills in order to obtain, create, maintain and/or advance your employment.

- GOAL CM5 Integrate changing employment trends, societal needs, and economic conditions into your career plans.

The biggest issue that counselors face is adequately covering all three domains, and the biggest issue in a career pathways system is finding enough time to adequately cover the Career Management Domain.[9]

The Role of Career Counseling in Programs of Study

Guidance counseling and academic advisement systems should help students plan for complete sequences of coursework that lead to graduation and enrollment in postsecondary programs within the Career Pathways of their choice. Systems should include career awareness tools and coursework plans encompassing both Program of Study (POS) and academic prerequisites for graduation and POS completion. Plan development should include students, parents, and academic and Career Technical Education (CTE) teachers and should be updated regularly throughout students' education. Guidance

---

9 http://associationdatabase.com/aws/NCDA/pt/sp/guidelines

counseling and academic advisement help students to make informed decisions about which POS to pursue. The Carl D. Perkins Career and Technical Education Act of 2006 (Perkins IV) supports developmental career counseling by treating it as an integral component of POS. To fulfill their intended role in POS, counseling and academic advisement systems should:

- Follow state and/or local guidance and counseling standards, such as the National Career Development Guidelines.

- Ensure that guidance, counseling, and advisement professionals have access to up-to-date information about POS offerings.

- Provide information about postsecondary education and career options, including prerequisites for particular POS.

- Offer resources that help students identify their career interests and aptitudes and select appropriate POS.

- Provide information and resources that will enable parents to help their children prepare for college and careers, including workshops on college and financial aid applications.

- Offer web-based resources and tools for obtaining student financial assistance.

- Encourage students to expand their portfolios while in high school by participating in volunteer, work-based, and paid opportunities to provide real-life experience in their chosen fields.

- Include students, parents, and guidance and academic and CTE staff in initial and ongoing planning and process.

Career counseling should be a progressive system that spans from pre-K to adulthood. The system should have counselors as the linchpin but involve others in helping students achieve their career goals. Members of the counseling team could include:

- Counselors — Serve as team leaders and facilitators

- Teachers — Assist in the process of integrating career information into the curriculum framework

- Administrators — Are critical for the program to be a part of the school improvement process

- Employers—Ensure that the program is on target with the knowledge and skills needed and support work-based learning activities

- Parents—Model attitudes and knowledge that affect students' career choices

- Community—Provide mentors and work-based learning activities

Teachers, school staff members, representatives of community-based organizations, and employers should all have a role to play, but the counselor is the central source of cohesion and stability in the system. School counselors can serve as the catalysts for change in their schools by:

- Helping monitor the progress of **ALL** students (not just a select few).

- Serve as a **LIAISON** between students, families, the community, and the school system.

- Provide **LEADERSHIP** in assessing schools' needs and collaborating with others to develop solutions.

- Help bridge the gap between **ACADEMIC AND CTE** educators at the secondary and postsecondary levels.

Working together, the members of the counseling community can follow these steps in helping students prepare for careers:

- *Help students find their passions*—The system should help students figure out what is important to them. Students will need to figure out their interests, values, skills, and strengths.

- *Crosswalk passions to Career Clusters™*—Match interest and strengths (passions) to the broad career clusters.

- *Help students be college and career ready*—Students should follow plans of study (updated often) that have "road maps" (course sequences) that prepare the students academically for the clusters.

- *Help students choose careers*—As students become more aware of their passions and the careers within clusters that interest them, they will need guidance on which careers are in high demand and provide high wages.

Counseling Curriculum Spanning Pre-K to Adult

Counseling in a career pathways system should be a progressive system that starts as soon as possible and continues through adulthood. There are usually four steps in this progressive system:

1. *Elementary Grades* — Career awareness should be the focus of the elementary grades.

2. *Middle School* — Middle schoolers should have the opportunity to begin to explore careers and begin the process of developing individual learning plans that will be updated throughout their academic careers.

3. *High School* — High school focuses on preparing for careers and applying knowledge and skills sets to chosen Career Cluster™ areas.

4. *Postsecondary* — Postsecondary narrows the focus to specific career fields. Applying knowledge and skills sets within career areas should be continued and managed.

Individual Learning Plan — At the core of every career pathways career development system is the individual learning plan (may be called something different in your state, e.g., individual career plan, graduation plan). The individual learning plan is a personalized document that students develop with their counselors and/or counseling teams to chart their progress toward their academic and career goals during each school year, to ensure that they are on the path to graduation, and to determine what resources and tools are required for success in their chosen career pathways after graduation. The individual learning plan can be electronic. Each school must determine how and when individual learning plans will be accessed by students and updated. The individual learning plan could include:

- Career goals
- Programs of study (course sequence)
- Interest inventories
- Postsecondary plans
- Work-based learning experiences
- Resumes
- Test scores

- Grades
- Examples of work (work portfolios)
- Other

Individual learning plans need to be "owned" by the student and updated frequently. They should be living documents/files that are at the core of the career development system. There should be regular opportunities to plan and assess student progress in the course sequence that meets the prerequisites for enrollment in post-secondary as well as academic requirements for graduation in their career pathways.

Overcoming Challenges

Some observers feel that delivery of career guidance and counseling in K-12 may now be less effective than at any time in the past half century. Increases in academic standards, challenging socio-emotional needs, and budget constraints have left less time and fewer resources to devote to career guidance and counseling.

Changes in the workplace have also created new challenges. The workplace has transitioned from the apprenticeships, multi-generation family businesses and farms, and lifelong careers of the past to a broad range of fluid scenarios in which most people have multiple career options and will change careers, even several times, over the course of their working lives. Consequently, career education is no longer a simple academic exercise or a series of isolated activities but a long-term exploration of self and how to make a happy and successful transition into the world of work. It is less about charts and graphs and earning potential than it is about matching interests, talents, aptitudes, and skills to potential careers. The volatility of the modern labor market has created the need for a better educated, more skilled, and more flexible employee who understands that career training is a lifelong process.

In 1988 the William T. Grant Foundation (http://www.wtgrantfoundation.org/Home) explored a looming crisis for "the forgotten half," the 20 million non-college-bound American students who were "in danger of being caught in a massive bind that can deny them full participation in our society." A decade later, the American Youth Policy Forum (www.aypf.org) released *The Forgotten*

Half Revisited, a study about youth leaving high school unprepared to compete for high-skill, high-demand jobs. The study noted that in the ten years since the W. T. Grant Foundation report, a comparable population of young people had lost even more ground in job preparedness.

In February 2011, the Harvard University Graduate School of Education released a report titled *Pathways to Prosperity,* which provides a bleak picture of the ill-preparedness of our youngsters and young adults. (See Chapters 2 and 3.) While job opportunities in areas that require at least some postsecondary education have risen dramatically in number and percentage of the overall labor market over the past 25 years, employers in increasing numbers are sounding the alarm that new workers lack the skills to be successful in careers. The problem is more pronounced in minority communities in metropolitan areas, which are more likely to experience high rates of generational poverty, higher-than-average unemployment and high school dropout rates, and significantly lower postsecondary matriculation and graduation rates.

For many American youngsters, "going to college" is something everyone does right after high school, but too few appreciate the life-long advantages in earning power and quality of life that a college education provides. For too many, the connection between college and career is unclear. Moreover, although the overwhelming majority of students profess the desire and intention to go to college, many lack the commitment and understanding necessary to prepare for and succeed in college. Our young people accept the popular mantra that "to be successful you must go to college," but far too few successfully make the transition from intention to action.

In spite of the extensive resources that have been made available to increase the number of Americans with college degrees, (1) by 2008 fewer than 40 percent of Americans under 28 years of age had earned associate degrees or higher, (2) under 60 percent of college graduates were working in careers that required college degrees, (3) in 2009 approximately 85 percent of college graduates moved back home to live with parents, and (4) African-Americans and Hispanics were quickly losing ground to Caucasians and Asians in college going and graduation attainment (College Board). College surveys of student majors reveal high rates of change and confusion about the relationship between what students do in college and getting degree-worthy jobs after graduation. Clearly there has been a loss of career development focus, and the K-12 education system is not as well prepared for the global economy of the 21st-century as it should and could be.

A veritable alphabet soup of professional and research organizations has joined the effort to define and implement successful career development programs, including ASCA, the National Career Development Association (NCDA), the National Board of Certified Counselors (NBCC), and, more recently, the National Office for School Counselor Advocacy (NOSCA), among others. Despite those efforts, three pitfalls continue to prevent the majority of students from gaining access to high-quality career development experiences.

First, career guidance and counseling is still not taken seriously enough in K-12 education. Schools rarely look for creative ways to blend academic and career objectives and develop students that are college and career ready. Most still look at interest, skill, aptitude, and personality inventories as separate and isolated activities and make no effort to interweave the results of those activities into academic subjects in ways that enhance written and oral communication skills and overall student performance. Inventories are the first step towards identifying a career pathway and the course sequence that one will take. The historical and economic contexts of careers provide real-world perspective and show how students' school years prepare them for their work years.

Second, most schools still present the traditional college experience as the only pathway to success. Students are rarely informed of the plethora of high-paying, high-demand, high-skill career opportunities that are accessible to them through technical training or apprenticeships. The "college for all" philosophy also implicitly fosters the belief that careers in skilled trades are intrinsically less valuable than careers that require college degrees. While math, literacy, and science attainment continues to decline in this country, along with declining or stagnant high school and college graduation rates, European countries such as Germany, Switzerland, Finland, and Denmark are achieving superior results by offering rigorous academic curricula combined with career preparation pathways after grade 9 or 10. Those countries have also been successful in developing partnerships in which business and industry are willing to invest heavily in time and money to prepare the next generation of workers.

Third, our K-12 system operates under the assumption that education, especially attainment of college degrees, naturally leads to good career choices. The reality is otherwise. High percentages of American students enter college undecided as to the majors they will study, and many change their majors after enrollment. Entering college without the benefit of up-to-date career information and exploratory experiences can, at the very least, lead to confusion about what to study and can add years and crippling debt to the college experience. On the other hand, students who have had a comprehensive and progressive career guidance and development system starting in elementary school and continuing through high school are prepared and eagerly await their postsecondary education and training.

Recommendations

Most states have made available free to all schools and all students online access to college and career assessments and information. Perkins IV funding is available to all states to support comprehensive CTE. Those and many other resources are widely available, but their full utilization depends on widespread recognition of the fact that career education is integral to student achievement and not only can but must be central to the K-12 experience. Following are twelve recommendations that promote career guidance and counseling in schools.

1. **Develop a system with counselors as the facilitators** — Every school district should have a system of career development activities where all educators are career counselors and the counselor is the facilitator.

2. **Use the language** — Encourage teachers to use the language of careers in the classroom and, whenever possible, illustrate academic concepts with work-based examples.

3. **Develop subject-to-subject and grade-to-grade crosswalks** — Career development should not be limited to annual career fairs or other isolated events. Rather, it should be an ongoing process in which school counselors help teachers open lines of communication that enable them to collaborate on assignments

across subject areas and plan developmental activities that build across grades.

4. **Bring career inventories into the classroom** — Schools often find it difficult to reserve time to administer inventories and review results with students. Providing students with opportunities in core academic courses to research, write, and present findings builds skills without conflicting with core academics.

5. **Partner with business, industry, and all levels of postsecondary education** — Provide students opportunities to interact with role models that can help create imprints of purpose and success. The deeper and more consistent the relationship between students and life after high school the more effective teachers will be in helping students understand the importance of their studies.

6. **Get students out of the school building** — Students need opportunities to see and experience college and the workplace. Visiting colleges and worksites removes mysteries and misgivings and eliminates misunderstandings about access. It can also create excitement and provide opportunities to establish mentoring and role model relationships.

7. **Create formal Career Pathways with multiple exits** — Create rigorous contemporary career classes linked to dual enrollment, articulation, and industry certification opportunities.

8. **Create a culture that values work** — Work provides purpose and contributes to a positive self-image and sense of self-worth. Schools and districts should put in place programming and processes that encourage students to consider what it means to find one's "place" in the workforce and that help students to see that the value of one's work is determined by far more than the socioeconomic status attached to how much it pays.

9. **Involve students in work-related experiences** — Volunteering, job shadowing, internships, and apprenticeships are some of the many structured activities that provide experiences that help students understand what the workplace expects from employees and what types of work they would enjoy as adults.

10. **Teach students that career development is a lifelong process** — Students and workers of the future must be helped to understand that, because of rapid changes in the marketplace, career exploration and training must continue throughout their lives. As job categories change, become obsolete, and/or are created, retraining in allied or new fields will be a necessity.

11. **Counselors and educators must stay informed about career trends** — Any professional whose role involves advising students should understand the nature and direction of the labor market. For example, one new trend in community college and technical school education is called *responsive education*, in which industry works as a partner to identify short-term labor market needs and colleges respond with education programs designed to meet those needs. Training for industry is constantly being "retooled" to meet local needs, and professionals who advise students must stay abreast of that trend to help students understand education and career options.

12. **Expose students to advanced technology** — Students must be given an opportunity to become comfortable with general workplace technology, where appropriate, to learn specialized technology especially with digital individual learning plans.

Career guidance and counseling should prepare students to make informed career decisions through (1) awareness and understanding of qualities that contribute to success on the job, (2) the ability to use data and other resources to support decision making, and (3) an awareness of the training and postsecondary requirements for success. Career development is a lifelong process in which an individual defines and refines life and work roles. It includes awareness of interests, skills, attitudes, talents, and abilities and how they develop and change throughout the educational experience. This process provides the framework in which students explore a variety of educational and occupational opportunities, identify a career pathway, learn the realities of the workplace, and identify both the technical skills and individual attributes they will need to succeed in the world of work.

Career development starts with awareness, exploration, and practice and matures in the form of sound decision-making based on knowledge of the workplace and well-chosen high school to postsecondary education/training plans of study in a career pathways system. From high school through adulthood, students expand knowledge, skills, and attitudes through practice and application. Career development integrates experiences and helps prepare students for the changing academic needs and skill requirements of a fast-changing workplace, make good decisions about the career development process, and become lifelong learners who can adapt to the world of work.

Resources

American School Counseling Association, (1953–present). www.schoolcounselor.org

College Board, (1900–present). www.collegeboard.org

National Board for Certified Counselors, (1982–present). www.NBCC.org

National Career Development Association, (1913–present). www.NCDA.org

National Office for School Counselor Advocacy, College Board (2008–Present), www.advocacy.collegeboard.org

SECTION IV CHECK-UP

After reading the **DELIVER** section chapters, complete this initial formative assessment to determine where your schools, colleges, and region stand regarding the organization and structures needed to support career pathways implementation, evolution, and sustainability. How you rate your readiness may indicate the need for a deeper analysis, including a comprehensive self-evaluation and external evaluation.

DELIVER Checklist	NA	Disagree			Agree	
	NA	−2	−1	0	1	2
(1) The curriculum has been built upon standards (common core, technical, employability, national, state, and/or industry) in a chosen Career Pathway.						
(2) Instructors (including academic, Adult Basic Ed, etc.) have been provided training so that courses are being applied to the world of work and taught contextually.						
(3) There are opportunities for horizontal teaming (academic/technical, workforce, academic, remediation, student affairs, and categorical programs) for educators in a particular pathway.						
(4) Learners develop career and education plans upon entering pathways and revise the plans as needed.						
(5) There are student services available such as tutoring, career counseling, career exploration and planning, flexible schedules, financial aid, and job placement.						
(6) There is a systematic and seamless process for secondary students to earn college credit for postsecondary courses taken in high school, transfer HS credit to any two- or four-year institution in the state, and transfer credit earned at a two-year college to any other two- or four-year institution in the state.						

Section V. Ensure

CTE is a results-driven system that demonstrates a positive return on investment.

Within Career Technical Education (CTE) there have always been heart-warming stories of student success. The lack of solid and consistent data that supports the argument for CTE policy and funding support has generally been CTE's Achilles' heel.

The past several years of longitudinal study reports have begun to turn that around and to give CTE the data it needs for self-improvement and for legislative support. CTE's attention to results is improving the system.

The certifications chapter discusses the role of certificates and certifications and their incorporation into program delivery, as well as their utilization in support of the postsecondary completion agenda. The chapter on using data presents the case for data as a tool for decision-making and support in CTE programs.

POS Framework Components Supported
Technical Skills Assessments
Accountability and Evaluation Systems

Certificates and Certifications

John Foster

Credibility

This chapter discusses the role of certificates and certifications as the culmination of technical training programs. Typically the awarding of a certificate or certification is the final event in the training process. It is important that we keep the timing of the event in mind because, in most cases, the individuals being assessed for certificates or certification have little or no practical (performance) experience in the technical areas they are preparing to enter. They are being assessed on the basis of standards formulated by experts in their particular industries.

People who pursue technical certificates and certifications generally fall into four categories:

- Secondary students coming through either private or public technical training programs

- Postsecondary students (two-year, four-year, or apprentice)

- Dislocated workers (or adults who are changing careers)

- People who are already in the workplace (i.e., incumbent workers)

Certificates and certifications are both based on content standards derived from industry, typically job and task analyses. Yet certificates and certifications are not the same thing.

A *certificate* reflects knowledge and skills acquired through a training program administered specifically for the purpose of awarding the certificate. A certificate is awarded only once and does not require periodic renewal. A certificate program typically yields an assessment report that is detailed enough to be used for improvement of instruction, whereas a certification program typically yields only pass/fail results (i.e., according to whether the candidate has met the cut score or not).[1]

The purpose of a typical *certification* process is to verify training and experience by assessing the currency of associated knowledge and skills. Most certifications are time-limited and must be retaken every three to five years. A typical certification program involves assessment of the candidate's knowledge of relevant content and his or her ability to demonstrate the skills embedded in the content. Participation in assessment for certification usually requires meeting eligibility requirements such as minimum hours of training, minimum experience, or payment of certification fees. Certification also requires that test-takers achieve pre-established cut scores.

Following are definitions of key terms related to certificate and certification programs.

- *Subject matter experts* are people who have specialized knowledge, experiences, and credentials pertaining to technical occupations or industries. The development, delivery, and assessment of a program might involve input from multiple subject matter experts. If the program is to be deemed credible, the contributing subject matter experts must first be deemed credible, as determined through an unbiased evaluation process. Factors to be considered in establishing the credibility of subject matter experts are diversity of experience (how broadly they have been involved in their occupations), length of time in their occupations, and professional affiliations (a clear sign of commitment to their fields).

- *Credibility*. A program is *credible* if its claims of rigor, relevance, and currency are accurate. In most cases, the final test of credibility is the culminating event, the assessment, which typically assesses areas such as the subject matter expert's expertise,

---

1 More detailed information regarding the standards for certificates and certifications can be found in ANSI standards ASTM E 2695-09 and ANSI/Io/IES 17024. The ISO 10667-2 requirements "assessment development for service providers" will also shed light on this topic.

program content, whether the program enables the student to meet applicable occupational standards, psychometrics, presence or absence of bias, effectiveness of delivery, security (e.g., of personal and proprietary information), and, lastly, the currency of the program (i.e., the extent to which it reflects recent developments in the occupation or associated laws and regulations).

- *Assessment* is the largest part of the certificate and certification process. Both people and things (e.g., training facilities) can be assessed. This chapter focuses on assessment of worker competence. Technical assessments are most credible when they test two aspects of the training process: (1) "head skills" (the student's overall knowledge of processes, terminology, tools and equipment, and regulations and codes, as well as the ability to read and interpret technical data); and (2) on-the-job performance (manipulation of tools and equipment in performing tasks associated with an occupation). The latter is often referred to as *performance assessment*.

- *Standards* are guidelines that define what a student should know and be able to do after completing a training program. Some are established prior to and independently of the development of training programs. Others are established by subject matter experts as part of the program development process. (This is common in programs that focus on emerging occupations.) Standards are sometimes referred to as blueprints, in that they delineate simple-to-complex sequences of skills that applicants must acquire to be deemed competent.

- A *certificate* is an official document attesting to the truth of stated facts—e.g., dates and places of births or deaths, marital status, health status, completion of academic courses or programs, or (our focus here) competence to practice certain professions. A common example is a high school diploma or GED.

- *Certification* is the process of attesting to the authenticity of something or someone. Occupational certifications are typically issued by professional associations such as the Society of Manufacturing Engineers or by companies such as Cisco™ or Microsoft™. Certifications must be periodically renewed and thus require ongoing education.

- *Licensure* is usually conferred by state agencies or boards. Licensure is a normal requirement when a state has determined that there is a need to protect its citizens from hazards in areas such as sanitation, health, or transportation. Fields in which states typically issue licenses are cosmetology and nursing.

- A *credential* is a certified document awarded to an individual to indicate that he or she has met recognized standards on an assessment of knowledge and skills. Credentials may or may not require periodic renewal. Many different types of credentials are awarded or offered by different agencies and organizations. Understanding the different characteristics of each type of credential and the "doorway" they provide to those who earn them can be confusing. The U.S. Department of Labor's Employment and Training Administration (ETA) defines a credential as a qualification or competence issued to an individual by a third party with the relevant authority or jurisdiction to issue such credentials. ETA's guide utilizes the following categories:

  1. Educational diplomas, certificates, and degrees;

  2. Registered apprenticeship certificates;

  3. Occupational licenses (typically awarded by state government agencies);

  4. Personnel certifications from industry or professional associations; and

  5. Other skill certificates for specific skill sets or competencies within one or more industries or occupations (e.g., writing, leadership, etc.).[2]

- An *occupationally specific certificate* is tied to a classification of instructional program (CIP), a standard occupational classification (SOC), a *Dictionary of Occupational Titles* (DOT) code, and more recently the O*NET codes. These types of certificates are very specific (example: wind turbine technician) and align tightly to standards or blueprints based on a thorough job and task analysis. NOCTI (formerly the National Occupational

---

2 Employment and Training Administration Advisory System, U.S. Department of Labor, *Training and Employment Guidance Letter no. 15-10,* 2010 (http://wdr.doleta.gov/directives/attach/TEGL15-10acc.pdf).

Competency Testing Institute) assessments are an example of this type of certificate.

- *Industry-specific association-sponsored certificates* are awarded by associations that sponsor training programs designed to enhance worker employability or improve their status within their industries. Expected performance standards are typically established by the sponsoring associations. The approximately 1600 industry-specific certifications and certificates currently offered across the country differ *substantially* in motivation and quality. To ensure credibility, any new program should adhere to the guidelines established by at least one of these organizations: the American National Standards Institute (ANSI), the American Society for Testing and Materials (ASTM), the American Education Research Association (AERA), the American Psychology Association (APA), and the International Organization for Standardization (ISO).

- *Business-sponsored credentials* pertain to and bear the trademarks of individual businesses. These may also vary considerably in credibility. The most widely recognized examples are in information technology, for example, Cisco™, Microsoft™, and Adobe™. One simple way to gauge the credibility of these types of programs is to look for separation between the training and assessment components. If the instructor who administers the assessment is the same person who performs the training, the certification may be legally indefensible.

As you can see, several overlapping terms are used to describe certificates and certifications, so it is important to bear in mind their differences. Even more important, people who pursue these certificates and credentials should be very aware of the credibility they offer.

Evolution

Ultimately the integrity of credentialing comes down to the individuals involved and the goals of each credentialing entity. Most credentialing entities start out with altruistic goals and the desire to solve problems, but some evolve in the direction of diminishing credibility. The following section offers a brief look at the evolution that has occurred in the credentialing process.

Some of the early pioneers in credentialing were apprenticeship programs, in which tasks were codified so that they could be replicated. As unionization crept into apprenticeship programs nationwide, workers were increasingly expected to carry out uniform, replicable tasks. Employees who completed training programs were more strongly positioned in collective bargaining, and employers could highlight the skills of their employees in marketing their products. Both employee and employer benefited from standardized training that enabled the employee to acquire *verifiable* skills. However, as with the business-sponsored credentials described in the preceding section, these programs provided too little firewall between training and certification. In other words, because the organizations that provided the training benefited from the certification of their trainees, they would always have an interest in making the assessment too lenient.

On a track running parallel to individual training via apprenticeship programs, and later vocational schools, was industry's development of certifications. In their early days, these certifications dealt more with one's ability to use proprietary products. In some cases, the training for these certifications arose to prevent workplace injuries. In other cases, it stemmed from the need to limit the population of workers within particular industries, thus maximizing the perceived value of the services they provided.

With the implementation of the Vocational Education Acts of 1963, the need for vocational instructors became critical and along with it the need for a way to certify instructors. Many states established regional training centers called area vocational technical schools (often called area technical centers today). Tasked with providing technical education to secondary and sometimes postsecondary students, these new centers struggled to find competent instructors. Traditional teacher certification did not meet the need for instructors who were competent to deliver industry-specific curricula in ways that would meet the needs of employers in specific locales. As certification of students became increasingly normal, there arose a need for a means to certify *instructors*.

The common factor in the multiple streams of this evolution was the need for standardization. As Eli Whitney (American inventor best known for his invention of the cotton gin) proved in his efforts to standardize the manufacture of rifle parts, standardization is the bedrock of production manufacturing. When parts are uniform in their specifications and quality, the end result is predictably good. It is not suggested that teachers are interchangeable parts in an assembly line, rather, that standardization is necessary to achieve high quality in the training and education of our technical workforce. This is why standards and assessment have become increasingly pervasive themes throughout the education community. The pervasive interest in standards and assessment is partly driven by federal legislation. Since the 2001 passage of *No Child Left Behind* (NCLB), we have increasingly seen standardized student assessment as a measure of school quality. With NCLB, systems were put in place in several states that, rightly or wrongly, connected student outcomes on standardized tests to teacher and school performance. Again we see recognition of the need for a "body" (in this case, states monitored by the Federal Government) whose role is to attest to the quality of teaching.

ETA has listed four attributes of educational and workforce credentials that strengthen the value of credentials to individuals. These attributes are industry recognition, stackability, portability, and accreditation. Though the focus of these attributes is on the value of the credentials to the individual, the attributes still provide valuable information when deciding what programs to utilize in education settings.

The last and most important note in this section on evolution deals with the Perkins Act. Since its beginning in 1984 as the Carl D. Perkins Vocational and Technical Education Act, the legislation has aligned vocational education to industry. However, the alignment was historically based on local economics and local employers, just as general education was aligned to local communities. The act has been reauthorized several times, most recently as the Carl D. Perkins Career and Technical Education Improvement Act of 2006 (Perkins IV). Whereas NCLB mandated universal end-of-program *academic* assessment, Perkins IV calls for technical skill assessments that are aligned with industry-recognized standards and encourages universal end-of-program assessment for *CTE* programs. Though the regulatory requirements are vague and implementation has been slow, schools in states that receive Perkins dollars are encouraged, where appropriate and applicable, to institute systems of third-party end-of-program assessment based on industry standards. As the years of Perkins IV have ticked by, states have implemented systems that contain both certificate and certification programs that are tied to industry standards and are typically listed as "accepted" on state-approved lists. Some states have developed customized assessment programs as well.

Essentially there has been and continues to be a general belief that certificates and certifications provide a way to attest to program quality, but as with many beliefs, "the devil is in the details." Is the program credible? Are the standards credible? Are they really reflective of workforce needs? In every worthwhile program, the answer to these questions is yes.

Value of the Process

One of the reasons there are so many opinions about certificates and certifications is that a variety of groups benefit from them. Though no one would disagree with the statement that accountability and data have increasingly become a focus of educational research, news, and commentary in recent years, it is still important to note whose lens one is using. Some of the current attention to accountability and data use may be driven by regulatory requirements, some by the need for classroom improvement, and some by the demands of society as a whole. Everyone agrees that metrics are important, but answering the question "important to whom?" is complicated. This section reviews the value of certificates and certifications for various groups.

People typically value industry credentials according to the sectors they represent and the range and levels of the credentials that can be obtained within those industries. For example, a safety certification issued by the Occupational Safety and Health Administration (OSHA)has value for workers in certain fields, but it is not intended to be representative of all of its holder's knowledge and skills, and it is not considered a particularly high-level credential. When people pursue credentials such as the OSHA safety certification, they typically have two goals in mind: first, to get jobs or improve their standing in their current jobs and, second, to acquire (and be able to prove that they have acquired) knowledge and skills. Achievement of the latter goal takes the form of lists of relevant processes, tools, equipment, concepts, and terminology with which the trainees have become familiar through their training programs.

For the educator or trainer, those lists, when viewed in aggregate, provide data that can be shared with constituents and supervisors as evidence of success or as a rationale for adding tools or equipment. The data can also provide information that is useful in improving instruction and focusing curriculum for given groups. Viewed over a period of years, the data reveals longitudinal trends that can provide a basis for systematic improvement.

Many CTE programs around the country interpreted Perkins IV mandates to mean that all CTE graduates must have industry certifications. If that were even possible, it would provide a means for all CTE graduates to certify their skills to employers, and their teachers could proudly boast, "Sixty percent of my students acquired the XYZ certificate!" However, there are flaws in this scenario. What data do teachers have as a result of their students taking certification exams? How would teachers use assessment data to improve their programs and move students from 60 percent to 80 percent, and how would teachers know what steps to take in seeking systemic improvement? Fortunately, data provides a way to make program improvements that help students achieve goals and help educators make informed decisions about ways to improve their programs. Therefore, it is critical that schools select certificate or certification programs that can deliver sufficiently gradient data.

For the economy, the certificate or certification process theoretically provides an engine that speeds the employment process and enables employers to determine whether the credentials of incoming employees are sufficient. Therefore in theory, when the "big picture" of assessment data is provided, economists and labor market analysts can begin to make connections between the supply and demand sides of our economy.

Among the chief benefits to society of a credentialed workforce is confidence. We naturally look for licensed tradespeople. We look for the Automotive Service Excellence (ASE) logo on display at our car dealership because this assures us that the people who work on our vehicles have been tested and proven competent by a third party. This credibility is similar to seeing physicians' medical degrees, board certifications, and state practitioner licenses on the walls in their offices. It gives patients (especially new patients) confidence in the skills of their physicians.

The Systems

As we look at our current credentialing system, we should consider motive, credibility, and perception. Earlier in this chapter we defined terminology associated with certificates and certifications. In this section we describe some of the levels of certificates and certifications.

- *Industry certifications.* Many industry certification programs are created by professional associations to benefit themselves and their members. Because of the inherent self-interest involved, be sure to look beneath the surface when making decisions about how much weight to give any industry certification. Be sure to discuss the value of the certification with other representatives of the industry outside of the group that administers it. Is this something that is really valued by employers, or is it just something to add to a resume? Is this credential required for employment? Does it turn up in "help wanted" ads or web-based searches? Is it really needed or merely "nice to have"? In other words, who really cares?

  Remember too that in many industry certification programs, the same people do the training and the testing, which makes those programs less than completely credible. A certifying body in which the instructors and testers are the same people—and the curriculum and assessments were developed by the entity that administers the program—is suspect, unless there are very clear firewalls between training and assessment. Other questions regarding the use of certifications have to do with the availability and use of data. Typically, a certification system delivers only pass/fail results. Rarely is any further data reported. When that happens, the instructor receives no information that would enable him or her to improve the program, change the curriculum, share with constituents and the CTE community, or know whether regulatory requirements are being met.

- *Industry-based certificate* programs answer more questions for consumers of information in the education sector than do most other kinds of programs. The assessments tied to industry-based certificate programs provide detailed reports on the students who take part in them—information that is useful to teachers, administrators, and policymakers. In addition, some industry-based certificate programs address (or can be customized to address) relatively broad areas of content rather than only narrowly focused areas. Programs such as those sponsored by NOCTI are rigorously reviewed and updated on a regular basis and are tied to all applicable standards within a given industry.

- *State licensure* programs such as those mentioned earlier in this chapter are typically governed by the states in which they are administered, usually by state-selected contractors. Most state licensure systems consist only of the assessment component and not the training component. Because this automatically establishes a firewall between the training and assessment components, the credibility of state licensure systems is relatively high. State licensors serve the public by instilling confidence in the individuals delivering services. This is why state licenses are so often publicly displayed on the premises of entities that deliver services to the general public.

- *Pathway assessments* are a relatively recent development resulting in part from the work of the National Skill Standards Board (NSSB). Established by the U.S. Department of Labor, the NSSB was tasked with establishing national standards in broad categories of industry. Some of the efforts of the NSSB can be seen in the success of certification programs such as the Manufacturing Skill Standards Council (MSSC), which certifies manufacturing workers. While the NSSB worked to establish standards for industry, the U.S. Department of Education worked concurrently to determine the education requirements for similar Career Clusters™ and Career Pathways. Though much of the work of the NSSB was discontinued, the work carried out on the education side continued forward for several years. The culmination of this work was the establishment of 16 Career Clusters™ into which 79 Career Pathways could fit. All jobs listed in the *Dictionary of Occupational Titles* and other categorization mechanisms are in some way associated with those 79 pathways. Unlike typical certificate or certification assessments, which assess a person's understanding of specific tools, equipment, and processes, pathway assessments focus on the ten knowledge and skill statements associated with every cluster. These knowledge and skill statements pertain to areas such as entrepreneurship, getting along with others, ethical values, and broad technical skills. To our knowledge, NOCTI is the only body that administers this level of assessment.[3]

- *Foundation-level (soft skill) certificates* are "stepping stones" to more skill-specific technical credentials. Employers are often willing to provide substantial technical training to lower-level employees if they will first undergo the steps necessary to demonstrate good soft skills, such as coming to work on time, working effectively in teams, and exercising personal responsibility.

- *Business-specific certificates* usually focus on software packages or particular types of hardware. Business-specific certificates are typically narrow. They often do not attempt to cover all aspects of any particular industry, though they may, in fact, be important for advancement within industries. People who are considering these types of programs should first check for substance and credibility and make sure the programs are valued by employers.

Considerations for Education

For most people, certificate programs that use third-party industry-based assessments are the most efficient means of demonstrating qualification for employment. A credible certificate program delivers valid and reliable details about the knowledge and skills a person possesses. Although in some sectors (notably information technology), individuals are better served by *certification* programs, there is more to consider than potential benefits to the individual. The CTE community has to look at the benefits of all aspects of any particular program, not just those that impact the individual. If the decision — certificates versus certifications — impacts only the individual, and the cost of training is being borne by that individual, the decision is clearer and involves fewer criteria. However, the decision on certificates versus certifications does not typically impact only the individual and thus should be evaluated from multiple viewpoints. A *certificate* assessment

---

3 Certificate information can be found at www.nocti.org.

can deliver detailed data about an individual's competency and abilities. It can also provide details to potential employers, teachers, instructional institutions, states, and/or national governments. The beginning of this chapter notes that the key to understanding certificates and certifications is in the credibility of the assessments tied to those programs. Following is a list of potential criteria for selecting assessments related to certificates and certification systems:

- Do the majority of the certificate or certification standards and competencies align with the technical components in one's Program of Study?

- Is a performance component available to assess hands-on skills; if not, is there a viable substitute?

- Are customized assessment options available to meet the needs of one's Program of Study?

- In addition to a total score on a certificate assessment, do the score reports provide detailed information that can be used as a basis for instructional improvement?

- Are the score reports able to provide easily identifiable individual and group strengths, as well as areas needing improvement?

- Can the resulting score report options be aligned to national academic standards?

- Are resulting pre-post-test score comparisons or competency-level reporting available?

- Do the score reports provide normative data for comparison purposes (e.g., criterion-referenced and/or norm-referenced scores)?

- Are there professional development opportunities for teachers and administrators to learn how to interpret and use data?

- Are both online and paper/pencil delivery options available for the certificate assessment?

- Are accommodations for persons with disabilities available?

- Is personalized technical support and customer service readily available?

- Does the cost of the certificate or certification assessment include user training, supplemental administration materials, score reports, and technical support?
- Are there site license or administration or membership/subscription fees in addition to the cost of the certification or certificate assessment?
- To use the assessment, must the school/staff be certified or endorsed by the testing organization? Is there a cost involved?
- Are preparation tools available?
- Is the certificate or certification development process based on reputable industry testing standards?
- Is the certificate or certification based on industry-recognized technical standards?
- Is the organization that developed the process reputable and recognized?

To summarize, the two major components of certificate and certification programs are training and assessment. Both are derived from standards assembled by recognized industry experts. Since the assessment portion is typically the component that yields data, that component is typically used as a metric for success and the awarding of the credential. Credibility is determined by the quality of the subject-matter experts who develop and validate the standards. These experts are entrusted with specifying required tasks and the levels at which they must be performed. The assessment should closely reflect those standards. Organizations that facilitate this process for industry-specific processes must ensure that the performance on the assessment is closely tied to performance expected in the field. The stability and consistency of such performance is called reliability.

CTE educators are under constant pressure to move quickly to ensure that their programs are connected with industry credentials. Weighing the pros and cons of each program and its associated standards is critical. We hope this chapter has given you increased knowledge of terminology, systems, and history, but above all tools that will help you in selecting the type of credential to use.

Resources

American Educational Research Association. (2009). The Standards for Educational and Psychological Testing, Part I: Test Construction, Evaluation, and Documentation. Washington, DC., AREA.

American National Standards Institute. (2012). Assessment service delivery: Procedures and methods to assess people in work and organizational settings, Part 2. Washington, DC, AREA.

Carl D. Perkins Career and Technical Education Improvement Act of 2006. (2006). Public Law 109-270 (Perkins IV).

Davenport, R. (2006). Credentialing and Certification. *T+D Magazine*, 60(5), 60-61.

Foster, J., & Pritz, S. (2006). The Certification Advantage. *Techniques: Connecting Education & Careers*, 81(1), 14-20. <http://www.thefreelibrary.com/The+certification+advantage.-a0140655787>.

Harvard Graduate School of Education. (2011). *Pathways to Prosperity: Meeting the challenge of preparing young Americans for the 21st century.* Cambridge, MA: Harvard Graduate School of Education. <http://www.gse.harvard.edu/news_events/features/2011/Pathways_to_Prosperity_Feb2011.pdf>.

Hoyle, T. (2010). Credentials for Success: An Evolution in the IT Industry. *T+D Magazine*, 64(7). <http://www.astd.org/Publications/Magazines/TD/TD-Archive/2010/07/Credentials-for-Success-An-Evolution-in-the-IT-Industry.aspx>.

Knapp, L. G., & Naughton, J. (2010). Certificate or Certification? That Is the Question. *T+D Magazine*, 64 (11), 54-59. < http://www.astd.org/Publications/Magazines/TD/TD-Archive/2010/11/Certificate-or-Certification-That-Is-the-Question.aspx>.

Lualhati, J.C. (2006). The ABCs of Certification Use. *Techniques: Connecting Education & Careers*, 81(1). <http://www.thefreelibrary.com/The+ABCs+of+certification+use%3a+by+learning+a+few+of+the+basics%2c...-a0140655789>.

Norland, E. (1990). Controlling Error in Evaluation Instruments. *Journal of Extension*, 28(2). <http://www.joe.org/joe/1990summer/tt2.php>.

No Child Left Behind Act of 2001. (2002). Public Law No. 107-110.

Using Data for Decision-Making, Accountability, and Evaluation

Dean Folkers, Hope Cotner, Pradeep Kotamraju,
and Kurt Geisinger

*If you don't know where you are going, you'll
probably end up somewhere else.* —Yogi Berra

This chapter discusses both the historical and emerging roles of accountability and evaluation in the development and implementation of Programs of Study (POS), shares insights on the broader implications and uses of data to achieve successful outcomes, and provides examples of successful state and local data collection and reporting systems.

Why Data Collection, Accountability, and Evaluation Are Necessary

Being called upon to give an account for the success or failure of programs can stir strong emotions, including fear. But accountability in education should be seen in an entirely positive light. It is a necessary tool for getting the best possible results. More specifically, the results of good data collection can:

1. Establish baselines for improvement initiatives;
2. Show progress toward goal accomplishment and focus future goal setting;
3. Provide for informed planning, priority setting, and decision-making;

4. Focus efforts on student learning and student success;

5. Form the basis for creativity, imagination, and vision;

6. Help to ensure proper alignment of budgets to priorities;

7. Provide the basis for solid reporting;

8. Provide a foundation for collaborative efforts;

9. Supply the information needed for effective stakeholder communication and public relations; and

10. Provide a solid footing for the entities that are being held accountable.

Accountability for educational outcomes should be viewed within the context of how the data that it requires can help us improve in understanding our students, communicating effectively to parents, and informing and educating taxpayers about their investments. Chapter 11 discusses the age-old question posed by students, "Why do I have to learn this?" The best way to prepare for that question is to arm yourself with data about graduation rates, employment rates, salaries earned, and the quality of life achieved by students from your community who performed well in school. If we are not held accountable for program outcomes, we often neglect to collect that data.

Numerous other justifications for accountability (and the data collection that it requires) could be cited. Consider, for example:

• While schools generally have widespread community support, in times of stress, such as when budgets are tight or bond referenda are under consideration, school boards and administrators must be able to make a strong case for continued or enhanced support. Consider how much more compelling that case would be if school leaders could display data showing a direct correlation between school programs and the health of the local economy.

• Future state and federal support for Career Technical Education (CTE) is dependent upon the availability of data showing the positive impact of programs and services that receive supplemental funding through these sources.

• Data is necessary to communicate effectively with and win the support of business and industry.

Education Accountability in the 21st Century

The demand for accountability in education has become a "hot topic" especially during the last decade. Accountability has been the subject of much discussion[1] and the focus of several pieces of legislation, including No Child Left Behind (NCLB), its successor, the Elementary and Secondary Education (ESEA) Acts, and the Carl D. Perkins Career and Technical Education Act of 2006 (Perkins IV) for CTE as enforced by the U.S. Department of Education Office of Vocational and Adult Education (OVAE).

The standard method of meeting today's accountability requirements is for state education agencies (SEA) to collect data from local education agencies (LEA), such as school districts and postsecondary institutions, and assess the majority of K-12 students. This data is then summarized to determine whether the LEAs and SEAs are meeting pre-established targets. The collected information and the results from associated assessments must be provided to the relevant federal agencies for their consideration and review.

Evaluation Strategies and Trends

A common goal of both education and workforce development legislation is the development of *dashboard indicators* — dials (or indices) that decision-makers can use in evaluating programs. Dashboard indicators have been popular in industry and are becoming increasingly prevalent in education. One type of dashboard indicator is a formal assessment of what students have learned, including both knowledge and skills (academic and technical). A second type of dashboard indicator focuses on the flow of students through the system. A third type, not discussed in this chapter, involves following graduates and finding out how successful they are once they are employed in jobs related to their CTE experiences.

---

1 U.S. Department of Education, Office of Vocational and Adult Education, *Investing in America's Future: A Blueprint for Transforming Career and Technical Education* (Washington, DC, 2012); V. Schray, *Core Indicator Framework* (Washington, DC: U.S. Department of Education, Office of Vocational and Adult Education, 2000); U.S. Department of Education, *A Test of Leadership: Charting the Future of U.S. Higher Education* (Washington, DC, 2006).

NCLB dictated much of the development of the evaluation strategies used today to assess the extent to which students learn the material described in state-specific standards at the elementary and secondary levels in general education. Regional accrediting bodies now also require outcomes assessment for higher education, but higher education generally has far more flexibility in setting goals. However, even here there have been calls for more standardized approaches to accountability[2] involving carrots and sticks, particularly as the cost of higher education skyrockets and graduation and job placement statistics lag.[3]

Among the changes in accountability measures is a new focus on reading, mathematics, and science for all students. Under NCLB, students are required to take tests in reading and mathematics across seven grades (3–8 and one in high school). Starting in 2008, tests of science were required for students in three grades. As determined by the scores, each student was placed into one of four or five categories. All students (100 percent) were expected to be "proficient" at the end of their twelve years of schooling. Each state was required to develop its own content and skill standards for reading and mathematics for each of the grades for which testing was required and to establish standards of performance whereby students could be assigned to other levels (e.g., non-proficient, advanced). Performance data for cultural, ethnic, and racial groups also had to be provided separately. Schools that did not succeed in helping students reach proficiency status could face increasing sanctions. These sanctions span a range of possibilities, from assistance in improving outcomes to the dismissal of teachers and administrators. The underlying justification for the tests is based on two beliefs: that the tests will improve the academic performance of all students and that measurement-driven instruction leads to high performance by schools, teachers, and, ultimately, students.[4]

---

2 U.S. Department of Education, *A Test of Leadership.*

3 M. Bloom, "Obama Proposes New Race to the Top, This Time, for Higher Ed" (National Public Radio, January 27, 2012) (http://stateimpact.npr.org/ohio/2012/01/27/obama-proposes-new-race-to-the-top-this-time-for-higher-ed/).

4 D.M. Koretz and L.S. Hamilton, in R.L. Brennan (Ed.), *Educational Measurement* (4th ed.) (pp. 531–578) (Washington, DC: ACE/Macmillan, 2006).

During the 1980s and 1990s, one type of testing that was increasingly popular was performance assessments. This type of testing, also known by other names (e.g., authentic assessments), represented a significant departure from multiple-choice tests. In general, this type of testing included essay examinations, laboratory experiments, oral presentations, and hands-on performance tasks involving higher-order thinking and applied skills. Teachers appreciated the tasks because they were closer to the type of instruction they provided. Students *constructed* responses rather than selecting them from lists of multiple choices. By the early 2000s, however, most states had returned to multiple-choice testing. The performance tasks took too long to test, could not be scored without the judgment of experts (which incurred considerable expense), produced less than completely reliable results, and were not clearly generalizable to other tasks.[5] Thus, these task-based measures came to be seen as burdensome, expensive, and of dubious technical quality. They play a continuing role in CTE, but they must be administered effectively to be useful.

The advent of NCLB brought *standards-based testing* into existence. This approach began with the development of statewide standards in reading and mathematics, then aligned the curriculum and instruction to those standards, and finally developed measures parallel to the standards. Public accountability was ensured by the visibility of the numbers of students who reached each level of academic performance. The tests impacted schools more strongly than students, although some states required high school graduation tests in addition to grade-level tests, making the process high-stakes indeed. Alternate assessments provide reasonable testing accommodation for students with disabilities and English-language learners.

Perkins IV and CTE Accountability

Perkins IV provides funds to states to assist them in providing high-quality CTE. Each state that receives federal funds must develop a plan for the use of and prioritization of funds. The plan must describe how LEAs will receive funds, what the funds can be used for, funding priorities, and strategies for accountability and evaluation. If the plan is approved, the state must implement it, and this includes collecting

---

5 Koretz and Hamilton.

and reporting the performance and evaluation data set forth in the federal law.

Perkins IV devotes a complete section to accountability. The purpose of Perkins accountability requirements is, according to the Act, "to establish and support State and local performance accountability systems . . . to assess the effectiveness of the State and the eligible recipients of the State in achieving statewide progress in career and technical education and to optimize the return on investment of Federal funds in career and technical education activities." Clearly, the Perkins IV intent for accountability applies to each state as well as local programs that utilize federal dollars. The Act identifies specific areas that, at a minimum, are to be measured, including:

- student attainment of challenging academic content standards,

- student attainment of career and technical skill proficiencies, including student achievement on technical assessments that are aligned with industry recognized standards,

- retention in postsecondary education, or

- transfer to a baccalaureate degree program.

The Act identifies reporting expectations the states must provide to show how they are addressing the Act and its provisions. One must read the Act to fully comprehend the importance of being held accountable for intended results when receiving federal dollars and to be cognizant of the provisions directed by each state-level office. The burden of accountability is squarely on each state. As entities at the local level receive Perkins IV funds, the burden is then shared among those who directly implement programs and services.

A new element in the Perkins IV accountability framework is *technical skills assessments*, which were designed to indicate how well CTE students are doing. Also, the development, refinement, and sustenance of *Programs of Study* (POS) — the lynchpin of Perkins IV — requires new thinking about ways to measure the engagement, achievement, transition and completion outcomes of students enrolled in POS. This topic is covered more fully later in the chapter.

Data Quality

Obtaining high-quality data has been an elusive goal over the years, but progress continues to be made at the federal, state, and local levels. The Data Quality Campaign (DQC), which began in 2005, focuses on improving the quality and use of educational data collected from early childhood, K-12, postsecondary, and workforce systems. DQC sets forth 10 elements that states should use in developing data systems:

1. Statewide student identifiers
2. Student-level enrollment data
3. Student-level test data
4. Information on untested students
5. Statewide teacher identifiers with a teacher-student match
6. Student-level course completion (transcript) data
7. Student-level SAT, ACT, and Advanced Placement exam data
8. Student-level graduation and dropout data
9. Ability to match student-level P-12 and higher education data
10. A state data audit system

As states develop systems of integrated data and alignment, local school districts must accept the responsibility of providing student-level records. The initial transition in most states continues to evolve, but technological advances, the use of standard protocols (e.g., the *schools interoperability framework* [SIF]), and political considerations will continue to move implementation forward. The infusion of financial resources has also expedited the development of the systems.

The U.S. Department of Education's funding of the State Longitudinal Education Data Systems (SLDS) has been one such effort to help states better manage and use student educational data.[6] Efforts to improve data systems and accountability under Perkins IV are documented on the Peer Collaborative Resource Network website (http://cte. ed.gov), which provides information on the NCLB academic achievement measures, the Statewide Longitudinal Data Systems (SLDS), the

---

6 Data Quality Campaign, *Statewide Longitudinal Data Systems Grant Applications Summary of Key Findings* (Washington, DC: U.S. Department of Education, Office of Vocational and Adult Education, 2009) (http://www. dataqualitycampaign.org/files/SLDS_Grant_Analysis_Summary.pdf).

Common Education Data Standards (CEDS), and the P-20/Workforce integrated data systems being built within states.

K-20 Statewide Systems

States are constantly seeking ways to support longitudinal data collection activities and improve student outcomes as they continue to build and use statewide longitudinal data systems. New expectations—to do more than ever before, and to do it with less—require systemic changes and recalibration of the K-12 education system to the goal of graduating every student *college and career ready*. As is the case with any large-scale overhaul, data collection systems are required at every stage.

Following are state profiles of promising practices in the creation of longitudinal data collection systems.

Maryland

- Establishing a statewide vision to build and use data systems while protecting privacy
- Established Maryland Longitudinal Data System Center Governing Board to:
  - Provide general oversight
  - Ensure public transparency
  - Establish policy and research agenda
  - Oversee privacy and security policies and implementation.[7]

Kentucky

Kentucky's Department of Education built on the success of the K-12 statewide longitudinal data systems and the systems developed independently by the Council on Postsecondary Education and the Education Professional Standards Board to create a P-20 statewide data resource.

- The system links data from pre-school, P-12, educator preparation and certification programs, CTE, postsecondary and adult education, and other sources.

---

7 http://www.dataqualitycampaign.org/recognition_program/2010

- Participating agencies individually control what data is shared, what analytic functions use that data, and who has access to data.

- The goal is for Kentucky's P-20 data system to reflect the interests of all educational agencies and provide state and local policymakers with the information necessary to improve the system.

The Data Quality Campaign reports that "the Kentucky Council on Postsecondary Education developed a series of reports that the state shares with high schools to provide information on their graduates' readiness and performance in Kentucky postsecondary education. These succinct, easy-to-read and easy-to-interpret reports are now used by educators and policymakers to stimulate discussion and help provide transparency so that parents, school boards, the media and students can understand how well their schools' students perform in college."[8] The reports include the number who graduated and subsequently enrolled in postsecondary institutions and their level of college and career readiness. Information included in the readiness reports also includes:

- High school performance

- In-state postsecondary enrollment characteristics

- ACT score distributions of college-going students

- Colleges and universities attended and college majors

Because the reports provide information at the building level, individual Kentucky schools are able to know the subsequent paths of their graduates, compared to district and state averages.

Florida

Florida's K-20 Educational Data Warehouse (EDW) is widely recognized as a model integrated data system.[9]

---

8 http://www.dataqualitycampaign.org/resources/field_profiles/HSfeedback

9 Information in this section was adapted from www.dataqualitycampaign.org and the website of the Florida Department of Education (http://www.fldoe.org/).

The EDW system:

- Integrates data extracted from multiple sources at the state level.

- Provides a single repository of data concerning students in the K-20 public education system as well as facilities, curriculum, and staff.

- Contains information on students (demographics, enrollment, courses, test scores, financial aid, awards, employment, curriculum), staff members (demographics, credentials, instructional activities) and educational institutions.

- Is linked through the Integrated Education Data Systems (IEDS) to the Florida Education and Training Placements Information Program (FETPIP) with a single pathway to the information through the Sunshine Connections Business Intelligence (BI) Portal.[10]

The policy and programmatic questions that have been addressed through the use of linked data include:

- What kinds of jobs did former students from various education levels attain, what were their earnings, and how did their employment experiences reflect the needs of the state's economy?

- How could job information on graduates better inform programmatic and budgetary decisions throughout the state?

- How could job information be integrated into K-20 funding decision processes?

- How are the linked data being used?

In Florida, the data has been used to inform the legislative funding processes (performance based budgeting and funding) for education; justify program offerings utilizing jobs information; and support initiatives and reporting requirements related to public assistance reform, correctional education, and children in foster care.

The system has helped foster closer collaboration between educators and employers at all levels. For example, using linked data from FETPIP, FLDOE was able to identify Florida employers that were

---

10 For more on Florida EDW, visit http://edwapp.doe.state.fl.us/.

employing a substantial number of high school dropouts. The findings led the Commissioner to reach out to these employers to develop strategies to re-engage these students and place them in adult education programs.

The next step is to develop mechanisms that can be used in conjunction with FLDOE's statewide longitudinal data systems to predict how elements of the K-20 education system and the workforce development system combine to provide stable, family-supporting upwardly mobile employment opportunities for students and people who are already in the workforce.[11]

Tennessee

Tennessee's Consolidated Management Activity Tracking System (CMATS) is an online data collection and reporting system.

CMATS:

- Is designed to enable adult education and workforce development agencies to share data on clients served in WIA Title I and Title II programs.

- Contains adult education data beginning 2003–2004.

- Allows tracking of students through multiple phases of learning and work.

- Allows for sharing of data across agencies in the Department of Labor (name, address, etc.) as well as employment data.

- Interfaces with the TN GED database and records weekly GED attainment. Adult education programs can share data with each other (assessment scores, previous attendance records, goals, notes, etc.).

- Provides real-time data reporting and review, and the data can be viewed by anyone in the state with permission.[12]

---

11 Data Quality Campaign, "Using Linked Data to Drive Education and Training Improvement" (http://dataqualitycampaign.org/files/UsingLinkedDataPaper-withMeetingNotes%5B1%5D.pdf).

12 Maryland Workforce Creation and Adult Education Transition Council, Promising Practices Research Brief 5: *Integrating Data Systems* (http://www.dllr.maryland.gov/adulted/aedoc-sribrief5.pdf).

Texas

In 2008 the Texas Education Agency initiated a study of the Texas Public Education Information Management System (PEIMS). The study resulted in a new direction and the creation of the Texas Student Data System (TSDS). A primary goal of the TSDS was to improve the capacity for data-driven decision making among key education stakeholders within the state: educators, parents, administrators, and policymakers.

The TSDS will leverage five major system components:

- District connections database;
- Certified PEIMS data store;
- Texas P-20 Public Education Information Resource;
- Business intelligence tools; and
- State-sponsored Student Information System.[13]

Using Data to Inform Decisions and Decision Makers

Businesspersons often use key indicator reports—data tables that condense large amounts of information into trend lines—as daily and periodic information on the short- and long-term health of their businesses. A typical data point for a manufacturer, for example, might include the resources expended in correcting manufacturing mistakes. That data is necessary to take corrective action. It is easy to see how the same approach could be translated to CTE programs and services. If students readily obtain jobs following completion of certain education programs and succeed at those jobs, the collected data support continuation of the programs.

To maintain support for CTE programs, it is essential to not only collect data but to be mindful of *how data are collected and displayed.* Legislators and state-level administrators rely on aggregated data from the local level in their decision-making. By ensuring that data is appropriate and accurate, LEAs play a critical role in securing continued public funding. Data collection is a prerequisite to all informed decision making, at both the state and local levels. Well-designed data

---

13 http://www.tea.state.tx.us/index2.aspx?id=7643&menu_id=938

collection systems that yield useful real-time reports are within the reach of CTE practitioners.

Which data should be collected? The National Research Center for Career and Technical Education (NRCCTE) at the University of Louisville suggests that CTE student success is observable in three areas that connect learning and work:

- *Engagement*—completion of high school and/or postsecondary programs;

- *Achievement*—both technical and academic achievement outcomes; the acquisition of industry credentials; and

- *Transition*—movement from high school to continued formal learning at the postsecondary level without the need for remediation and/or movement from education to the workplace.

POS student success is observable in the same three areas, with the adjustments indicated below:

- *Engagement*—defined as attending, focusing, and specializing in coursework and work-based learning within POS/Career Pathways;

- *Achievement*—defined as academic performance, skill development, and completing (graduating) school or college within a POS/Career Pathway; and

- *Transition*—defined either as high school graduates moving on to postsecondary education; moving to employment from postsecondary education; or, moving from employment back into education at multiple entry and exit points, as enabled by the student/worker's POS/Career Pathway.

Using Labor Market Data to Set Program Priorities

A key element in determining which POS should be promoted at the SEA and the LEA levels is labor market information. Recent reports[14] from the Center for Education and the Workforce (CEW), described in

---

14 A. Carnevale, N. Smith, J.R. Stone III, P. Kotamraju, B. Steuernagel, and K. Green, *Career Clusters: Forecasting Demand for High School to College Jobs 2008–2018* (Washington, DC: Center for Education and the Workforce, Georgetown University, 2011).

Chapter 2, indicate that (a) having a postsecondary education is now the norm for entry into many occupations; (b) while there are jobs for those with high school degrees or less, they are fast declining; and (c) even as jobs are disappearing from the middle, there exist significant shortages, particularly as the U.S. economy emerges out of the Great Recession.

The Career Clusters report by Carnevale et al. (2011) identifies which occupations are projected between 2008 and 2018 to meet at least one of the following: have the highest demand, are growing the fastest, pay a living wage,[15] show gender-based differences in employment patterns, and pay differently according to education requirements. Pertinent to this chapter is the fact that there are employment opportunities for workers across a broad range of educational levels, even those with high school diplomas or less. Nevertheless, occupations in general are undergoing a process of up-skilling, particularly those that require minimal education. From a POS perspective, the importance of strong high school CTE programs cannot be overstated.[16]

Table 1[17] projects that by 2018 the majority of workers with a high school diploma or less will find employment mainly in four clusters. "Middle skill" workers, i.e., those who attain associate degrees and beyond but less than bachelor's degrees, will earn higher wages and experience greater flexibility in choosing jobs (from seven clusters in the table). For workers with bachelor's degrees, opportunities will expand even further.

---

15 Carnevale et al. define $35,000 (2010$) as the Minimum Earning Threshold (MET). It is the absolute poverty-based definition of the earnings level that equals 150 percent of the federal poverty level (FPL) for a family of four. It can also be considered the wage level necessary to enter into the middle class.

16 J.R. Stone III and M.V. Lewis, *College and Career Ready in the 21st Century: Making High School Matter* (Teachers College Press, 2012).

17 Adapted from Carnevale et al., *Career Clusters*

**Table 1: High-Demand/High-Growth Clusters Paying
a Living Wage by Education Level Requirements
for Entry into Occupations: 2008–2018**

CLUSTER	High School or Less	Assoc. Degree or Some College	Bachelor's Degree
Hospitality and Tourism	◆	◆	◆
Manufacturing	◆	◆	
Architecture and Construction	◆		
Marketing, Sales, and Services		◆	◆
Health Science		◆	◆
Business, Management, and Admin.		◆	◆
Transportation, Distribution, and Logistics	◆	◆	
STEM			◆
Information Technology			◆
Government and Public Administration			◆
Finance			◆
Education and Training			◆

Table 2[18] lists the top six career clusters for persons at six educational award levels:

- High school participants
- High school concentrators
- High school graduates with less than one year of postsecondary education
- Persons who have completed at least one but less than two years of postsecondary education
- Holders of associate degrees
- Persons who completed two but less than four years of college

The table also identifies the top six clusters for all award levels.

18 Adapted from Carnevale et al., *Career Clusters.*

Table 2. Participation and Concentration of Workers with High School Diplomas and Postsecondary Middle Skills Working in CTE for Top Six Career Clusters by Award Type and Career Cluster

High School Diplomas		Postsecondary Middle Skills				
Participants	Concentrators	< 1 year	At least 1 but < 2 academic years	Associate degree	At least 2 but < 4 years	Total, all award levels
Business	Manufacturing, repair, and transportation	Health sciences	Health sciences	Health sciences	Health sciences	Health sciences
Communications and design	Business	Manufacturing, repair, and transportation	Consumer services	Business management	Manufacturing, repair, and transportation	Manufacturing, repair, and transportation
Manufacturing, repair, and transportation	Agriculture and natural resources	Consumer services	Manufacturing, repair, and transportation	Engineering, architecture, and science technologies	Consumer services	Consumer services
Consumer and culinary services	Consumer and culinary services	Protective services	Business management	Protective services	Public, legal, and social services	Business management
Computer and information services	Health sciences	Business management	Engineering, architecture, and science technologies	Computer and information sciences	Engineering, architecture, and science technologies	Protective services
Engineering technologies	Communications and design	Business support	Business support	Consumer services	Computer and information sciences	Engineering, architecture, and science technologies

The table shows five key facts:

1. Some Career Clusters are among the top six at both the secondary and postsecondary levels.

2. High school CTE students are going beyond the traditional, "old line" Career Clusters (agriculture and natural resources; manufacturing, construction, repair, and transportation) and are participating in less traditional, "new line" Career Clusters (business; computer and information sciences).

3. At the secondary level, students are choosing Career Clusters in which math and science knowledge requirements for employment are increasing, and many of these are in the "new line" Career Clusters (e.g., engineering technologies).

4. Health sciences ranks number one overall. It ranks first at four award levels and appears among the top six Career Clusters at the high school concentrator level. (Anecdotal evidence, on the other hand, suggests that well-rounded health sciences programs are very difficult to sustain at the secondary level.)

5. Some Career Clusters appear only on the secondary side (communications and design); some appear only on the post-secondary side (public, legal, and social services; protective services).

Tables 1 and 2 examine the Career Clusters from two points of view—employment opportunity by educational level and demand among CTE students. Taken together, the tables enable us to make two important observations.

1. Some Career Clusters span both the secondary and postsecondary educational levels while others appear only at the postsecondary level. (This is consistent with high school enrollment patterns. High school courses in business, for example, are common, while courses in protective services would be rare.) Career Clusters that span both levels and provide employment opportunities at multiple "exit points" are ideal candidates for the POS approach.

2. "New line" Career Clusters—the Career Clusters demanded by the new 21st-century economy (STEM, information technology, and engineering)—are rising in relation to the traditional, "old line" Career Clusters. And as stated previously

(though not evident directly from the tables), a certain amount of "up-skilling" is taking place in all Career Clusters. More and more students are pursuing—and more and more employers are demanding—skills that are founded on strong fundamentals in math and science.[19]

The preceding tables typify the information that SEAs and LEAs need to be able to align POS to employment opportunities, both now and in the foreseeable future. All decisions about POS should be informed by labor market demand and trends as well as the course-taking patterns of students. In making those decisions, SEAs and LEAs should also consider economic development priorities driven by labor market demand, not only in general but with respect to specific locations. This will enable the creation of a pipeline of qualified students to the places where they are needed. Success will depend to a large extent on the *coordinated* efforts of entities in economic development, education, and business/industry.

Other Data Sources

Other sources of data can be valuable in informing decision making and supporting program improvement, especially at the local level. These include, for example, surveys of the perceptions of community members, parents, and students; employer satisfaction surveys; measures of organizational climate; and surveys of levels of student engagement.

The Gallup Student Poll focuses on three indicators of student success: *hope* for the future, *engagement* with school, and *wellbeing*. These indicators have been shown to drive students' grades, achievement scores, retention, and future employment.[20]

- **Hope**—the ideas and energy we have for the future. Hope drives the attendance, credits earned, and grade point averages (GPA) of high school students. Hope scores are more robust predictors of college success than are GPA, SAT, and ACT scores.

---

19 Stone and Lewis, *College and Career Ready in the 21st Century.*
20 http://www.gallupstudentpoll.com/home.aspx

- **Engagement**—the involvement in and enthusiasm for school. Engagement distinguishes between high-performing and low-performing schools.

- **Wellbeing**—how we think about and experience our lives. Wellbeing tells us how our students are doing today and predicts their success in the future.

By measuring hope, engagement, and wellbeing, the Gallup Student Poll is helping create a more hopeful story about American education in which students and teachers get to do what they do best every day, students' wellbeing and success matter to the community, and students' personal wellness leads to success in school.

Using Data to Document Success

How much more effective are we when we use data to make programmatic decisions within education? NASDCTEc, in its 2011 brief titled *Investment in Career Technical Education: Linkages to Greater Earnings, Higher Employability, and Positive Benefit-Cost Ratio,* addressed the issue as follows.

> The use of accountability and data-driven decision making to support continuous improvement and effective implementation of CTE is a tenet of the National Association of State Directors of Career Technical Education Consortium's (NASDCTEc) vision for CTE. States and local CTE programs must enable themselves to (gather performance data and) showcase positive CTE results. Further, they must demonstrate the positive impact of CTE through return on investment (ROI) measured by fiscal returns or savings for government and employers, favorable societal impact, career benefits for individuals and a positive impact on regional, state or national economies.[21]

The NASDCTEc brief acknowledges the problems and costs associated with data-gathering and adds, "measuring improved quality of life can be done using a range of barometers and qualifiers. But diminishing resources and unavailability of longitudinal data—which would ideally follow students from K-12 education through postsecondary education and the workforce—limit many states and

---

21 http://www.careertech.org/file_download/08350a32-da59-490e-b4ad-ef2310bff36b

CTE programs from carrying out the complex analysis required to calculate ROI."

The Alliance for Excellent Education (AEE), a nonprofit organization, used a different economic model to calculate the economic impact of a high school diploma nationally and in each of the states. In its analysis, the Alliance was able to connect investments in education to the benefits enjoyed by society, which included increases in individual earnings, home and auto sales, job and economic growth, spending and investment, and tax revenue.

AEE's analysis provided a scenario of what would happen if each state's high school dropout rate was cut in half. The potential impact included:

- $7.6 billion increase in earnings
- $5.6 billion increase in spending
- $19 billion increase in home sales
- $741 million increase in auto sales

This work shows how a decrease in the number of high school dropouts would impact well beyond the individual, and provides a persuasive case for secondary education funding. The Alliance also produced similar statistics for each state.

Return on Investment Models

As noted earlier in this chapter, Perkins IV seeks accountability systems that optimize return on investment (ROI). Perkins is looking at ROI as a demonstrable positive return on the federal infusion of dollars. The NASDCTEc brief cited in the previous section addressed the issue as follows.

> At its most basic level, ROI measures how much academic achievement a program, school, district, or state achieves for each dollar that is spent on CTE. However, calculating an accurate ROI, and accounting for costs related to low-income, non-English speaking, and special education populations, is a sophisticated process. For example, the National Research Center for Career and Technical Education (NRCCTE) recently commissioned a study to address that intimidating issue. As a writer of the report, Kevin Hollenbeck explained, "It answers the question of how the program has changed

the lives of individuals who participated in it relative to their next best alternative." Through complex analysis, the study provided these outcomes that illustrate how secondary CTE programs in Washington State boost students' skills, productivity, likelihood of gainful employment and contributions to the local economy. The following outcomes related from the NRCCTE study provide compelling reasons to support CTE in Washington:

- After graduating from a high school CTE program, gradu-ates earn 38 more cents per hour, an average of $141 more per quarter, and are 4.1 percent more employable.

- Postsecondary CTE graduates can expect a 9.2 percent increase in employability short-term and a 6.7 percent longer-term increase.

- Secondary CTE students will see a longer-term net impact of $284 per quarter and postsecondary CTE students will experi-ence a longer-term net impact of over $1,000 per quarter.

- The public also benefits from CTE in Washington – the benefits of educating postsecondary CTE students are estimated to be more than double the cost to the public.

- The long-term benefits of educating secondary CTE students are even more substantial with a benefits-cost ratio of 8 to 1.

The Center for American Progress (CAP), a progressive Washington, DC-based think tank, produced a report early in 2012 to gauge the ROI for districts across the country. CAP examines "educational produc-tivity," which looks at the rate of student achievement based on the fiscal output of the system. A district that spends relatively little but produces high achievement has "high educational productivity."

CAP's data are displayed on an interactive website that allows for district-by-district comparisons on spending and academic achieve-ment. Data are available for most major school districts in the country, allowing users to view how districts with similar characteristics compare to one another. For example, CAP reports that two Wisconsin school systems of similar size that serve similar student populations get largely similar results on state exams—yet one spends an extra $8 million to run its school system. Being able to make this type of comparison benefits CTE schools that achieve stronger outputs than other local schools or schools with similar characteristics.

Arkansas and Minnesota have investigated the cost-saving potential of education programs for each state and released statistics that succinctly describe the rate of return for education:

- Arkansas: High school graduates or GED recipients earn an average of $8,860 more per year than non-high school graduates. $18 million is spent on CTE with an ROI of 43 percent.

- Minnesota: In FY 2004, Minnesota served 81,500 adult learners (38,663 being ESL). Minnesota spent $41 million in 2004, returning 3 to 5 times the expenditure back to the state in cash and savings.

NASDCTEc has collected additional information relative to ROI in CTE. Examples from Oklahoma, Tennessee, and Washington follow.

Oklahoma

In 2006, Oklahoma conducted a study of the lifetime income gains of the CareerTech centers' full-time program graduates and their impact on the Oklahoma economy. This study was updated in 2008 to include three job training programs and the Oklahoma Bid Assistance Network.

Benefits to individuals:

- Oklahoma workers who have completed CTE training earn an additional $2 per hour, or nearly 20 percent more, than workers with only a high school diploma.

- The average estimated hourly wage for students who completed full-time programs in FY02 was $10.47, or approximately 12 percent more that the estimated wage rate for workers of similar age but no education beyond high school.

- Wage rates are higher for adult completers ($12.46) than for secondary completers ($7.58).

- Based on all sources of income, CTE-trained workers earn nearly $4,100 more per year than those with no education beyond high school.

Benefits to the state:

- The cost/benefit analysis suggests that each group of full-time certificate program completers generates a total of $2.4 billion in direct and indirect benefits, including added income over the course of their working lives, added tax revenue, and the added output generated by operation of the programs themselves.

- The largest direct benefit to completers is the $1.1 billion wage gain, which generates an estimated $82.6 million in direct added tax revenue to the state and local governments.

- Through multiplier effects, an additional $74 million is expected to be paid by other workers statewide as their future earnings increase, for a total tax impact of $157 million over their working lives.

Tennessee

In 2006, the Tennessee Department of Labor and Workforce Development, the Tennessee Career and Technical Education Council, and the Tennessee Department of Education Division of Career and Technical Education commissioned a report titled *The Economic Impact of Secondary and Post-Secondary Career and Technical Education in Tennessee.*[22] One of the questions researched in the report was, "What is the public's return on investment?" The following points from the report's executive summary address that question.

- Secondary and postsecondary CTE in Tennessee has a cost/benefit ratio of 1:1.99, generating nearly double the benefits relative to the cost of operations.

- Secondary and postsecondary CTE produced a turnover ratio of 1:1.01, meaning that for every dollar earned by CTE clients, graduates, and completers, an additional $1.01 was generated for the state economy. The total number of jobs created or impacted by the programs was about 7,000.

- The cost/benefit ratio produced by CTE expenditures and earnings was 1:5.37, meaning that for every $1 expended on secondary and postsecondary CTE, $5.37 is returned to the state economy in direct earnings, increased productivity, and additional labor income and taxes. In total, over 16,000 jobs were created or impacted by those expenditures and earnings.

---

22 http://www.tennessee.gov/education/cte_council/doc/econimpact.pdf

Washington

In September 2006, the Upjohn Institute released a report, *Net Impact and Benefit-Cost Estimates of the Workforce Development System in Washington State*, authorized by the Workforce Training and Education Coordinating Board (WTECB) of the State of Washington.[23] The report noted the following benefits of the state's workforce development system:

Benefits to individuals:

- Long-term economic benefits for secondary school students include increased employment, wage increases by $0.59 per hour, hours worked increased by 35.5 hours per quarter, and earnings increased by about 13 percent.

- CTE completers who go on to postsecondary education have better economic outcomes than other high school graduates. In the short-term, CTE completers who do not go on to higher education have relatively higher earnings impacts than other high school graduates. But in the longer term, CTE completers who do enroll in higher education have better outcomes.

- In the short term, the average quarterly earnings for community and technical college job preparatory training students increased by about 25 percent and included increased employment impacts of 9.2 percentage points, hourly wage increases of $2.92, and increased hours per quarter of over 70 hours.

- Over the longer term, these students earned an average of just over $900 per quarter more than their comparison group counterparts due to an employment net impact of 6.7 percentage points, and hourly wage impact of $1.87, and an hours-of-employment impact of about 40 hours.

Benefits to the state:

- The increased earnings gains by community and technical college job preparatory training students were accompanied by a decrease in Temporary Assistance for Needy Families (TANF), Food Stamps, and Medicaid eligibility.

---

23 http://www.upjohninst.org/publications/tr/tr06-020.pdf

Using Data to Demonstrate Successful POS Implementation

Examples of successful POS implementation can be found all across the country at both the state and local levels. The successes demonstrate increased graduation rates, higher-than-average placement rates, increased postsecondary completion, and highly successful job placements for students participating in CTE. Specific examples from all 50 states are available via the State CTE Success Map,[24] which provides strong evidence from schools across the country at the district, school, college, and program levels and includes impressive results for students in the following areas:

- Secondary graduation rates
- College-going rates (two- and four- year)
- Postsecondary credential attainment rates

One snapshot of state success was featured in a recent *Lincoln Journal Star* article highlighting CTE in Nebraska (Journal Star 2012). According to reporter Margaret Reist, "Nebraska students who take CTE courses are less likely to drop out of high school, more likely to take honors or advanced placement courses and — especially for those seniors who take three or more courses — are significantly more likely to get diplomas."[25] The article goes on to provide the following CTE statistics for the 2010–2011 school year:

- 63 percent of students in grades 7–12 have earned at least one credit in a CTE course.
- 34 percent of seniors completed at least three courses in a single CTE area.
- 29 percent of seniors who have completed three CTE courses are eligible for the free- and reduced-lunch program, compared with 32 percent of all Nebraska seniors.

---

24 http://cteworks.careertech.org/state-examples/

25 http://journalstar.com/news/local/education/with-tech-schools-numbers-fly-in-the-face-of-stereotypes/article_de0be701-aa0f-5d21-a714-ba67c95c088f.html?utm_source=From+the+Director%3A+Nebraska&utm_campaign=Nebraska&utm_medium=email

- 17 percent of seniors who have completed three CTE courses are eligible for the gifted program, the same percentage as all high school seniors.

- 33 percent of seniors who have taken three CTE courses also have taken honors or AP courses, compared with 26 percent of all high school seniors.

- 0.4 percent of students in grades 7–12 participating in CTE courses dropped out of school, compared with 2.9 percent of students not participating in CTE courses and 1.3 percent of students overall who dropped out.

- 1 percent of seniors who had taken at least three CTE courses dropped out of school, compared with 4.83 percent of students who had not taken three CTE courses and 3.52 percent of all Nebraska seniors who dropped out.

- 99 percent of seniors who took at least three CTE courses graduated from high school compared with 82 percent of all Nebraska seniors.

Another state example comes from Tennessee, which publishes an online CTE Report Card showcasing the demographics and performance of students in the state.[26] The report provides an opportunity to highlight the successes of CTE in Tennessee in the 16 Career Clusters™ as well as the opportunity to examine local district and school performance.

Tennessee's state report card is but one example of public reporting that demonstrates how communication of CTE outcomes can lead to public engagement. Data used to inform the public can do more than validate the performance of students and teachers, justify investments in programs, and direct the prioritization of programming. Information based on high-quality data can also help promote and market the success of programs to constituents, future students, parents, and the community at large. Creative, strategic approaches to the communication of CTE success, rooted in high-quality data, provide an exciting possibility for the future.

---

26 http://www.tn.gov/education/cte/cte_report_card.shtml

Using the Programs of Study Self-Assessment Tool

As you examine the data gathering and reporting systems in place in your own community and state, consider adding the POS Self-Assessment tool referenced in earlier chapters to your "accountability toolbox." The document, *Programs of Study: Local Implementation Readiness and Capacity Self-Assessment*, prepared by MPR Associates, Inc., under contract to the Office of Vocational and Adult Education, U.S. Department of Education, provides guidance in preparation for meeting accountability standards. [27]

The document encourages programs to

be explicit with identifying the credential, certificate, and degree opportunities that exist upon completion of the program of study. Local applicants should be encouraged to illustrate multiple POS entrance and exit points, if appropriate. The level of detail required by the state approval agency may vary, but should at a minimum list the credential, certificate, and degree opportunities on a Career Cluster Plan of Study, if that is the chosen template for submission. Additional credential, certificate, and degree information may be requested to document the level of career guidance detail available to POS students. If the state approval agency is seeking to align POS with high skill, high wage, high demand career fields, the exit award for the POS may be important information. . . . Systems and strategies to gather quantitative and qualitative data on both POS components and student outcomes are crucial for ongoing efforts to development and implement POS. (p. 24)

Elsewhere the document states that:

Well-designed accountability and evaluation systems should:

- Include the "10 Essential Elements of a State Longitudinal Data System" identified by the Data Quality Campaign.

- Provide for administrative record matching of student education and employment data (i.e., Unemployment Insurance [UI] wage records).

---

27 http://cte.ed.gov/docs/POSLocalImplementationTool-9-14-10.pdf

- Yield valid and reliable data on key student outcomes (indicators) referenced in Perkins IV and other relevant federal and state legislation.

- Provide timely data to evaluate and improve the effectiveness of POS. (p. 9)

The document offers measurement criteria for examining local progress:

Accountability and Evaluation Systems
Self-Assessment Ranking of Current Implementation Status and Importance to Your Implementation

Rank your development and implementation progress for Accountability and Evaluation according to the measurement criteria listed. Determine the level that most closely aligns with the progress made toward Accountability and Evaluation development and implementation. The self-assessment is intended to be an authentic gauge of actual implementation. Results from the self-assessment can be used to target areas for technical assistance and professional development. An analysis of the level of importance can assist in establishing the priority and possible timeline for implementing technical assistance and scheduling professional development.

Implementation Characteristics	Current Status	Importance
Program data is regularly used and evaluated for planning, development, implementation, and improvement.	☐ None ☐ In Progress ☐ Operational	☐ Low ☐ Important ☐ Critical
The program has procedures and processes in place to ensure collection of valid and reliable longitudinal data.	☐ None ☐ In Progress ☐ Operational	☐ Low ☐ Important ☐ Critical
Performance data is used to monitor the college and career readiness of students incorporating longitudinal data systems elements across educational levels and into employment.	☐ None ☐ In Progress ☐ Operational	☐ Low ☐ Important ☐ Critical
Program data is disaggregated to analyze the performance of sub-groups.	☐ None ☐ In Progress ☐ Operational	☐ Low ☐ Important ☐ Critical
Program data is shared with faculty and analyzed for program and classroom improvement.	☐ None ☐ In Progress ☐ Operational	☐ Low ☐ Important ☐ Critical
The program fosters a culture of continuous improvement	☐ None ☐ In Progress ☐ Operational	☐ Low ☐ Important ☐ Critical
Overall Status Summary	**Current Status**	**Importance**
After considering each of the implementation characteristics, please rank: 1) your current status of POS Accountability and Evaluation Systems implementation; and 2) the level of importance this element has to your POS implementation. Transfer these rankings to the Self-Assessment Summary to compare the status and importance of this element to the other POS framework elements.	❶ None ❷ In Progress ❸ Operational	❶ Low ❷ Important ❸ Critical

4 ACCOUNTABILITY AND EVALUATION SYSTEMS
PROGRAMS OF STUDY: LOCAL IMPLEMENTATION READINESS AND CAPACITY SELF-ASSESSMENT

25

Accountability and Evaluation Systems—Implementation Capacity Analysis
Self-Assessment Reflection and Action Planning

In the section below, identify your current capacity assets in the area of *Accountability and Evaluation Systems* by responding to the question prompts. Give equal analysis to local capacity barriers, items of critical importance, and steps needed to remedy these capacity concerns.

State or Local Self-Assessment	Items of Critical Importance/Action Steps
• What's working well that is worth keeping? • What goals do you have to sustain and enhance the level of collaboration among the partners? • What strategies will you use to sustain the engagement of partnership members? • How will you know if your partnership is being successful?	• What will be new or needs to be revised? • What strategies will you use to address items identified as being of critical importance? • What are the indicators you will use to measure your improvement? • How will you know if you are successful? And when?
Notes	Notes

Conclusion

The opportunities to influence and inform decisions at the federal, state, and local levels using high-quality data are tremendous and extremely important. A critical piece of the process is not just the collection, storing, and reporting of data, but effectively using and communicating the data to support informed decision-making in pursuit of continuous improvement. When this is done well, the outcomes can positively impact lives and ultimately the economic prosperity of our country.[28]

---

28 The Perkins Collaborative Resource Network (http://cte.ed.gov/) offers additional resources that support POS implementation, accountability, and evaluation.

SECTION V CHECK-UP

After reading the **ENSURE** section chapters, complete this initial formative assessment to determine where your schools, colleges, and region stand regarding the organization and structures needed to support career pathways implementation, evolution, and sustainability. How you rate your readiness may indicate the need for a deeper analysis including a comprehensive self-evaluation and external evaluation.

ENSURE Checklist	NA	Disagree			Agree	
		−2	−1	0	1	2
(1) There are well-developed technical skill assessments that measure student attainment of technical skill proficiencies at multiple points during the Career Pathway.						
(2) The technical skill assessments are based on industry standards where available and appropriate.						
(3) Program data is collected and used for planning, development, implementation, and improvement of Career Pathways.						
(4) Performance data (incorporating longitudinal data systems across educational levels and into employment) is used to monitor college and career readiness of students.						
(5) Inventory/survey of the economic development and labor market needs of the community has been conducted.						
(6) Career Pathways provide employment opportunities for high-wage and/or high-demand careers.						

CONCLUSION

Getting Proactive: Career Pathways to Link Education and Economic Prosperity

Kimberly Green and Richard Hinckley

We firmly believe that today's Career Technical Education (CTE) holds the key to both the United States' regaining of its former competitive strength in the global economy and the roadmap to individual economic prosperity. It also provides many of the answers to the improvement of American public education. Our book title, *The Career Pathways Effect: Linking Education and Economic Prosperity*, was selected to reinforce this belief. While we have come a long way, as the many successful models of CTE implementation provided throughout this book show, we and all of education have much more to do to develop strong data-defendable programs and services that provide adoptable blueprints for education improvement.

Our intent was to provide you, as either new or seasoned CTE implementers and education supporters, the structure and vision of today's CTE as it has evolved into Career Pathways initiatives. With the policy, financial, and programmatic impetus of many federal and state agencies, as well as the work of many organizations, CTE enjoys tremendous support. This support also presents an incredible opportunity and responsibility.

This opportunity, for CTE to be a mainstream solution-builder and help our nation regain its competitive edge, is the result of hard work by many visionary leaders and groups. Progressive initiatives such as the Common Core State Standards, Common Career Technical Core, and efforts to elevate both college *and* career readiness are bringing together general education and CTE in inventive ways. These efforts showcase the necessity of collaboration among academic and technical education and secondary and postsecondary education and underscore the importance of connecting systems and breaking down silos and stereotypes. They also share a common goal—ensuring personal and national economic prosperity.

Career Pathways aligned to the POS design framework give us a more uniform and common approach to CTE that provides transportable models that ease adaptation and adoption. We have answers and now need to push forward for our nation, our youth, and ourselves. In chapter 3, our friend and colleague, Bill Symonds, wrote, "Many Americans despair that we can ever achieve this vision. Our dominant educational culture—which all too often demeans CTE—is deeply entrenched. Even so, we already have some outstanding examples of models that open up multiple pathways to success." Throughout the book, state and local initiatives are featured that can help us all learn from one another, build on each other's success, and together lift this nation.

The book is intended to challenge you, to arm you with research and models to learn from, and, most importantly, to spark action. As Debra Mills and Mark Whitney pointed out in Chapter 2, *The National Condition and Career Pathways,* the trend lines for American education, as benchmarked with a competitive world, are stark and sobering. We certainly do not know whether we have hit bottom, but we cannot wait to determine whether that is the case. We have to quit reinventing solutions and learn to appreciate the hard work of others and adapt it to our own community with its unique mix of people, politics, organizational structures, and business sectors. We must further break down barriers within the education community and find new allies. The allies exist, sometimes having never even been asked to help. And, in that vein, it is not always about waiting for funding to begin your work. Certainly, grants and external financial support can hasten new initiatives, but growing and then sustaining excellent CTE is about the people, the stakeholders, and the return on investment.

Call it Career Pathways or by other names, but use its power to make a difference in your state and in your community to transform lives, educational institutions, and whole industries, on the way to bolstering our economic prosperity.